MathFlare

Name: ___________________

Class: ___________________

Teacher: ___________________

<u>Introduction</u>

As parents and educators, we recognize the pivotal role mathematics plays in shaping a child's academic journey and future success. Yet, the path to mathematical proficiency can often seem daunting, fraught with challenges and complexities. That's where the transformative power of MathFlare Workbooks shine through, illuminating the way forward with clarity, precision, and purpose.

Introducing MathFlare Workbooks – a beacon of guidance, a testament to excellence, and a catalyst for achievement. Crafted with meticulous care and expertise, MathFlare Workbooks stand as paragons of educational excellence, designed to nurture young minds, ignite a passion for learning, and develop a deep-rooted understanding of mathematical concepts.

Picture this: your child eagerly delves into the pages of Mathflare Workbook, greeted by a step-by-step guide illuminated with vivid examples that demystify complex mathematical concepts. With each turn of the page, they embark on a journey of discovery, encountering thoughtfully curated practice questions that reinforce learning and hone problem-solving skills. And when they unveil the answers to those very questions, a sense of accomplishment blossoms within them – a tangible reward for their hard work and dedication.

MathFlare: Math Workbook 1st Grade

But MathFlare Workbooks are more than just tools for learning; they are pathways to comprehension, fostering a deep-seated understanding of mathematical concepts through a sequential, logical flow. From fundamental principles to advanced problem-solving strategies, every chapter builds upon the last, ensuring a robust foundation upon which future knowledge can be constructed.

As parents, we yearn for nothing more than to see our children thrive, to witness the spark of inspiration ignited within them as they conquer academic challenges with confidence and poise. MathFlare Workbooks serve as partners in this noble endeavor, offering not just practice questions, but the keys to unlocking a world of opportunity.

And for teachers, MathFlare Workbooks stand as invaluable allies in the quest to cultivate mathematical proficiency in the classroom. With answers readily available, instructors can focus on guiding and nurturing their students, confident in the knowledge that MathFlare Workbooks provide a solid framework upon which to build.

In the pages of MathFlare Workbooks, we find not just the promise of academic excellence, but the seeds of a brighter tomorrow. So let us embrace the power of mathematics, let us champion the journey of learning, and let us pave the way for a generation of young minds poised to shape the world. With MathFlare Workbooks as our guide, the possibilities are infinite, and the future, bright.

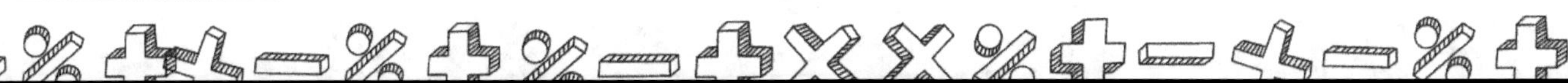

Table of Contents

MathFlare: Math Workbook 1st Grade

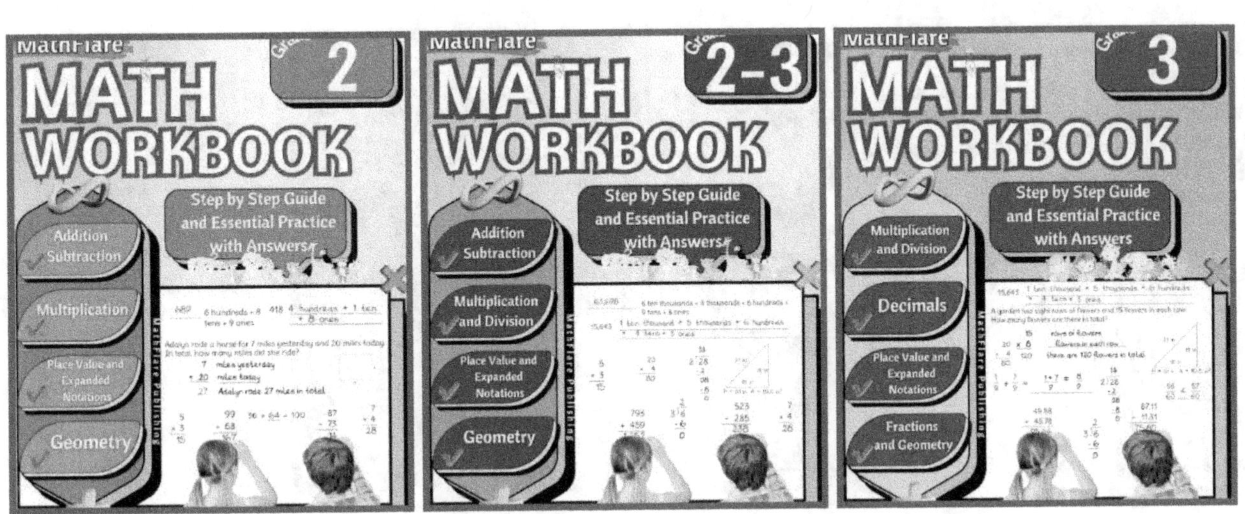

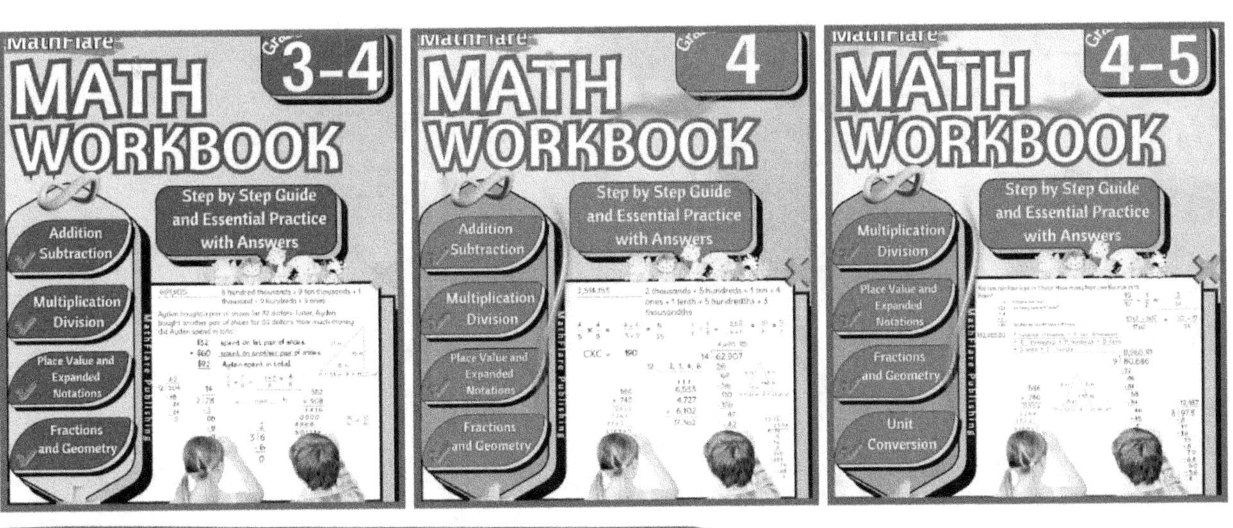

MathFlare: Math Workbook 1st Grade

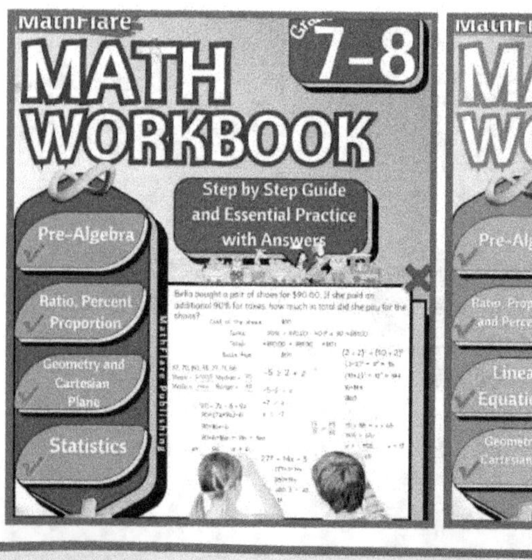

MathFlare: Math Workbook 1st Grade

Chapter 1

Counting and Numbers

Skip Counting

Skip counting is a fun and useful skill that helps us count faster by jumping over some numbers. It's a valuable tool for developing number sense and fluency in mathematics.

Count by 1 from 1 to 100

1	2	3	4	5	6	7	8	9	10
11	12	13	14	15	16	17	18	19	20
21	22	23	24	25	26	27	28	29	30
31	32	33	34	35	36	37	38	39	40
41	42	43	44	45	46	47	48	49	50
51	52	53	54	55	56	57	58	59	60
61	62	63	64	65	66	67	68	69	70
71	72	73	74	75	76	77	78	79	80
81	82	83	84	85	86	87	88	89	90
91	92	93	94	95	96	97	98	99	100

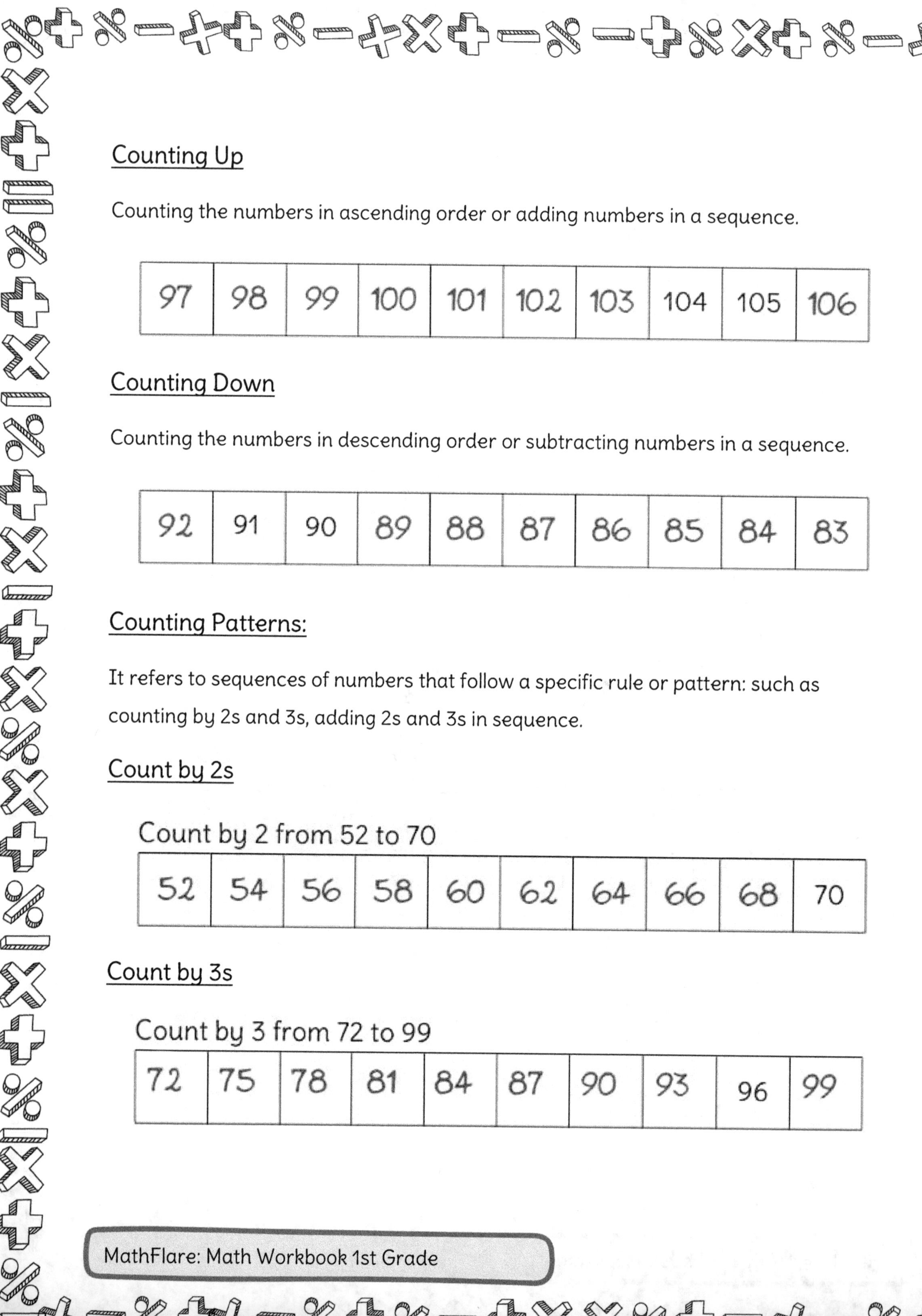

Counting Up

Counting the numbers in ascending order or adding numbers in a sequence.

97	98	99	100	101	102	103	104	105	106

Counting Down

Counting the numbers in descending order or subtracting numbers in a sequence.

92	91	90	89	88	87	86	85	84	83

Counting Patterns:

It refers to sequences of numbers that follow a specific rule or pattern: such as counting by 2s and 3s, adding 2s and 3s in sequence.

Count by 2s

Count by 2 from 52 to 70

52	54	56	58	60	62	64	66	68	70

Count by 3s

Count by 3 from 72 to 99

72	75	78	81	84	87	90	93	96	99

Skip Counting: Ascending

1) Count by 1 from 1 to 100

1								9	
	12							19	
					26		28		
						37			
		43				47			
52				56	57				
	63						68	69	
								79	
								89	
	92	93			96				100

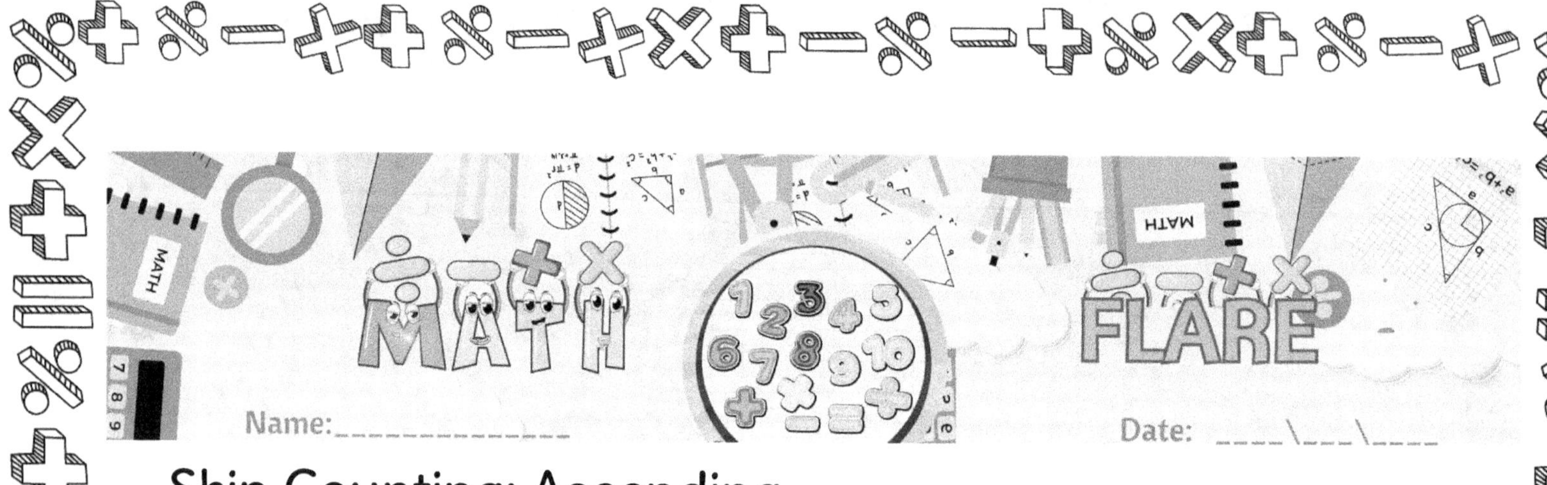

Skip Counting: Ascending

1) Count by 1 from 1 to 100

1								9	
			14			17			
		23							
				35					
				45					50
				55					
		64							
	92								100

2) Count by 1 from 1 to 100

								9	
1								9	
11			14			17	18		
			24						
		53							
				85					
	92							99	100

Skip Counting: Ascending

1) Count by 1 from 1 to 100

Count Up

Fill in the missing numbers by counting up.

1) | | | | | | | | 104 | 105 | |

2) | | 95 | 96 | | | | | | | |

3) | | | | | | | | 33 | 34 | |

4) | 18 | 19 | | | | | | | | |

5) | | | 33 | 34 | | | | | | |

6) | | | | | 80 | 81 | | | | |

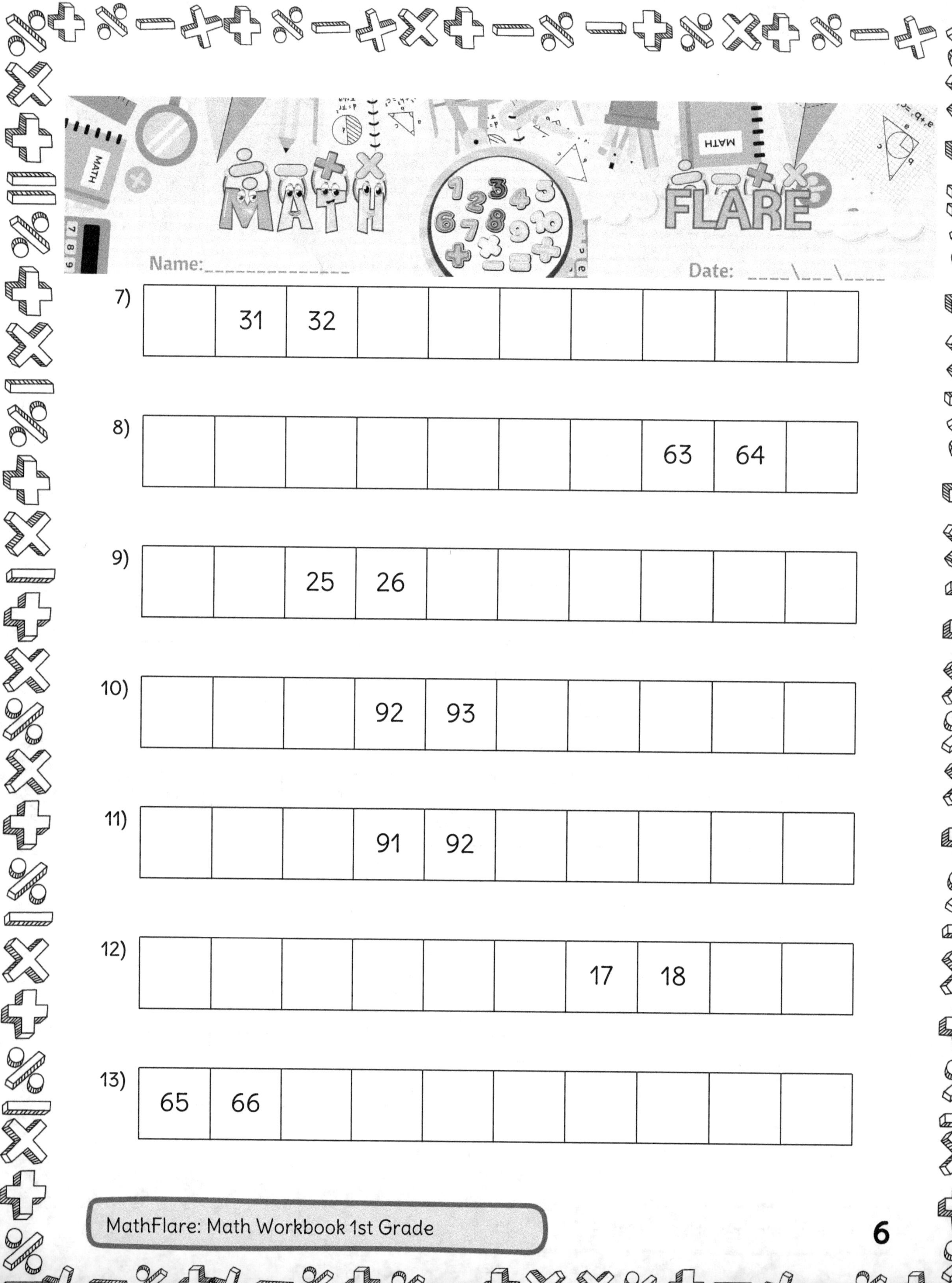

7)

| | 31 | 32 | | | | | | | |

8)

| | | | | | | | 63 | 64 | |

9)

| | | 25 | 26 | | | | | | |

10)

| | | | 92 | 93 | | | | | |

11)

| | | | 91 | 92 | | | | | |

12)

| | | | | | | 17 | 18 | | |

13)

| 65 | 66 | | | | | | | | |

14)

| | | | | | | | 69 | 70 | |

15)

| | | | | | 56 | 57 | | | |

16)

| | | | | 57 | 58 | | | | |

17)

| 94 | 95 | | | | | | | | |

18)

| 74 | 75 | | | | | | | | |

19)

| | | | | | | 14 | 15 | | |

20)

| | | | | 11 | 12 | | | | |

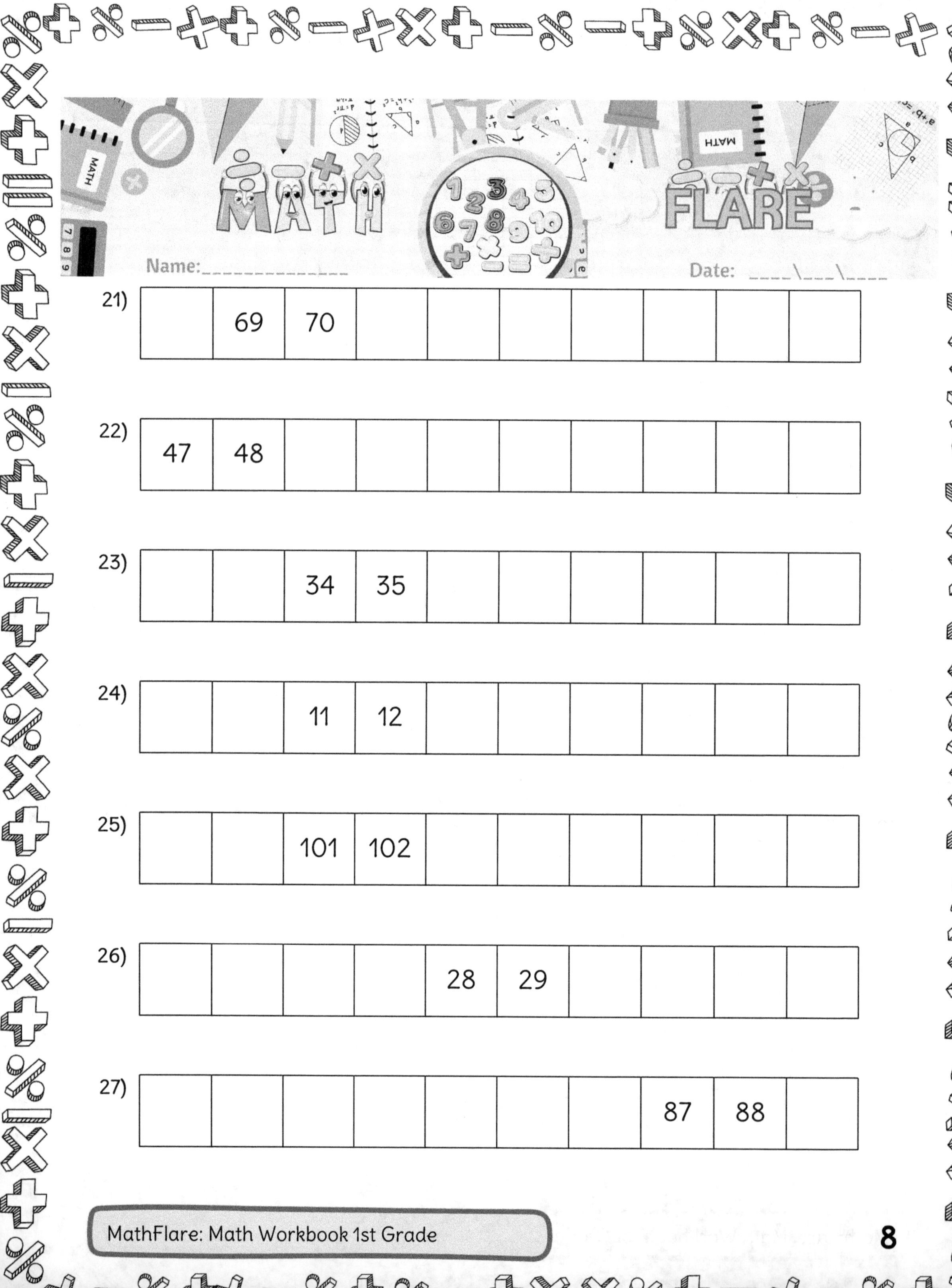

Name:___________________ Date: _______________

21) | | 69 | 70 | | | | | | |

22) | 47 | 48 | | | | | | | | |

23) | | | 34 | 35 | | | | | | |

24) | | | 11 | 12 | | | | | | |

25) | | | 101 | 102 | | | | | | |

26) | | | | | 28 | 29 | | | | |

27) | | | | | | | | 87 | 88 | |

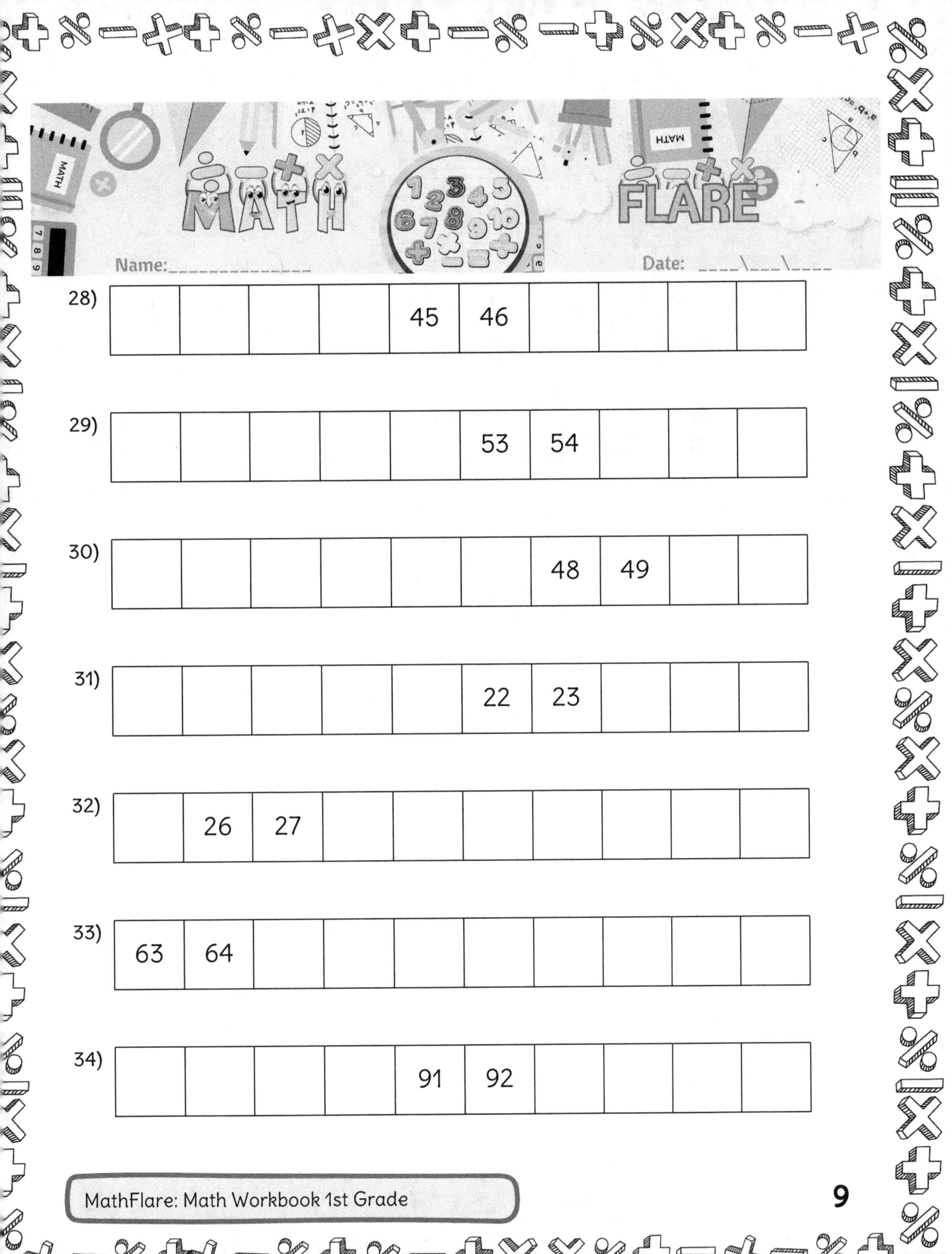

Name:________________   Date: _______________

28) | | | | | 45 | 46 | | | | |

29) | | | | | | 53 | 54 | | | |

30) | | | | | | 48 | 49 | | |

31) | | | | | | 22 | 23 | | |

32) | | 26 | 27 | | | | | | | |

33) | 63 | 64 | | | | | | | | |

34) | | | | | 91 | 92 | | | | |

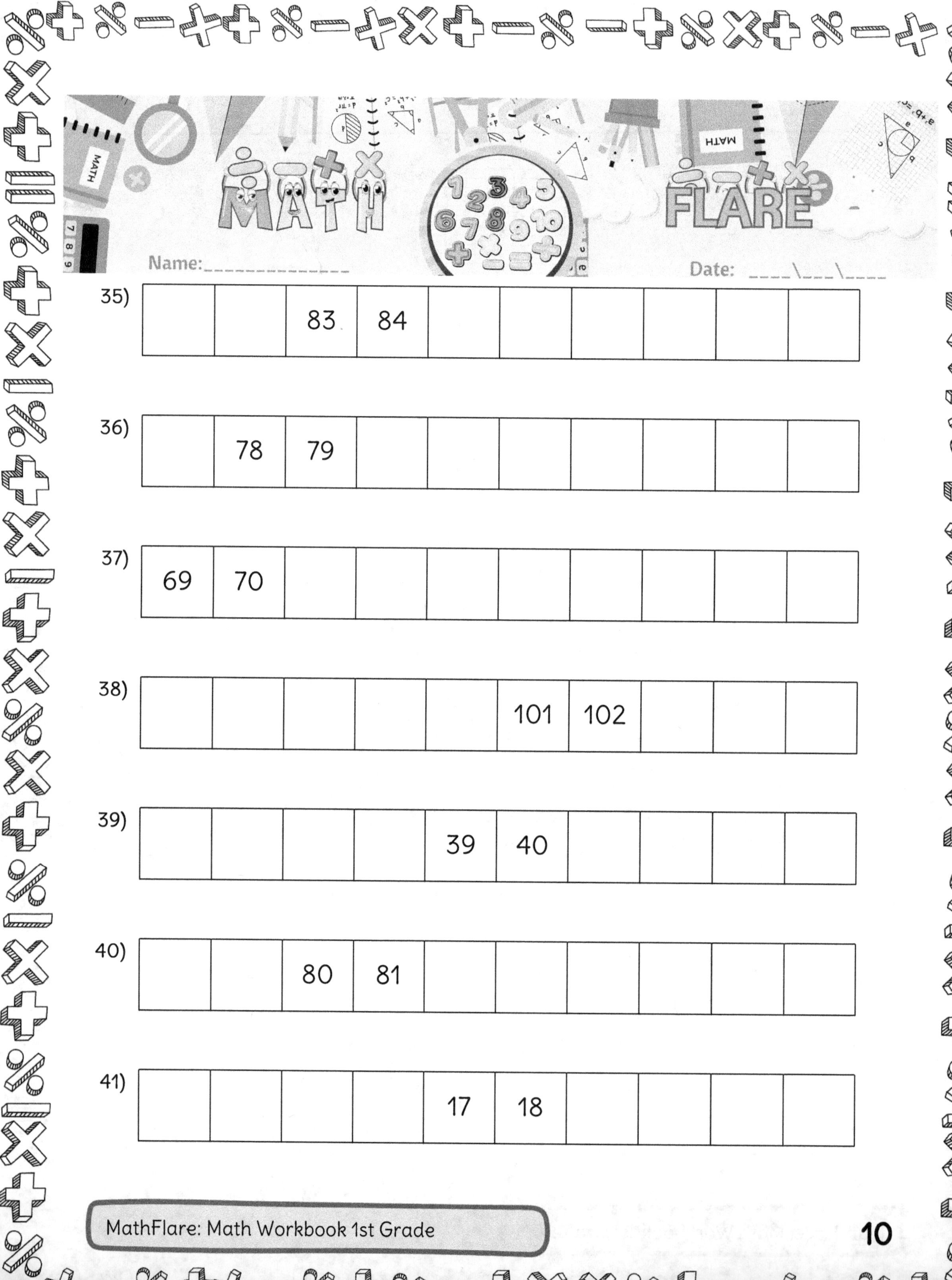

35)

		83	84					

36)

	78	79						

37)

69	70							

38)

					101	102		

39)

				39	40			

40)

		80	81					

41)

				17	18			

Name: ______________________   Date: ___ / ___ / ___

42) | | | | | | 34 | 35 | | |

43) | | | | | | | 101 | 102 | |

44) | | 12 | 13 | | | | | | |

45) | | | | | 58 | 59 | | |

46) | 51 | 52 | | | | | | | |

47) | | | | | | 21 | 22 | |

48) | 76 | 77 | | | | | | | |

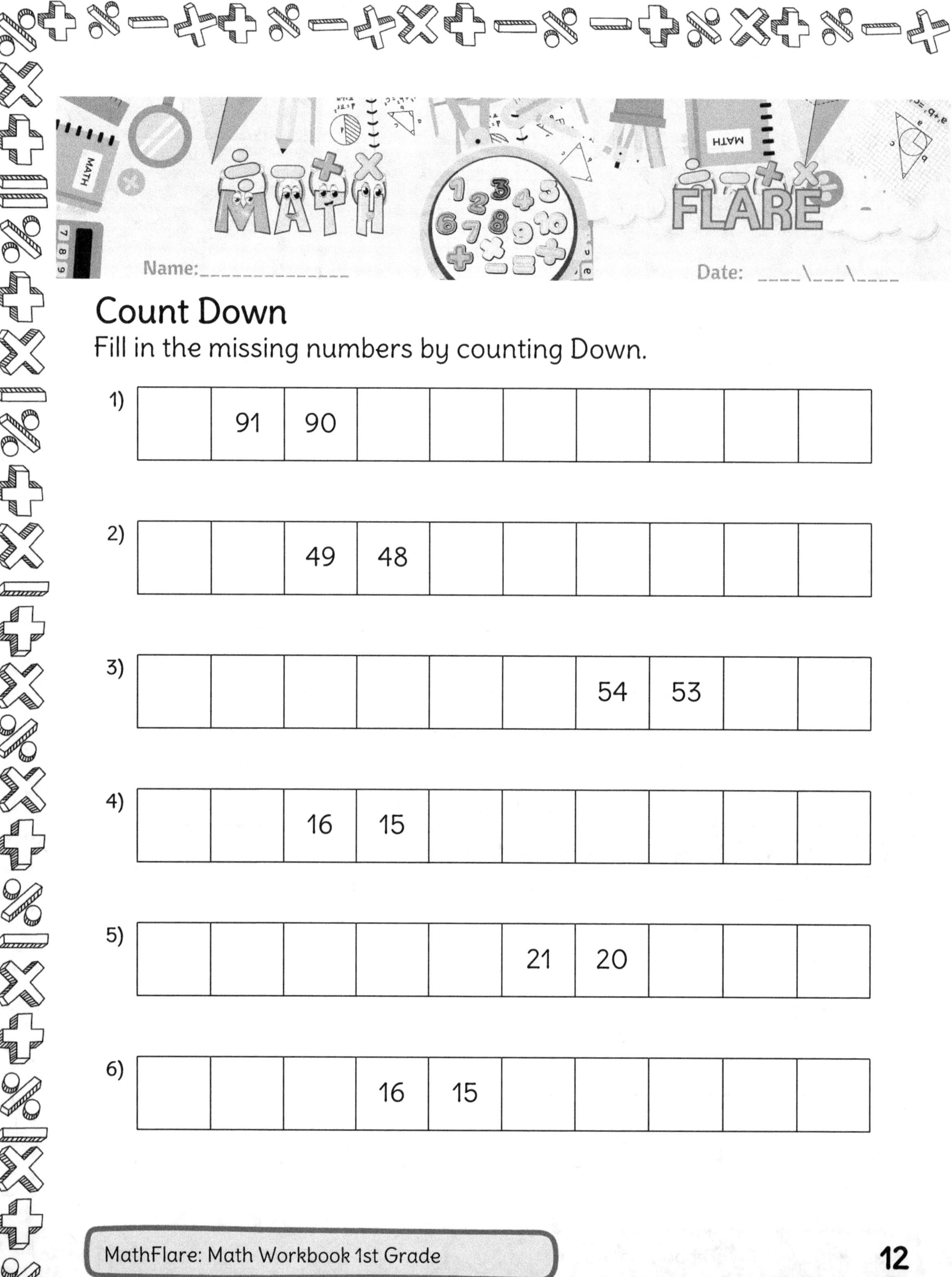

Count Down

Fill in the missing numbers by counting Down.

1) | | 91 | 90 | | | | | | |

2) | | | 49 | 48 | | | | | | |

3) | | | | | | 54 | 53 | | |

4) | | | 16 | 15 | | | | | | |

5) | | | | | | | 21 | 20 | | |

6) | | | | 16 | 15 | | | | | |

7)

| | | | | | | 26 | 25 | |

8)

| | | | | | | 83 | 82 | |

9)

| | | | | | | 8 | 7 | |

10)

| | | | | 29 | 28 | | | |

11)

| | | | | 32 | 31 | | | |

12)

| | | | | | 93 | 92 | | |

13)

| | | | 46 | 45 | | | | |

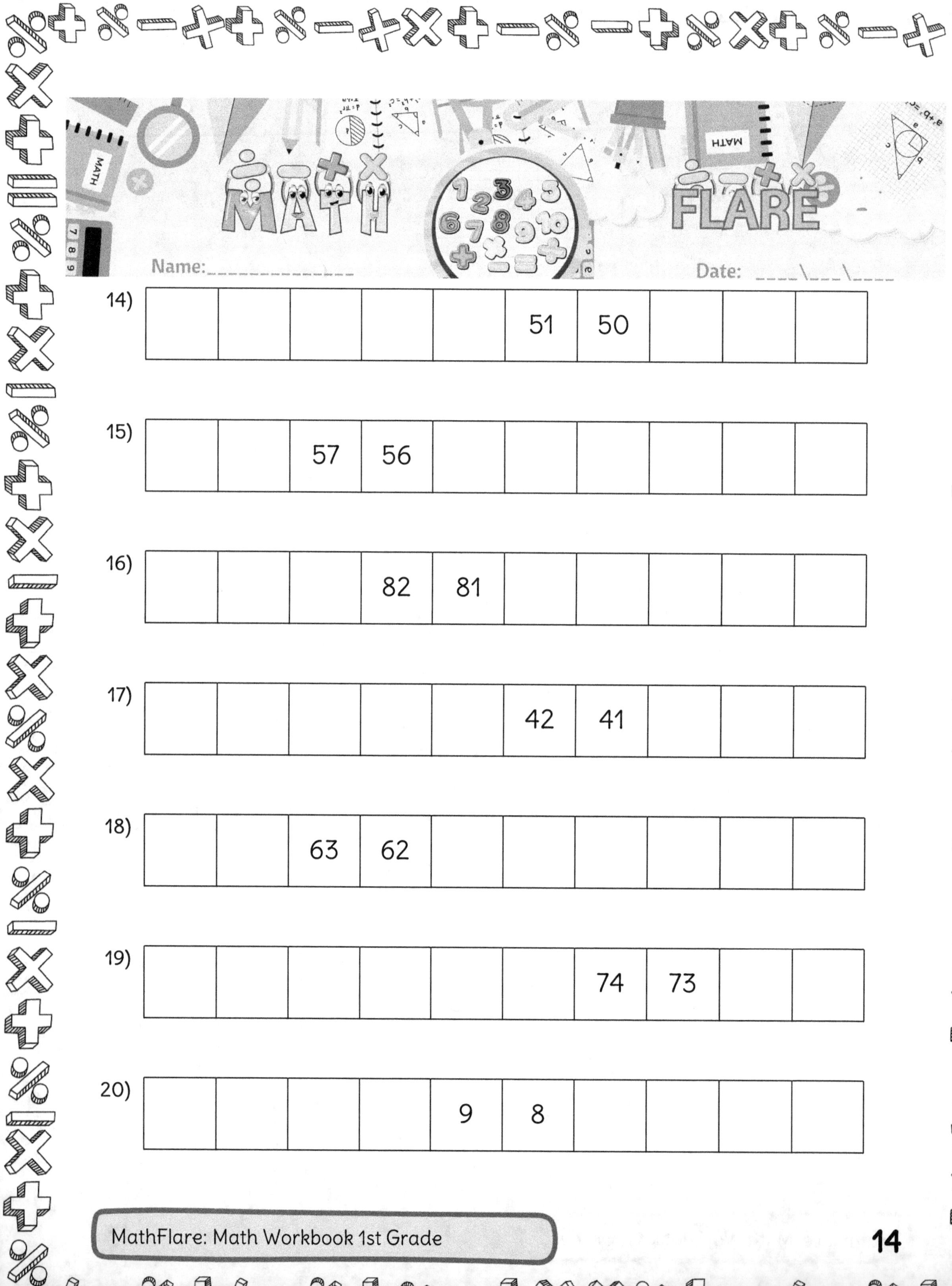

14)

					51	50			

15)

		57	56						

16)

			82	81					

17)

					42	41			

18)

		63	62						

19)

						74	73		

20)

				9	8				

Name: _______________________   Date: ___/___/___

21) | | | | | | 31 | 30 | | | |

22) | | | | 54 | 53 | | | | | |

23) | | | | | 84 | 83 | | | | |

24) | | | 43 | 42 | | | | | | |

25) | | | | 39 | 38 | | | | | |

26) | | | 52 | 51 | | | | | | |

27) | | | | | | | 79 | 78 | | |

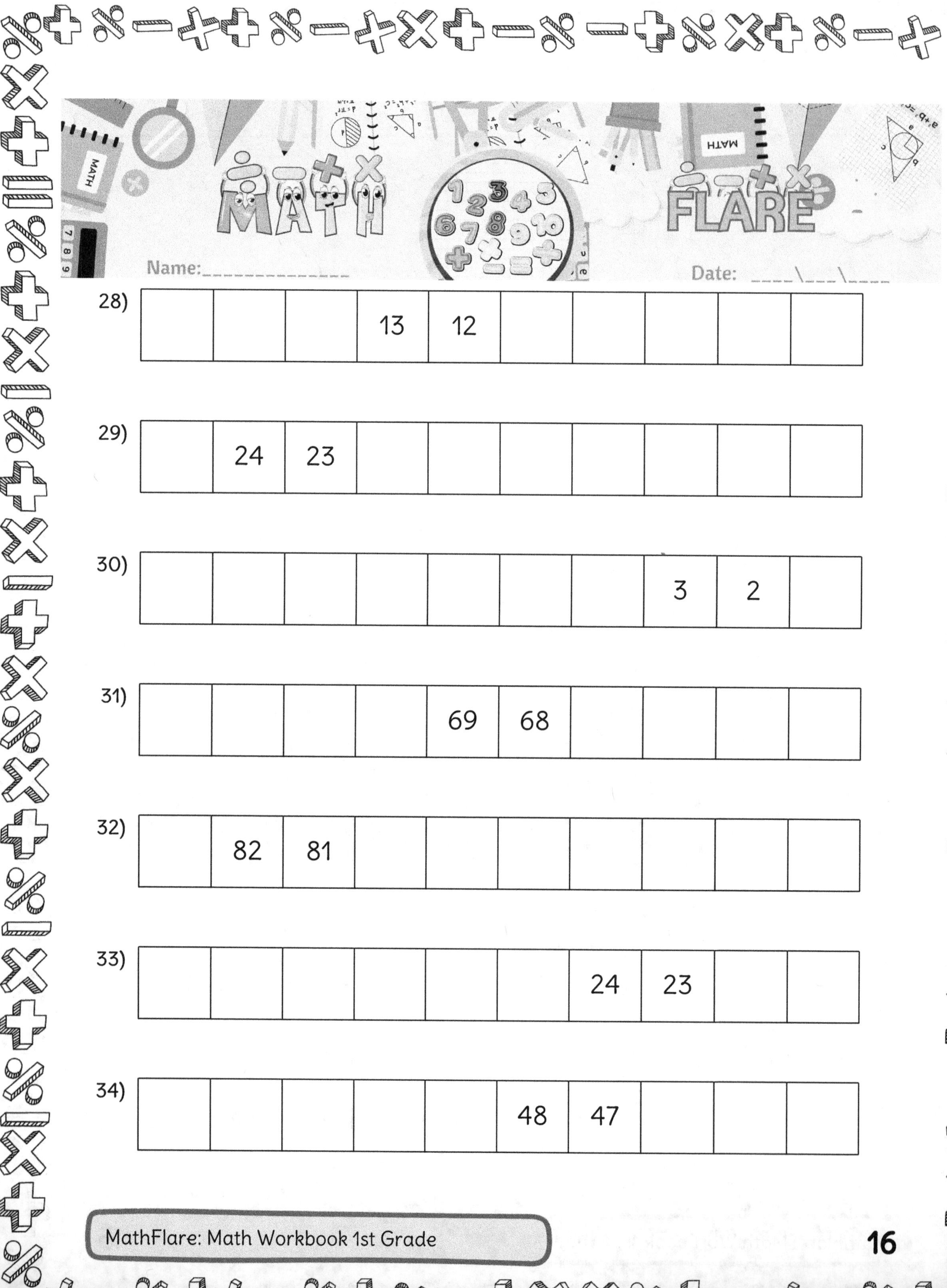

28) | | | | 13 | 12 | | | | |

29) | | 24 | 23 | | | | | | |

30) | | | | | | | | 3 | 2 |

31) | | | | 69 | 68 | | | | |

32) | 82 | 81 | | | | | | | |

33) | | | | | | | 24 | 23 | |

34) | | | | | | 48 | 47 | | |

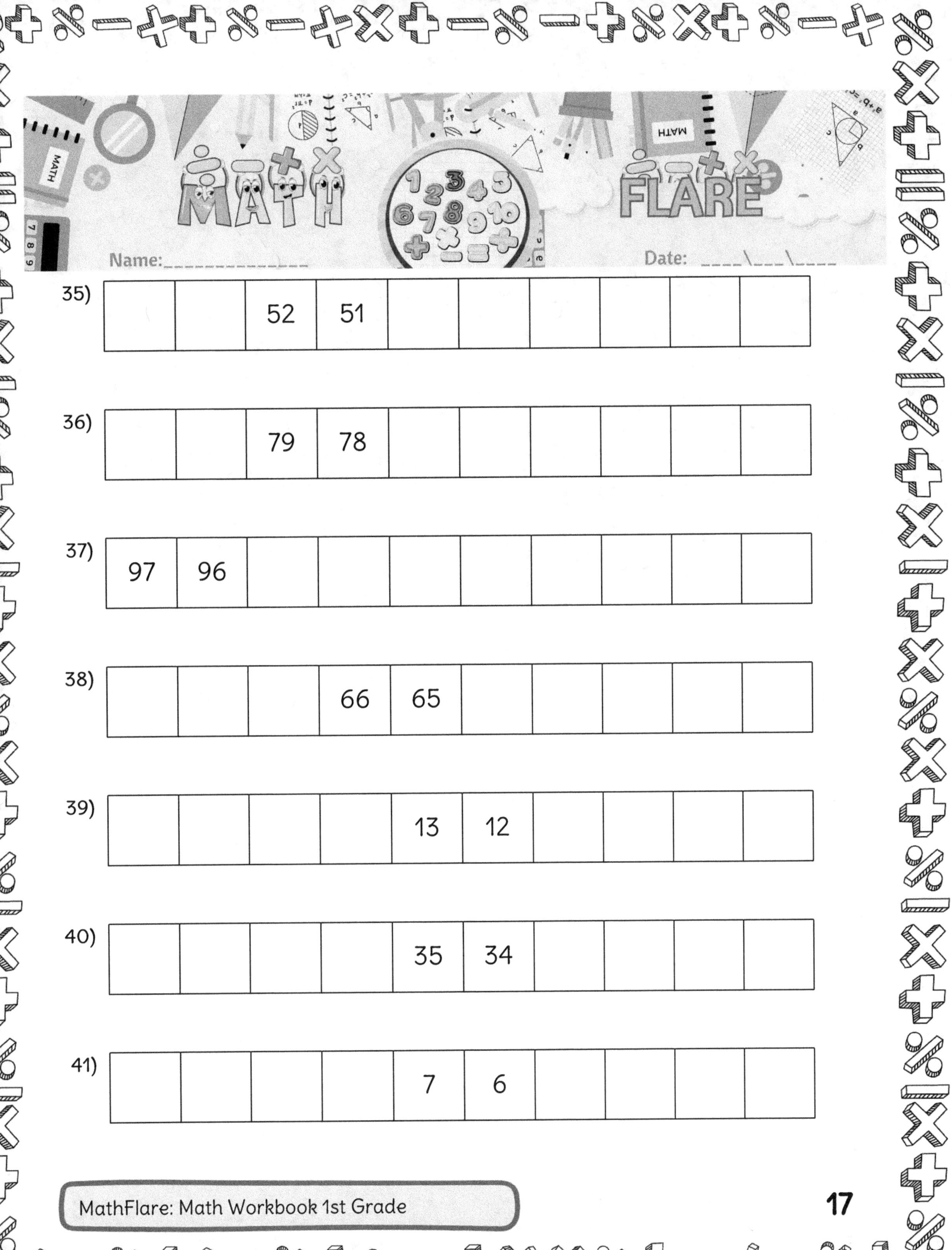

Name:________________   Date:____________

35)

		52	51						

36)

		79	78						

37)

97	96								

38)

			66	65					

39)

				13	12				

40)

				35	34				

41)

				7	6				

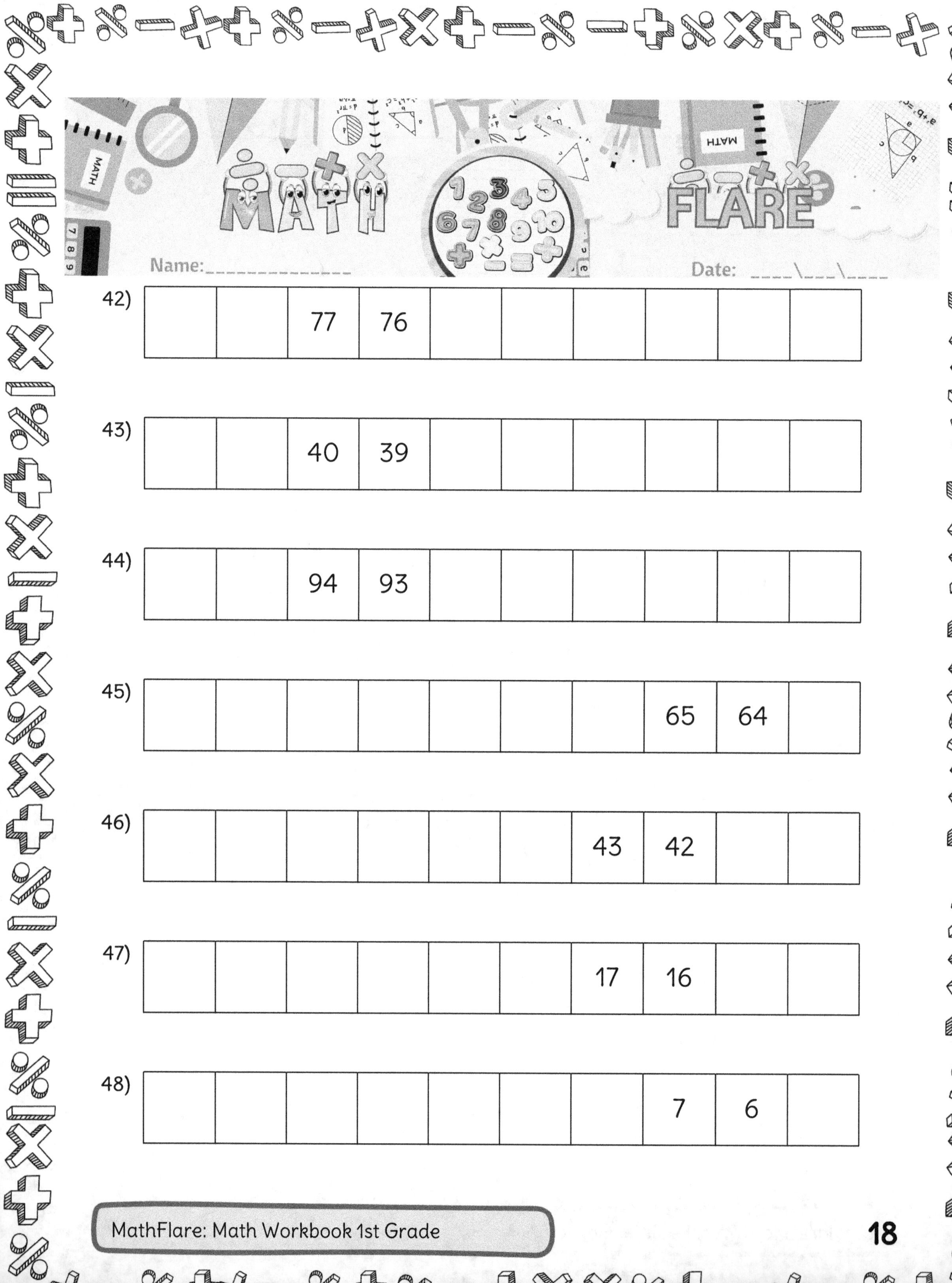

42)

		77	76						

43)

		40	39						

44)

		94	93						

45)

							65	64	

46)

						43	42		

47)

						17	16		

48)

							7	6	

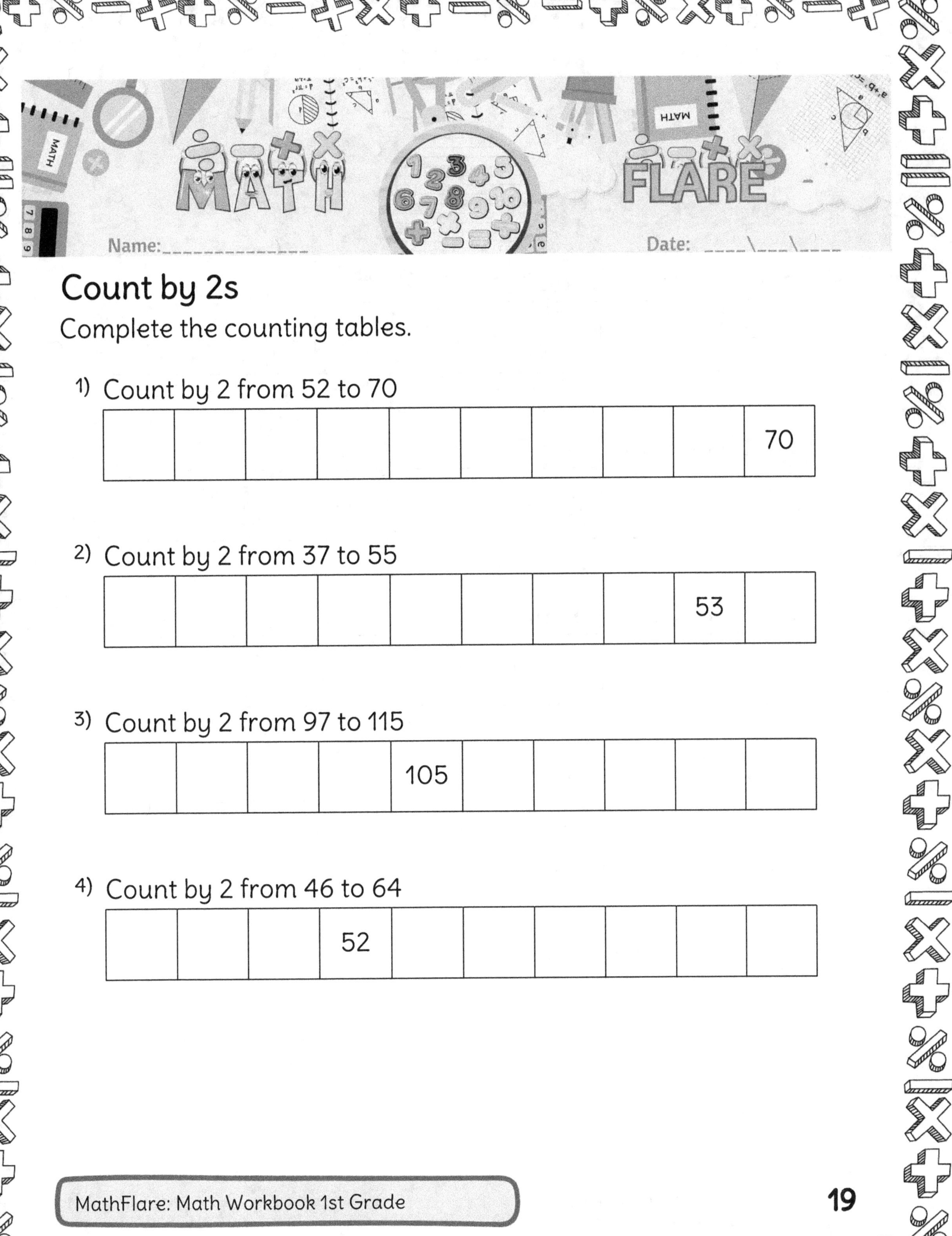

Count by 2s

Complete the counting tables.

1) Count by 2 from 52 to 70

									70

2) Count by 2 from 37 to 55

								53	

3) Count by 2 from 97 to 115

			105						

4) Count by 2 from 46 to 64

		52							

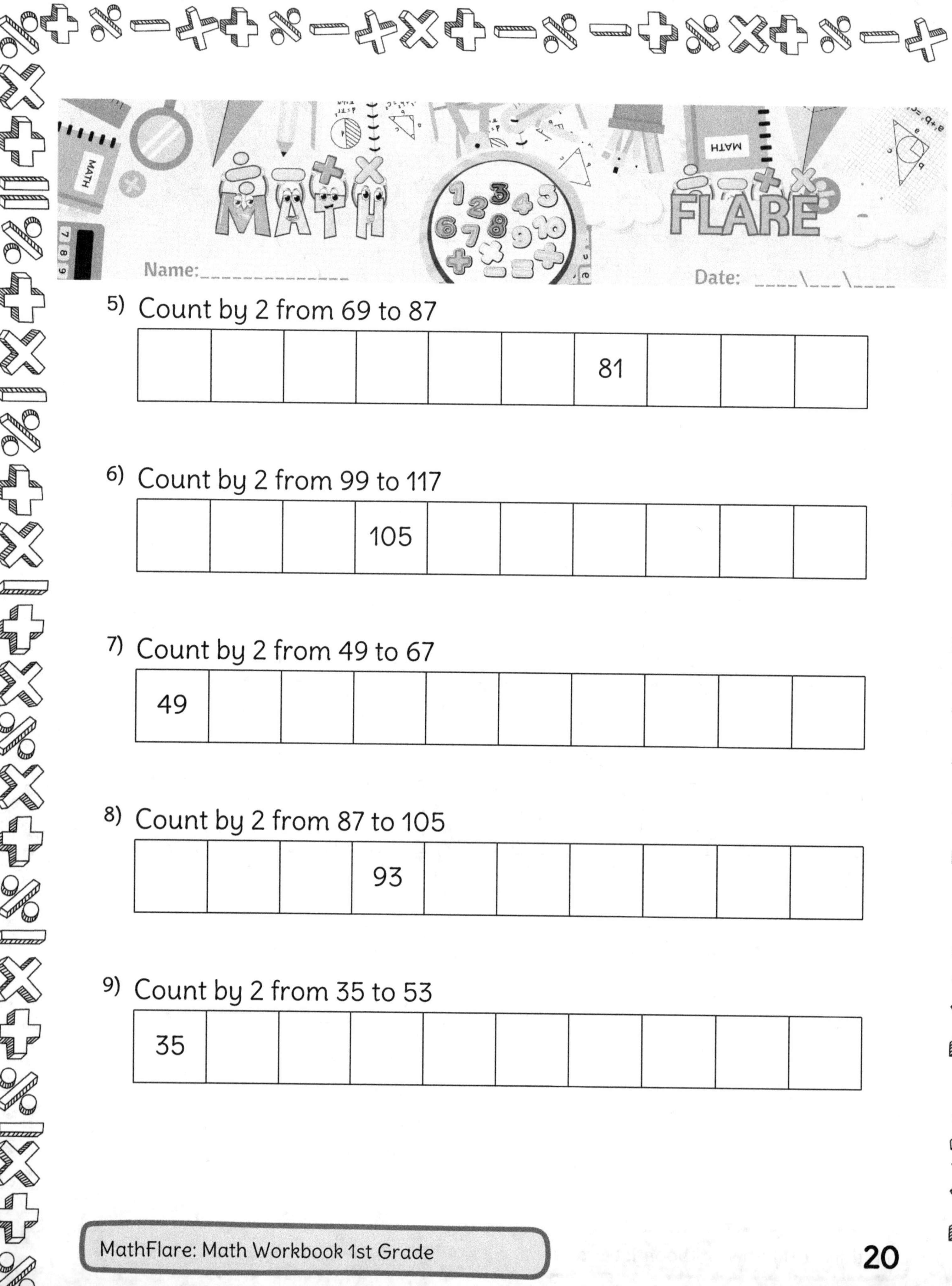

5) Count by 2 from 69 to 87

					81			

6) Count by 2 from 99 to 117

		105						

7) Count by 2 from 49 to 67

49								

8) Count by 2 from 87 to 105

		93						

9) Count by 2 from 35 to 53

35								

10) Count by 2 from 21 to 39

| | | | 27 | | | | | | |

11) Count by 2 from 80 to 98

| | | | | | | 92 | | | |

12) Count by 2 from 14 to 32

| | | 20 | | | | | | | |

13) Count by 2 from 50 to 68

| 50 | | | | | | | | | |

14) Count by 2 from 48 to 66

| | | | | 58 | | | | | |

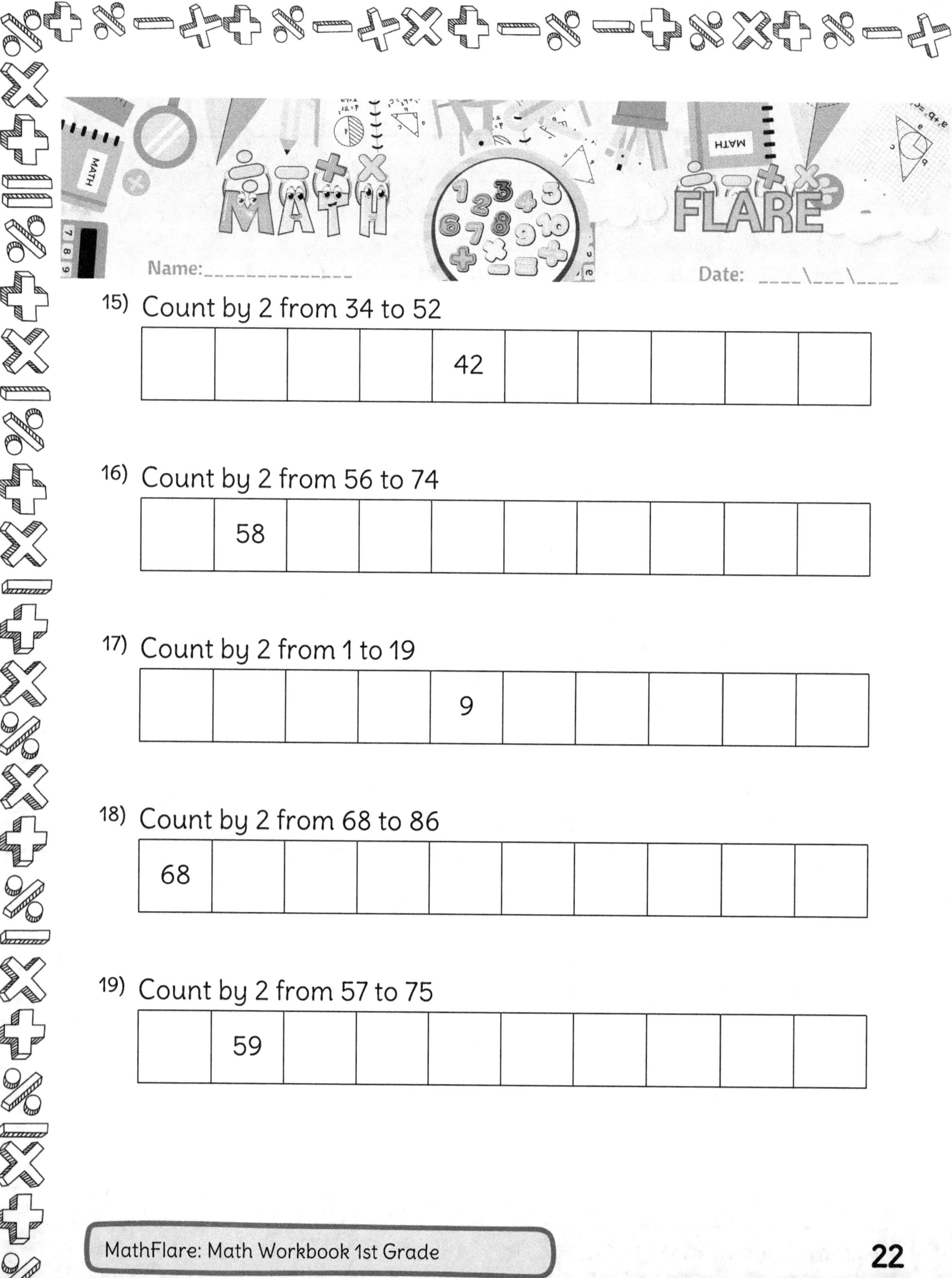

15) Count by 2 from 34 to 52

				42					

16) Count by 2 from 56 to 74

	58								

17) Count by 2 from 1 to 19

				9					

18) Count by 2 from 68 to 86

68									

19) Count by 2 from 57 to 75

	59								

20) Count by 2 from 86 to 104

						98			

21) Count by 2 from 60 to 78

					70				

22) Count by 2 from 26 to 44

									44

23) Count by 2 from 24 to 42

		28							

24) Count by 2 from 43 to 61

43									

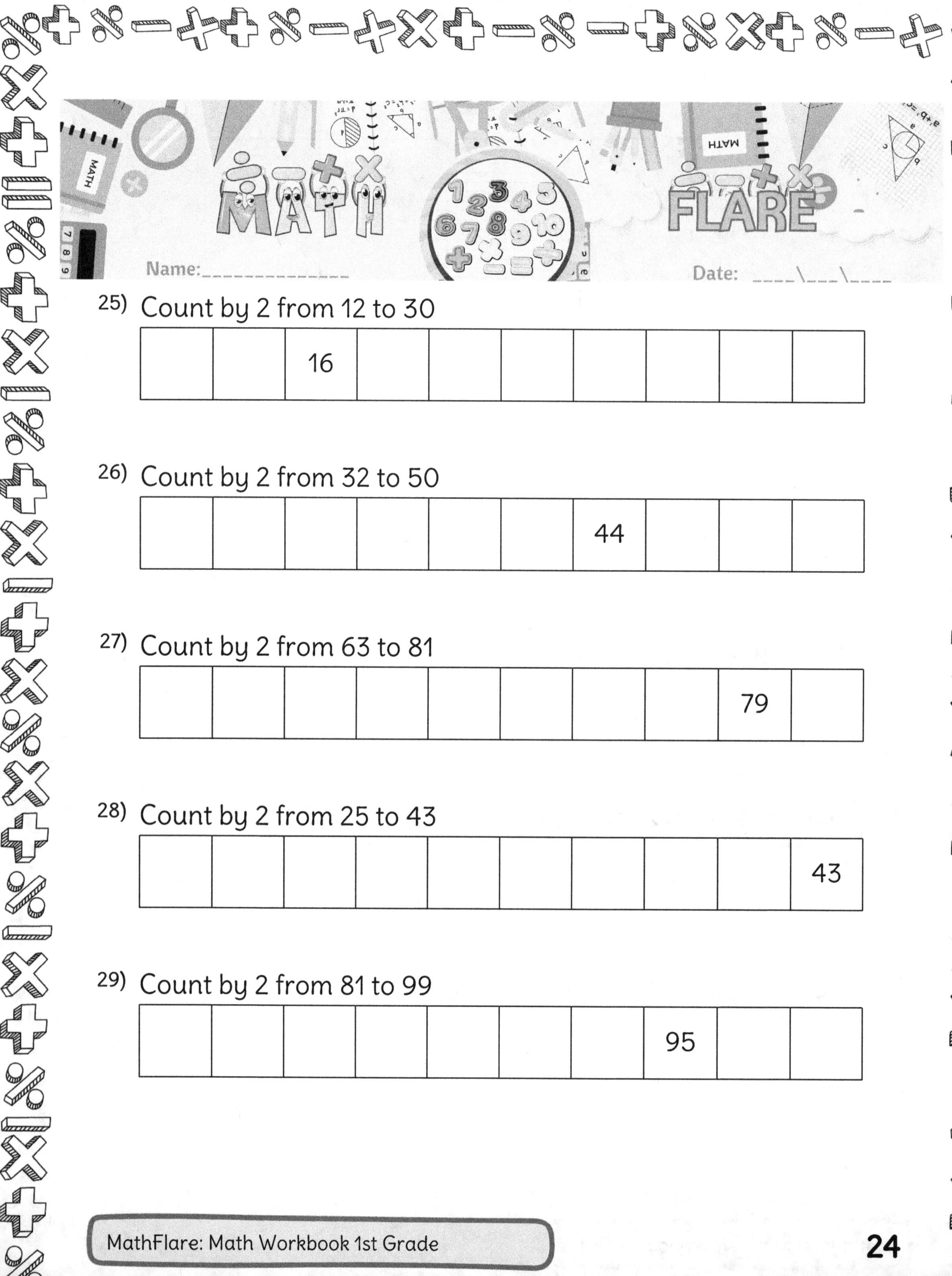

25) Count by 2 from 12 to 30

| | | 16 | | | | | | | |

26) Count by 2 from 32 to 50

| | | | | | | 44 | | | |

27) Count by 2 from 63 to 81

| | | | | | | | | 79 | |

28) Count by 2 from 25 to 43

| | | | | | | | | | 43 |

29) Count by 2 from 81 to 99

| | | | | | | 95 | | |

30) Count by 2 from 66 to 84

							80		

31) Count by 2 from 83 to 101

			89						

32) Count by 2 from 100 to 118

100									

33) Count by 2 from 94 to 112

94									

34) Count by 2 from 27 to 45

					37				

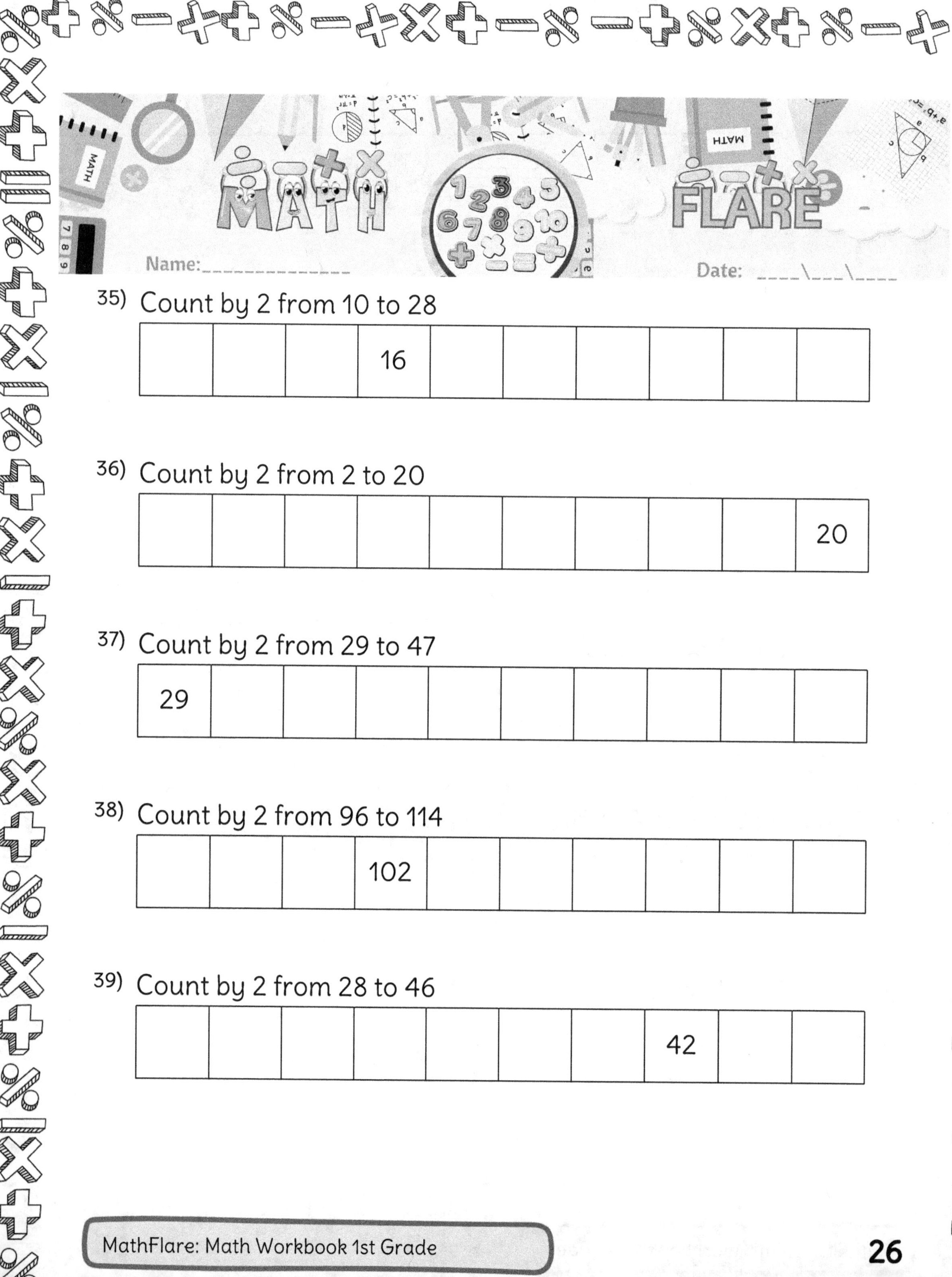

Name:_________________   Date: ____________

35) Count by 2 from 10 to 28

| | | | 16 | | | | | | |

36) Count by 2 from 2 to 20

| | | | | | | | | | 20 |

37) Count by 2 from 29 to 47

| 29 | | | | | | | | | |

38) Count by 2 from 96 to 114

| | | | 102 | | | | | | |

39) Count by 2 from 28 to 46

| | | | | | | 42 | | |

40) Count by 2 from 33 to 51

								49	

41) Count by 2 from 98 to 116

	100								

42) Count by 2 from 8 to 26

	10								

43) Count by 2 from 91 to 109

		97							

44) Count by 2 from 9 to 27

			15						

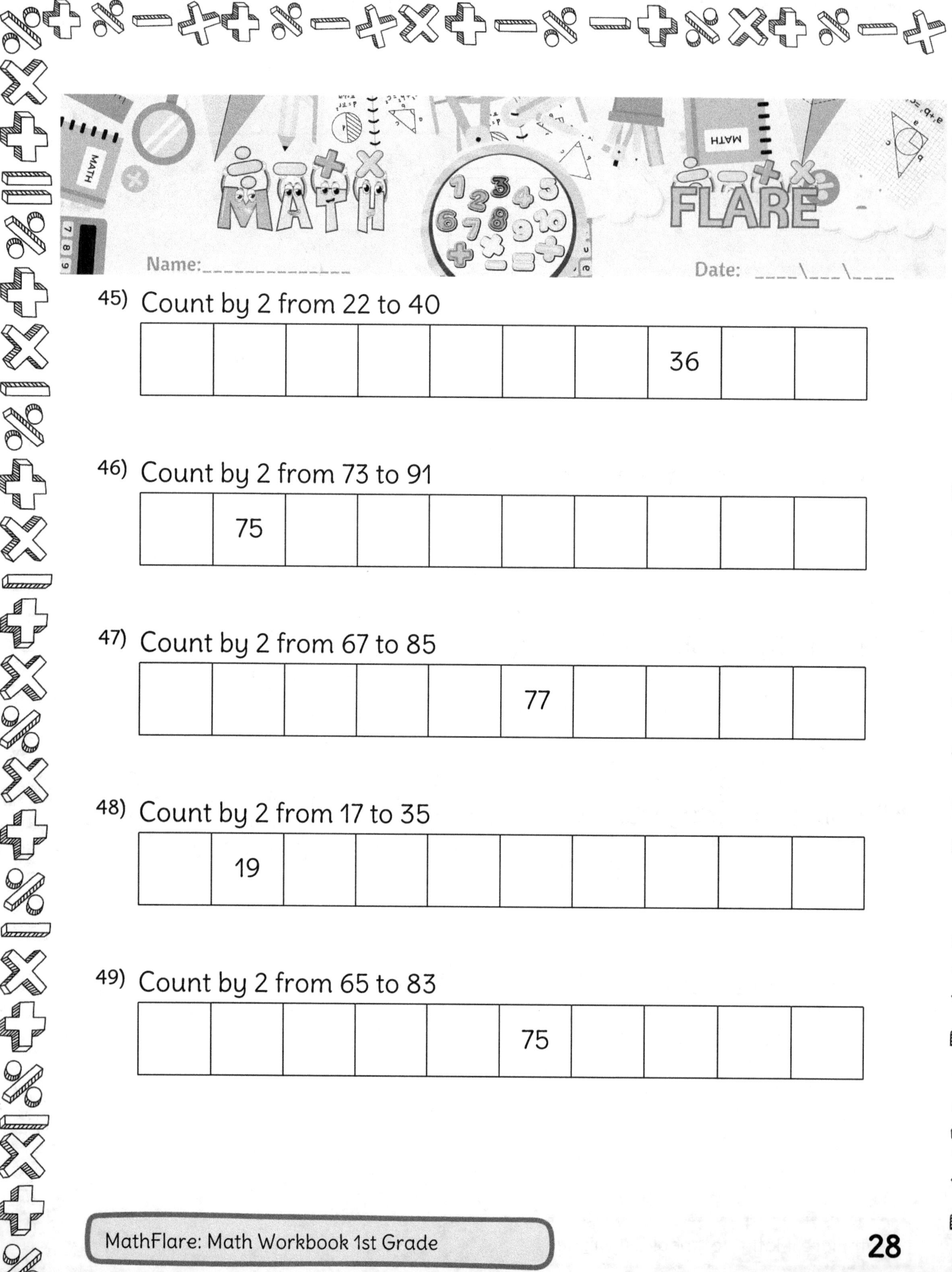

45) Count by 2 from 22 to 40

							36		

46) Count by 2 from 73 to 91

	75								

47) Count by 2 from 67 to 85

					77				

48) Count by 2 from 17 to 35

	19								

49) Count by 2 from 65 to 83

					75				

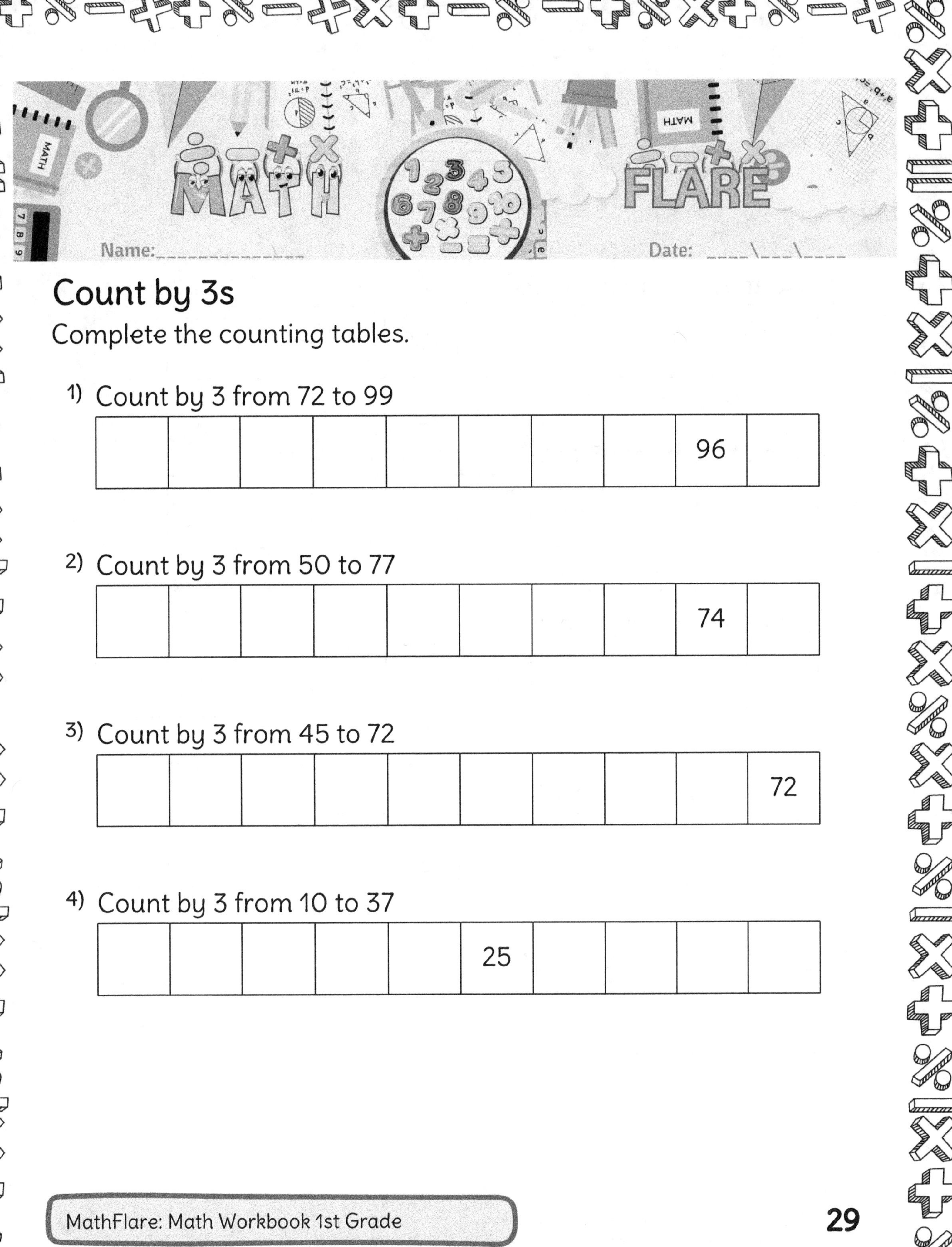

Count by 3s

Complete the counting tables.

1) Count by 3 from 72 to 99

								96	

2) Count by 3 from 50 to 77

								74	

3) Count by 3 from 45 to 72

									72

4) Count by 3 from 10 to 37

				25				

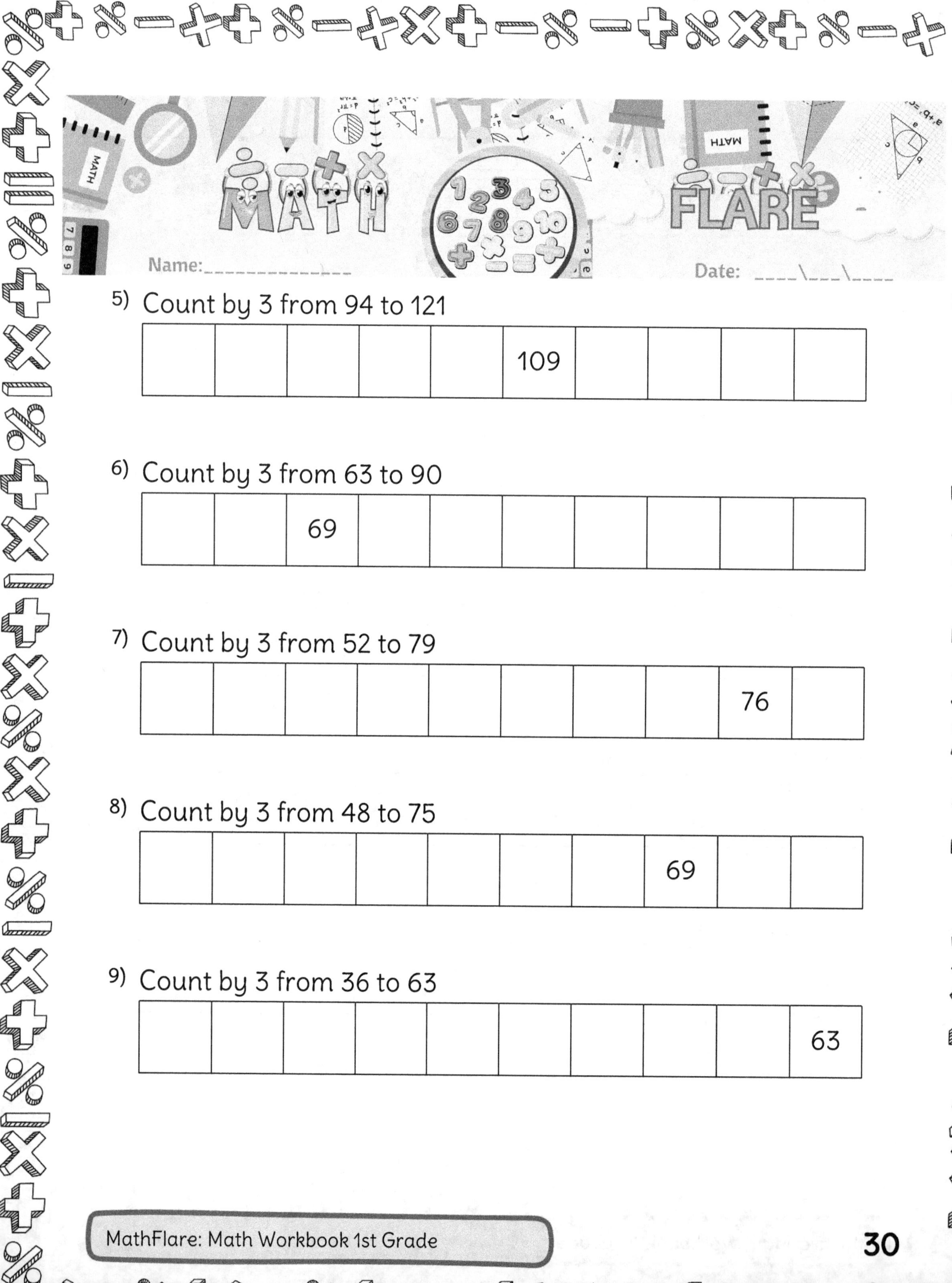

5) Count by 3 from 94 to 121

				109				

6) Count by 3 from 63 to 90

		69						

7) Count by 3 from 52 to 79

							76	

8) Count by 3 from 48 to 75

						69		

9) Count by 3 from 36 to 63

								63

10) Count by 3 from 28 to 55

					43				

11) Count by 3 from 83 to 110

			92						

12) Count by 3 from 90 to 117

							111		

13) Count by 3 from 73 to 100

								97	

14) Count by 3 from 30 to 57

							51		

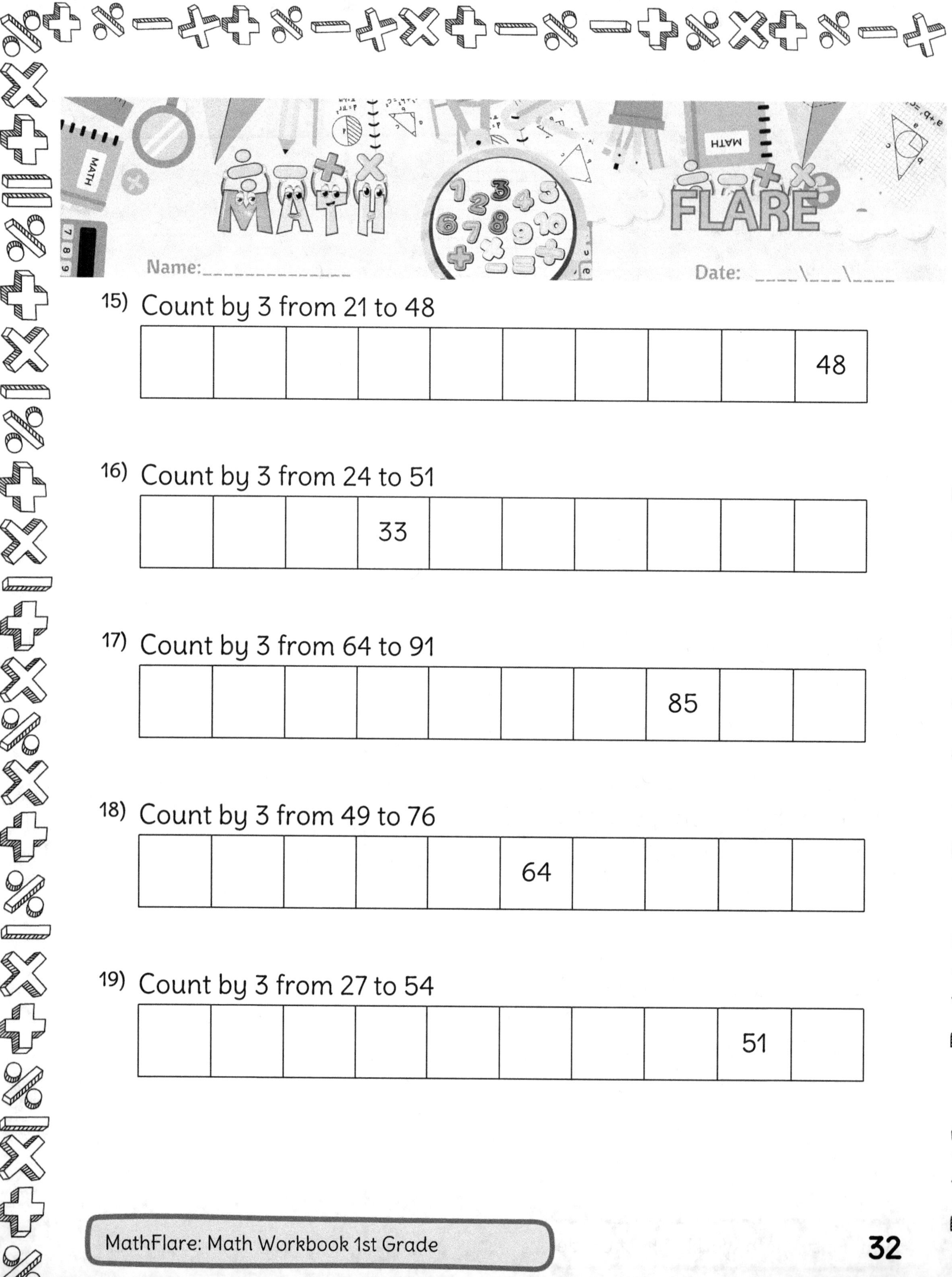

Name:______________________   Date: ____________

15) Count by 3 from 21 to 48

									48

16) Count by 3 from 24 to 51

			33						

17) Count by 3 from 64 to 91

							85		

18) Count by 3 from 49 to 76

					64				

19) Count by 3 from 27 to 54

								51	

20) Count by 3 from 12 to 39

| | | | | 24 | | | | | |

21) Count by 3 from 25 to 52

| | | | | | | | | | 52 |

22) Count by 3 from 65 to 92

| | | 71 | | | | | | | |

23) Count by 3 from 47 to 74

| | | 53 | | | | | | | |

24) Count by 3 from 37 to 64

| | | | | | | | 58 | | |

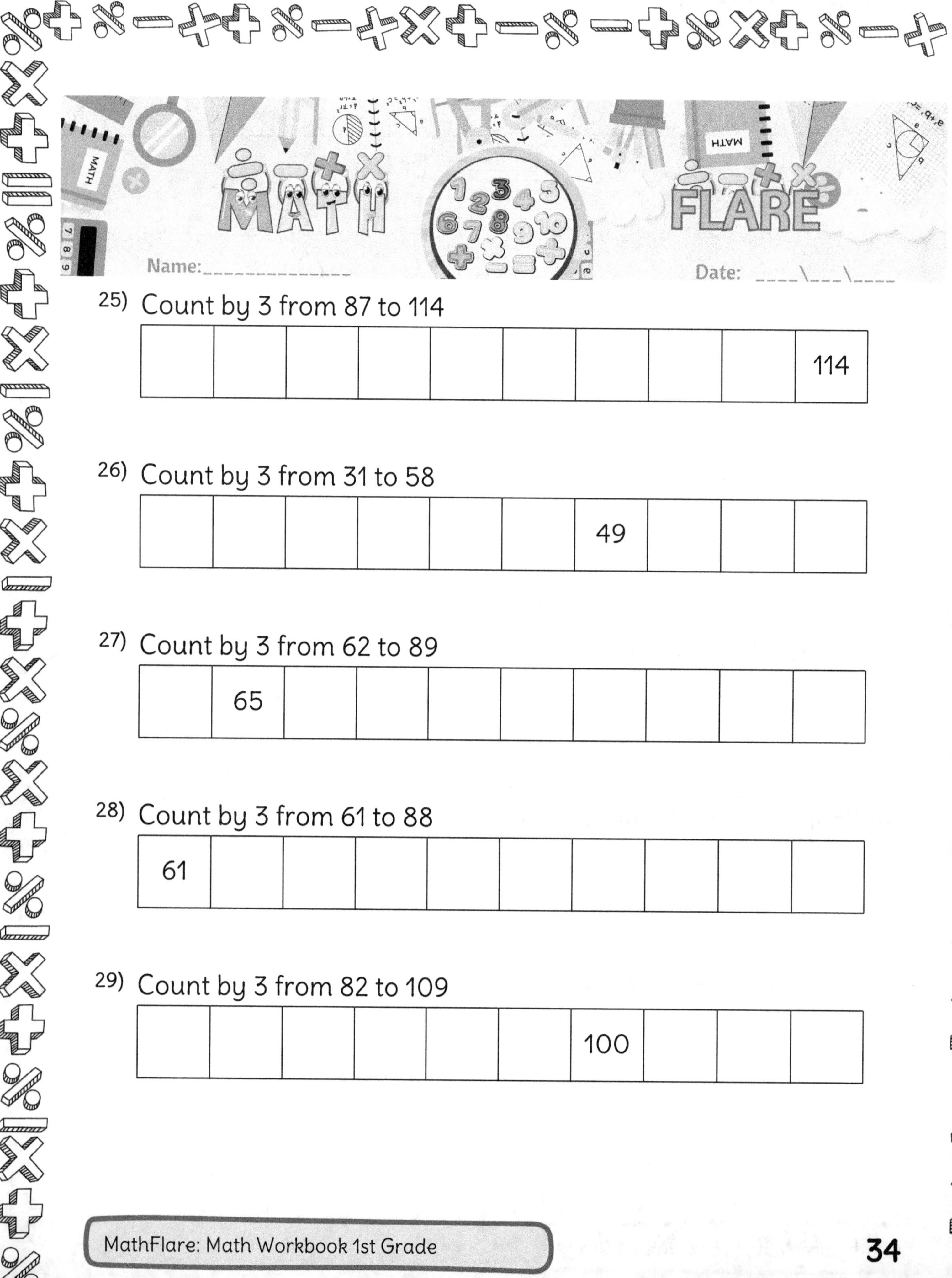

25) Count by 3 from 87 to 114

| | | | | | | | | | 114 |

26) Count by 3 from 31 to 58

| | | | | | | 49 | | | |

27) Count by 3 from 62 to 89

| | 65 | | | | | | | | |

28) Count by 3 from 61 to 88

| 61 | | | | | | | | | |

29) Count by 3 from 82 to 109

| | | | | | | 100 | | | |

30) Count by 3 from 15 to 42

15									

31) Count by 3 from 88 to 115

				103					

32) Count by 3 from 57 to 84

				72					

33) Count by 3 from 96 to 123

					114				

34) Count by 3 from 53 to 80

							77		

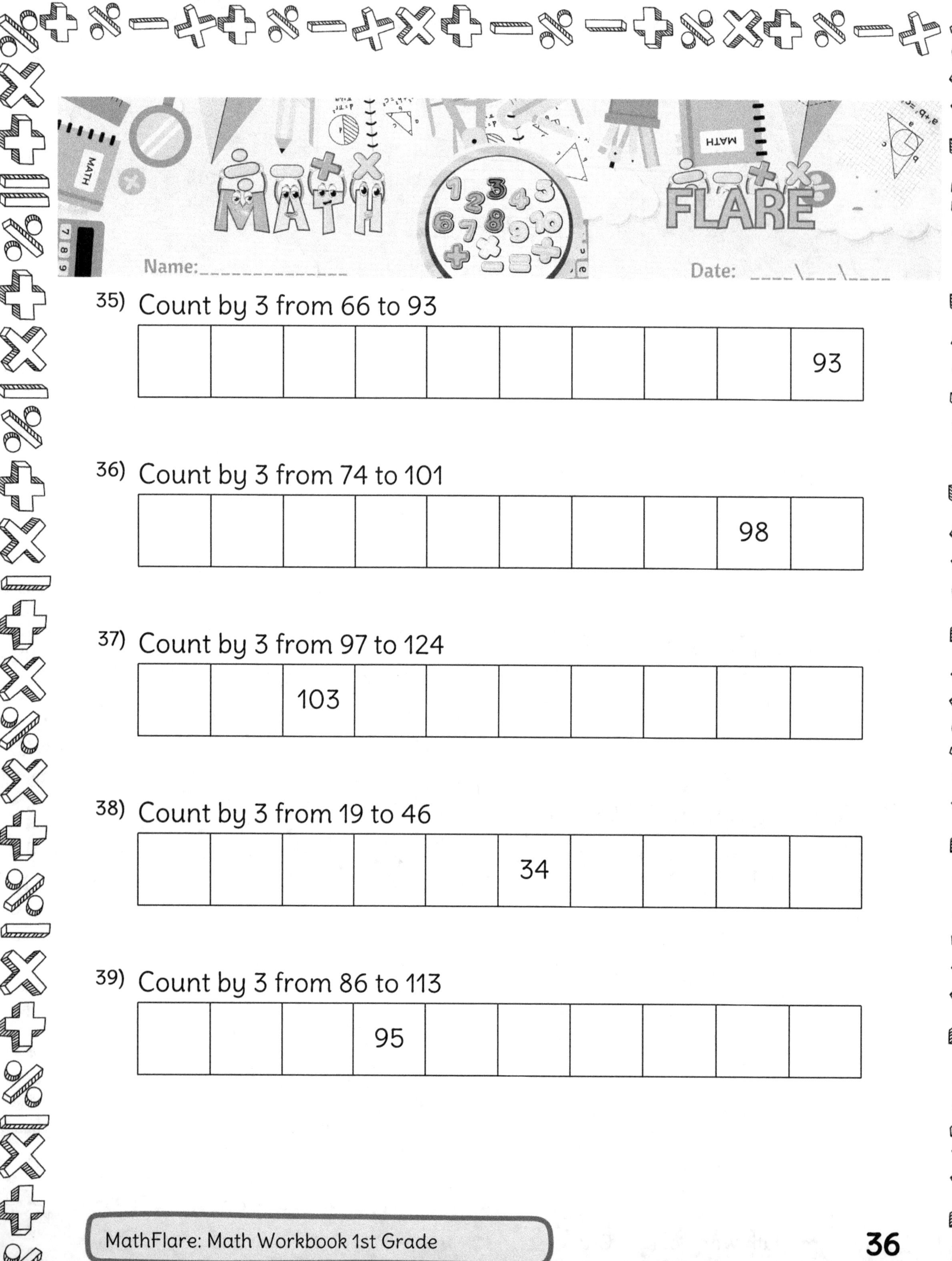

35) Count by 3 from 66 to 93

									93

36) Count by 3 from 74 to 101

								98	

37) Count by 3 from 97 to 124

		103							

38) Count by 3 from 19 to 46

					34				

39) Count by 3 from 86 to 113

			95						

40) Count by 3 from 26 to 53

			35						

41) Count by 3 from 22 to 49

			31						

42) Count by 3 from 89 to 116

				101					

43) Count by 3 from 93 to 120

	96								

44) Count by 3 from 32 to 59

32									

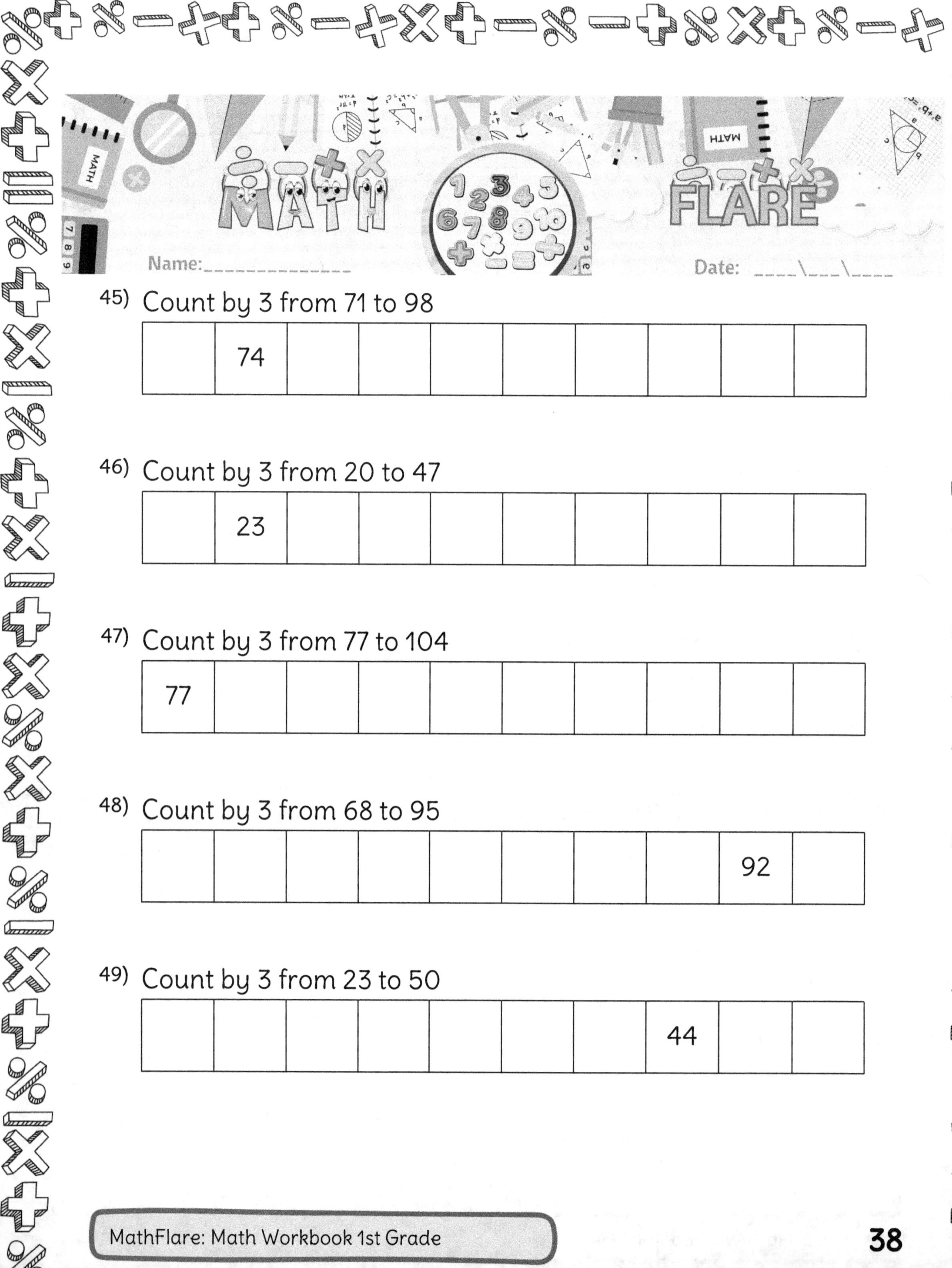

45) Count by 3 from 71 to 98

	74							

46) Count by 3 from 20 to 47

	23							

47) Count by 3 from 77 to 104

77								

48) Count by 3 from 68 to 95

							92	

49) Count by 3 from 23 to 50

						44		

Compare the Numbers

Add: > or < or = to make the following statements true.

1) 55 ___ 57

2) 43 ___ 100

3) 95 ___ 14

4) 22 ___ 27

5) 46 ___ 71

6) 52 ___ 7

7) 65 ___ 98

8) 67 ___ 11

9) 7 ___ 52

10) 31 ___ 4

11) 33 ___ 54

12) 87 ___ 33

13) 1 ___ 2

14) 21 ___ 60

Name:_______________   Date: _______________

15) 96 ____ 16

16) 60 ____ 91

17) 85 ____ 34

18) 19 ____ 33

19) 68 ____ 30

20) 41 ____ 80

21) 71 ____ 27

22) 37 ____ 38

23) 41 ____ 69

24) 39 ____ 80

25) 78 ____ 67

26) 64 ____ 48

27) 65 ____ 53

28) 100 ____ 2

29) 71 ____ 10

30) 99 ____ 94

Name:______________   Date: ____________

31) 93 ____ 62

32) 32 ____ 31

33) 11 ____ 61

34) 22 ____ 32

35) 80 ____ 35

36) 44 ____ 78

37) 12 ____ 52

38) 33 ____ 7

39) 17 ____ 49

40) 93 ____ 33

41) 63 ____ 42

42) 83 ____ 30

43) 52 ____ 12

44) 26 ____ 33

45) 34 ____ 18

46) 62 ____ 58

Name: _______________________ Date: _____ _____ _____

47) 31 ____ 47

48) 87 ____ 10

49) 95 ____ 7

50) 27 ____ 80

51) 47 ____ 8

52) 100 ____ 44

53) 23 ____ 87

54) 37 ____ 14

55) 20 ____ 94

56) 85 ____ 22

57) 18 ____ 67

58) 31 ____ 52

59) 80 ____ 2

60) 79 ____ 100

61) 36 ____ 90

62) 98 ____ 62

63) 73 ___ 86

64) 47 ___ 66

65) 65 ___ 24

66) 12 ___ 11

67) 22 ___ 13

68) 86 ___ 56

69) 42 ___ 40

70) 7 ___ 65

71) 76 ___ 13

72) 13 ___ 41

73) 34 ___ 40

74) 40 ___ 65

75) 16 ___ 36

76) 30 ___ 94

77) 28 ___ 28

78) 45 ___ 58

79) 10 ____ 39

80) 71 ____ 37

81) 41 ____ 72

82) 49 ____ 96

83) 82 ____ 75

84) 1 ____ 5

85) 81 ____ 75

86) 10 ____ 41

87) 95 ____ 15

88) 24 ____ 24

89) 77 ____ 58

90) 29 ____ 33

91) 47 ____ 83

92) 50 ____ 30

93) 94 ____ 19

94) 83 ____ 94

Name: _______________ Date: ____________

95) 69 ____ 29

96) 47 ____ 4

97) 69 ____ 70

98) 25 ____ 5

99) 64 ____ 18

100) 60 ____ 59

101) 40 ____ 36

102) 85 ____ 41

103) 27 ____ 90

104) 99 ____ 14

105) 5 ____ 22

106) 82 ____ 53

107) 11 ____ 39

108) 91 ____ 58

109) 23 ____ 20

110) 3 ____ 64

Name:________________   Date: ____________

111) 93 ___ 7

112) 37 ___ 52

113) 29 ___ 6

114) 72 ___ 26

115) 90 ___ 19

116) 60 ___ 60

117) 99 ___ 70

118) 93 ___ 12

119) 98 ___ 9

120) 4 ___ 5

121) 20 ___ 69

122) 90 ___ 48

123) 47 ___ 95

124) 94 ___ 30

125) 79 ___ 67

126) 83 ___ 45

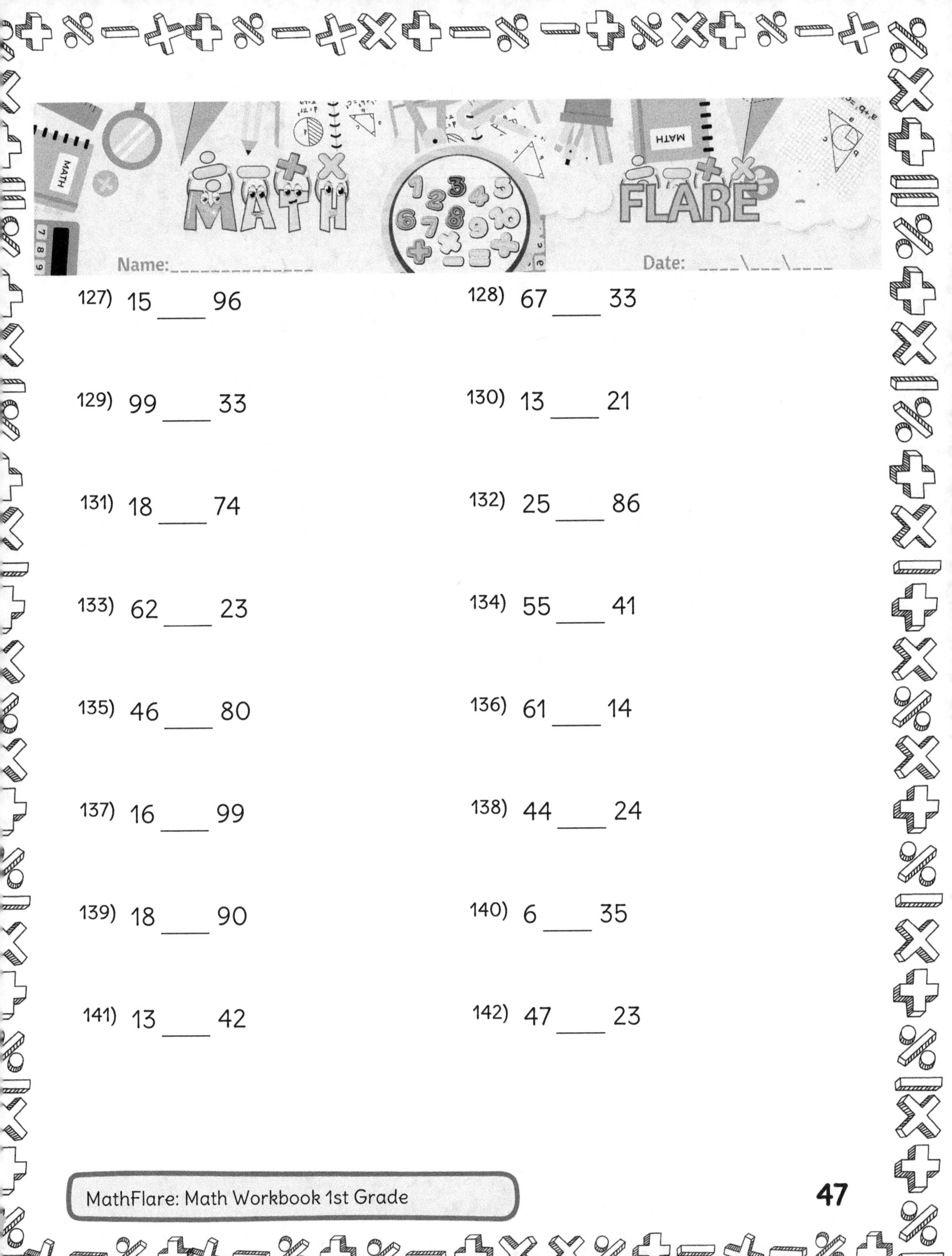

Name: _______________________   Date: ____ \ ____ \ ____

127) 15 ____ 96

128) 67 ____ 33

129) 99 ____ 33

130) 13 ____ 21

131) 18 ____ 74

132) 25 ____ 86

133) 62 ____ 23

134) 55 ____ 41

135) 46 ____ 80

136) 61 ____ 14

137) 16 ____ 99

138) 44 ____ 24

139) 18 ____ 90

140) 6 ____ 35

141) 13 ____ 42

142) 47 ____ 23

Name:_______________   Date: _______________

143) 37 ____ 15

144) 45 ____ 3

145) 4 ____ 61

146) 13 ____ 66

147) 96 ____ 84

148) 87 ____ 47

149) 45 ____ 4

150) 86 ____ 25

151) 41 ____ 54

152) 85 ____ 100

153) 7 ____ 69

154) 30 ____ 17

155) 52 ____ 44

156) 15 ____ 10

157) 28 ____ 78

158) 8 ____ 76

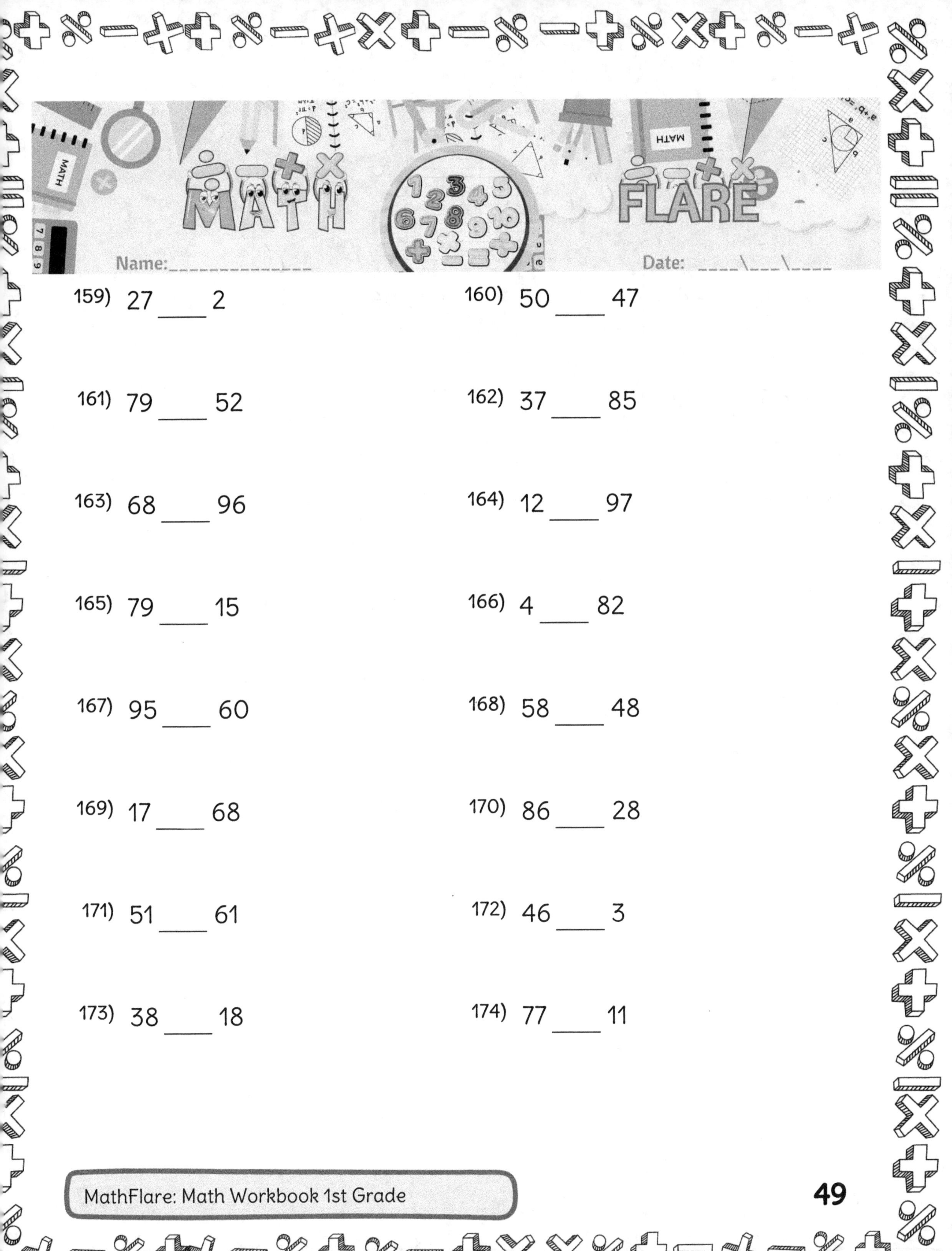

159) 27 ____ 2

160) 50 ____ 47

161) 79 ____ 52

162) 37 ____ 85

163) 68 ____ 96

164) 12 ____ 97

165) 79 ____ 15

166) 4 ____ 82

167) 95 ____ 60

168) 58 ____ 48

169) 17 ____ 68

170) 86 ____ 28

171) 51 ____ 61

172) 46 ____ 3

173) 38 ____ 18

174) 77 ____ 11

175) 21 ____ 44

176) 54 ____ 39

177) 46 ____ 89

178) 17 ____ 100

179) 33 ____ 11

180) 51 ____ 98

181) 5 ____ 56

182) 65 ____ 100

183) 6 ____ 47

184) 84 ____ 48

185) 19 ____ 80

186) 85 ____ 83

187) 62 ____ 51

188) 1 ____ 77

189) 58 ____ 1

190) 56 ____ 2

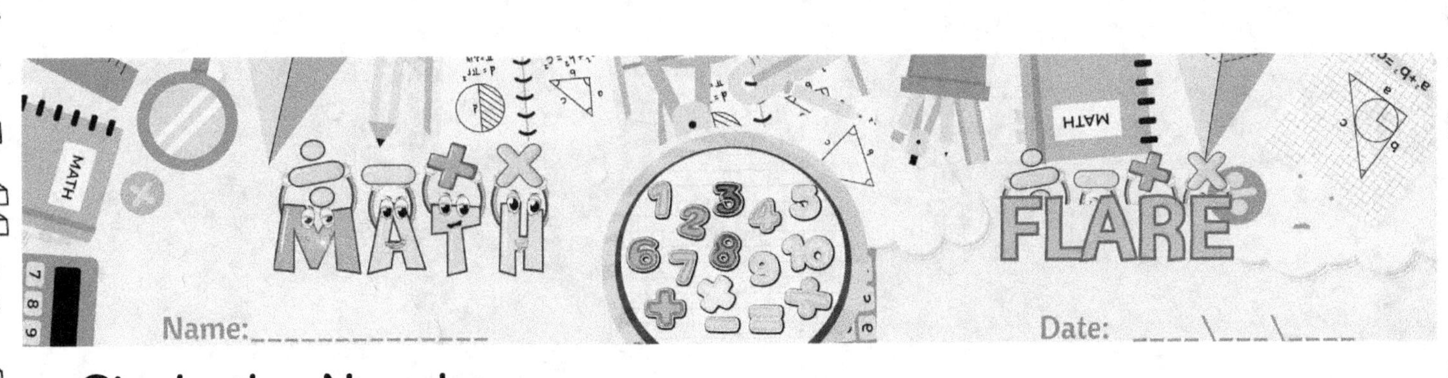

Circle the Numbers

Circle the smallest and biggest number in each group.

1) 26
8
89
17
87

2) 10
86
12
3
78

3) 59
95
85
84
74

4) 36
47
31
46
66

5) 84
34
27
74
11

6) 59
6
11
95
25

7) 69
60
55
8
80

8) 60
94
41
81
92

9) 2
73
12
16
85

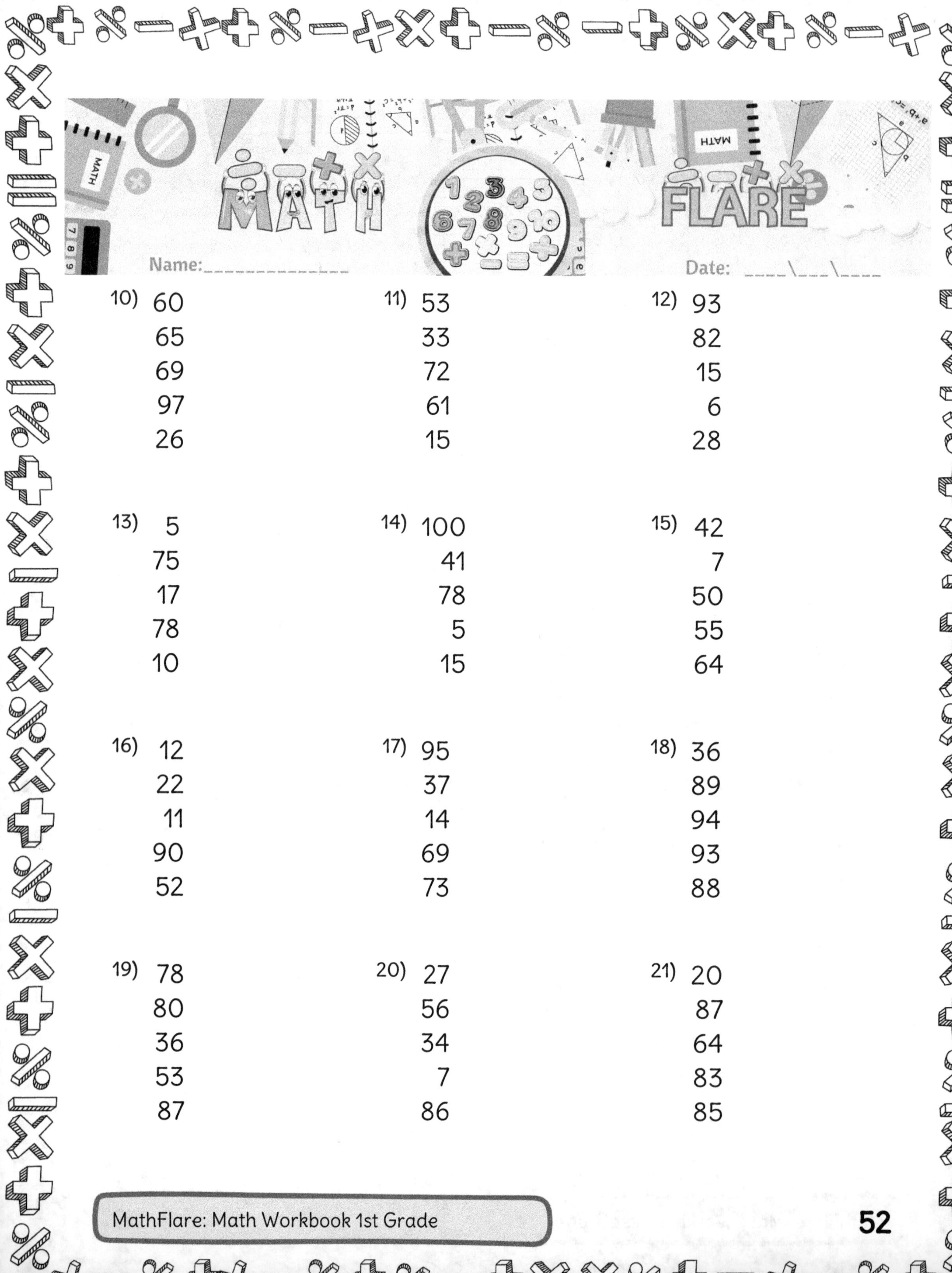

10)
60
65
69
97
26

11)
53
33
72
61
15

12)
93
82
15
6
28

13)
5
75
17
78
10

14)
100
41
78
5
15

15)
42
7
50
55
64

16)
12
22
11
90
52

17)
95
37
14
69
73

18)
36
89
94
93
88

19)
78
80
36
53
87

20)
27
56
34
7
86

21)
20
87
64
83
85

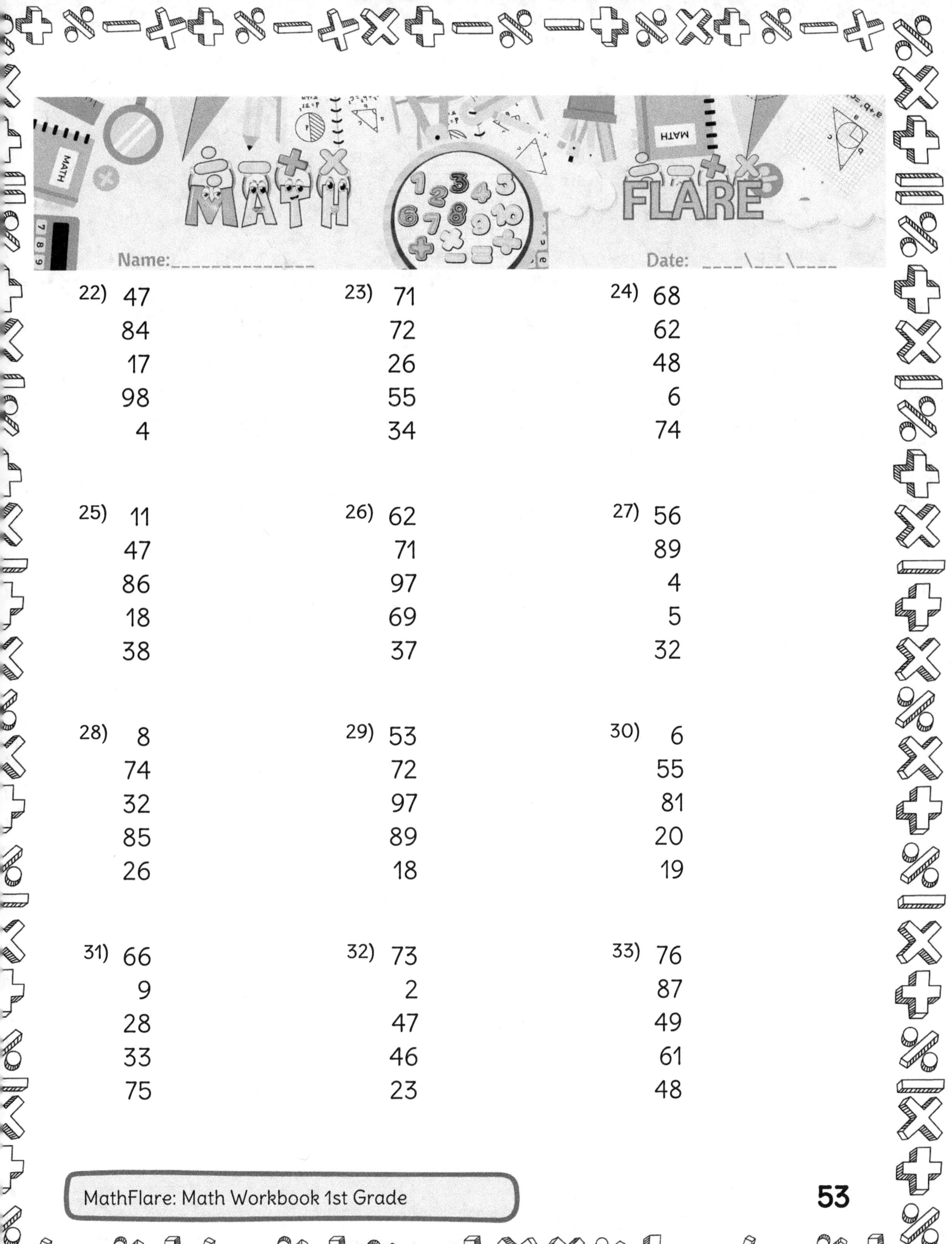

22)	23)	24)
47	71	68
84	72	62
17	26	48
98	55	6
4	34	74

25)	26)	27)
11	62	56
47	71	89
86	97	4
18	69	5
38	37	32

28)	29)	30)
8	53	6
74	72	55
32	97	81
85	89	20
26	18	19

31)	32)	33)
66	73	76
9	2	87
28	47	49
33	46	61
75	23	48

34)
82
69
21
24
27

35)
95
30
64
81
21

36)
40
51
97
1
32

37)
8
91
78
50
71

38)
48
61
71
31
59

39)
7
27
87
62
50

40)
67
24
36
42
38

41)
34
58
94
24
37

42)
45
47
13
36
23

43)
5
47
14
15
86

44)
9
100
90
21
98

45)
91
65
20
68
43

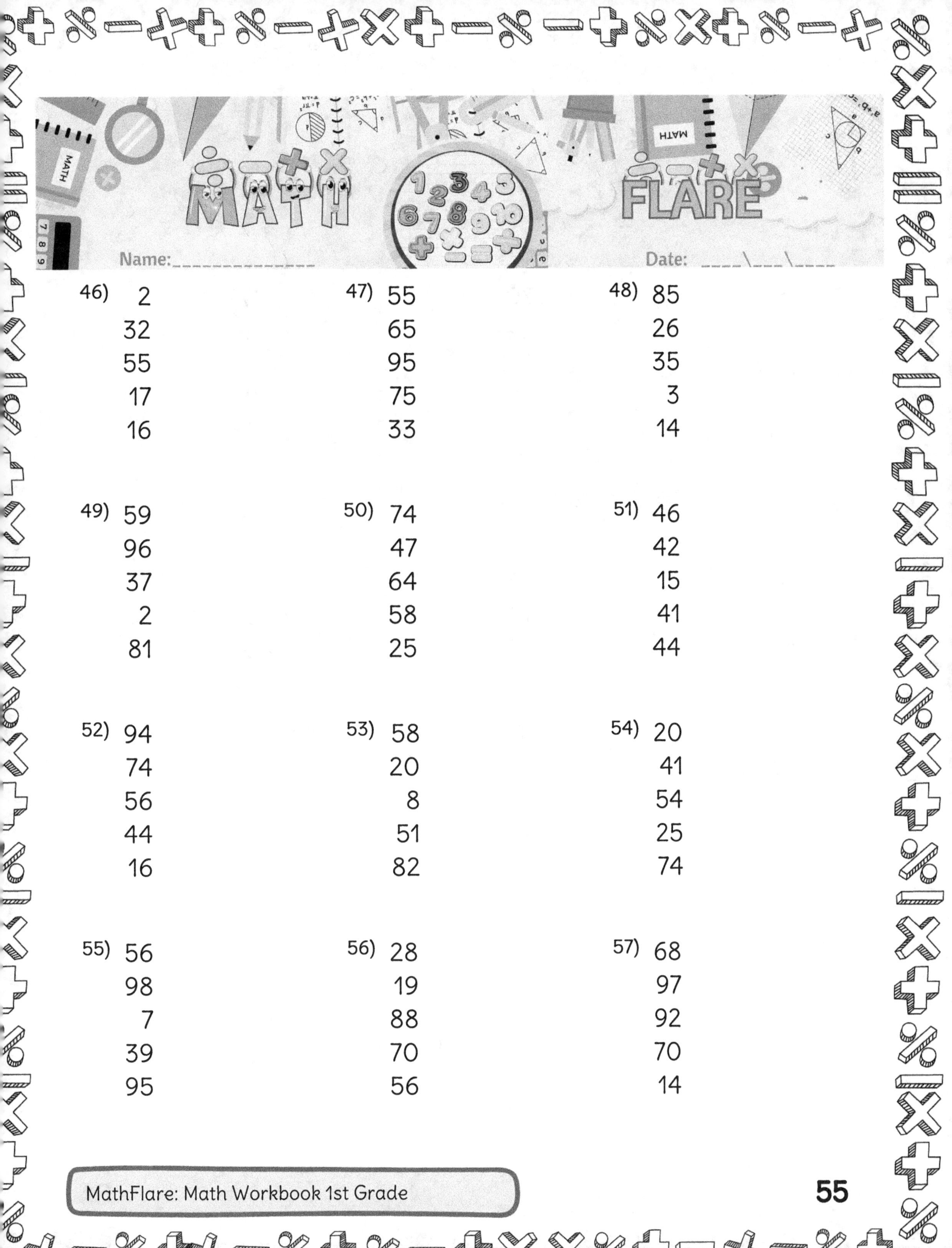

46)	2	47)	55	48)	85
	32		65		26
	55		95		35
	17		75		3
	16		33		14

49)	59	50)	74	51)	46
	96		47		42
	37		64		15
	2		58		41
	81		25		44

52)	94	53)	58	54)	20
	74		20		41
	56		8		54
	44		51		25
	16		82		74

55)	56	56)	28	57)	68
	98		19		97
	7		88		92
	39		70		70
	95		56		14

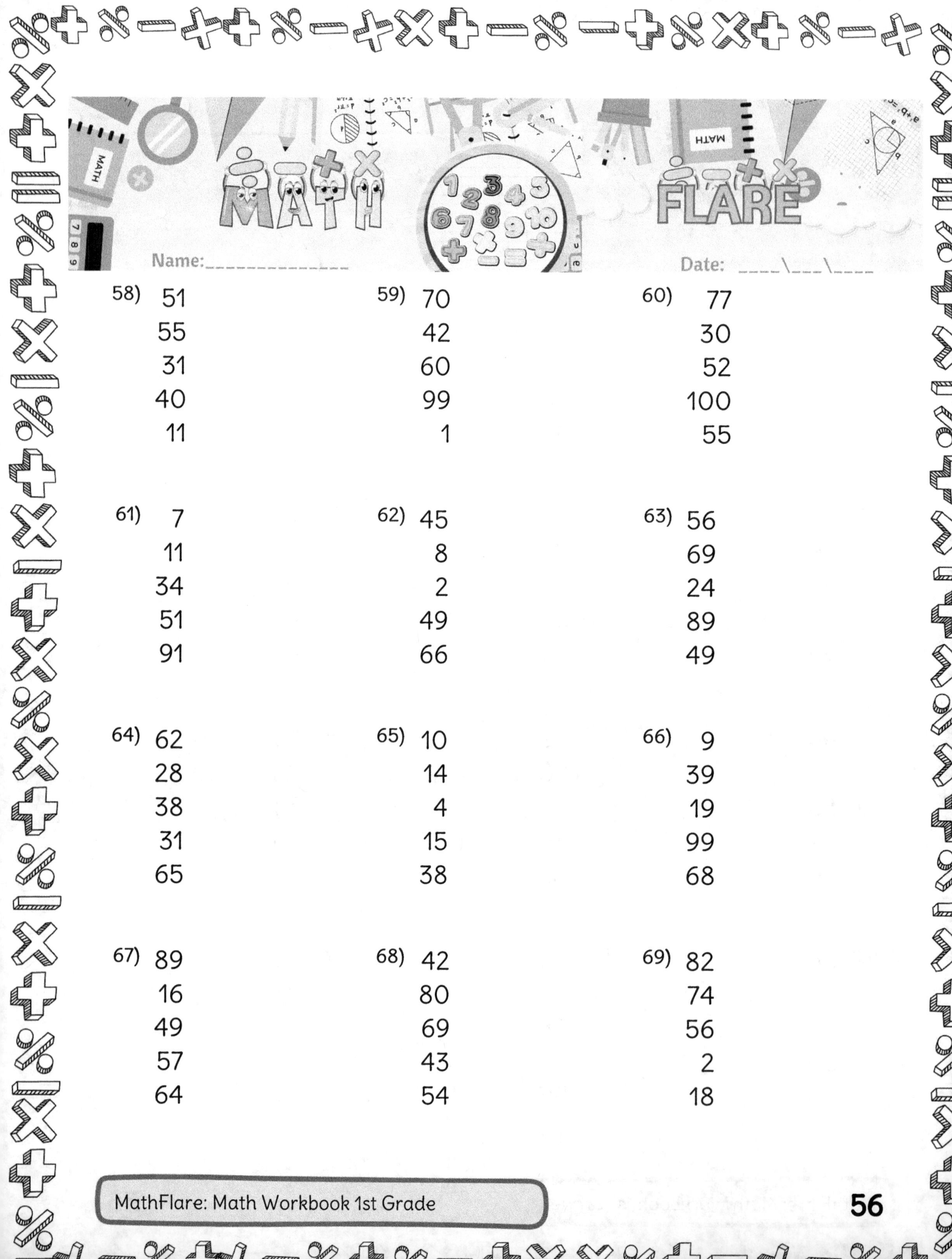

58)
51
55
31
40
11

59)
70
42
60
99
1

60)
77
30
52
100
55

61)
7
11
34
51
91

62)
45
8
2
49
66

63)
56
69
24
89
49

64)
62
28
38
31
65

65)
10
14
4
15
38

66)
9
39
19
99
68

67)
89
16
49
57
64

68)
42
80
69
43
54

69)
82
74
56
2
18

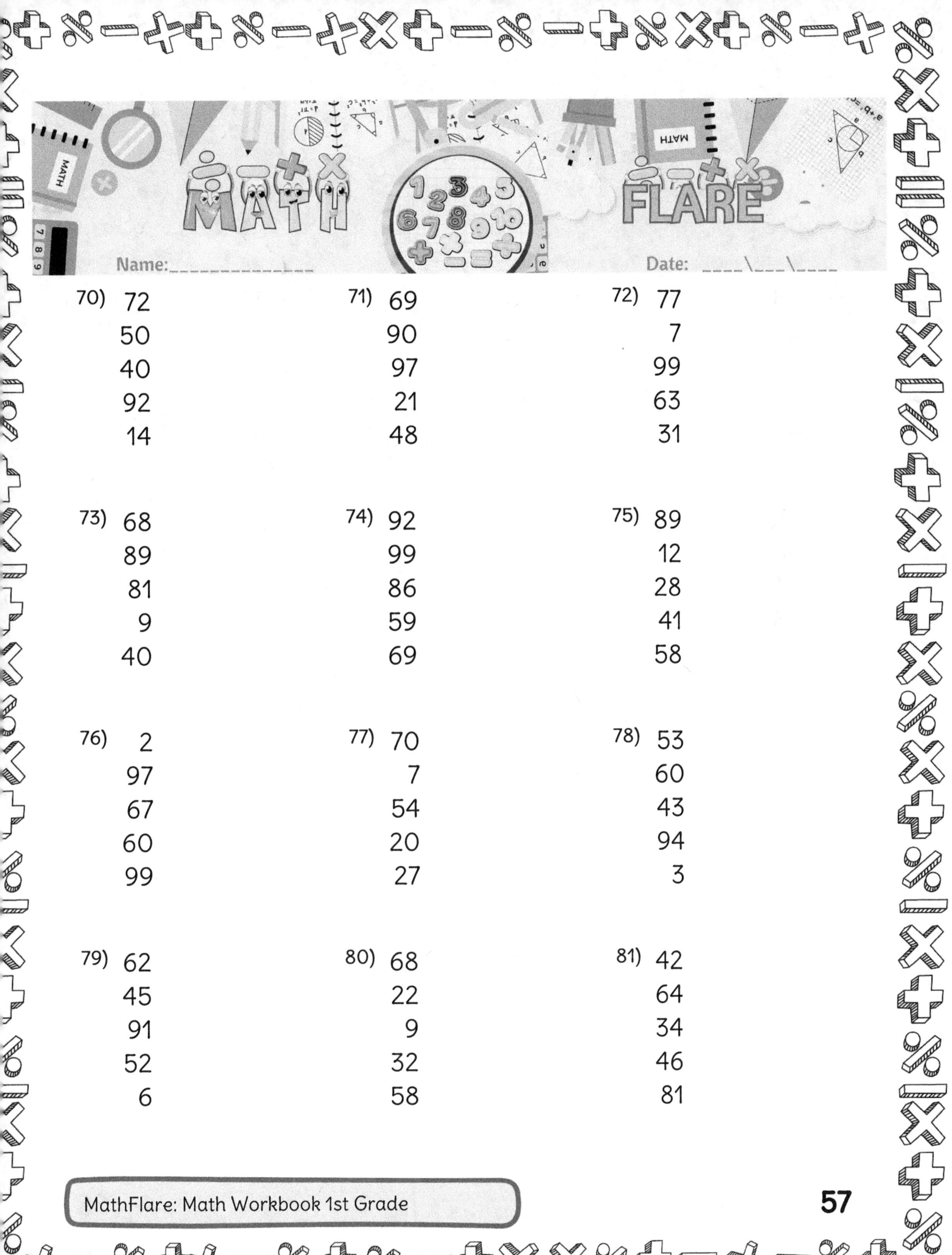

70)	71)	72)
72	69	77
50	90	7
40	97	99
92	21	63
14	48	31

73)	74)	75)
68	92	89
89	99	12
81	86	28
9	59	41
40	69	58

76)	77)	78)
2	70	53
97	7	60
67	54	43
60	20	94
99	27	3

79)	80)	81)
62	68	42
45	22	64
91	9	34
52	32	46
6	58	81

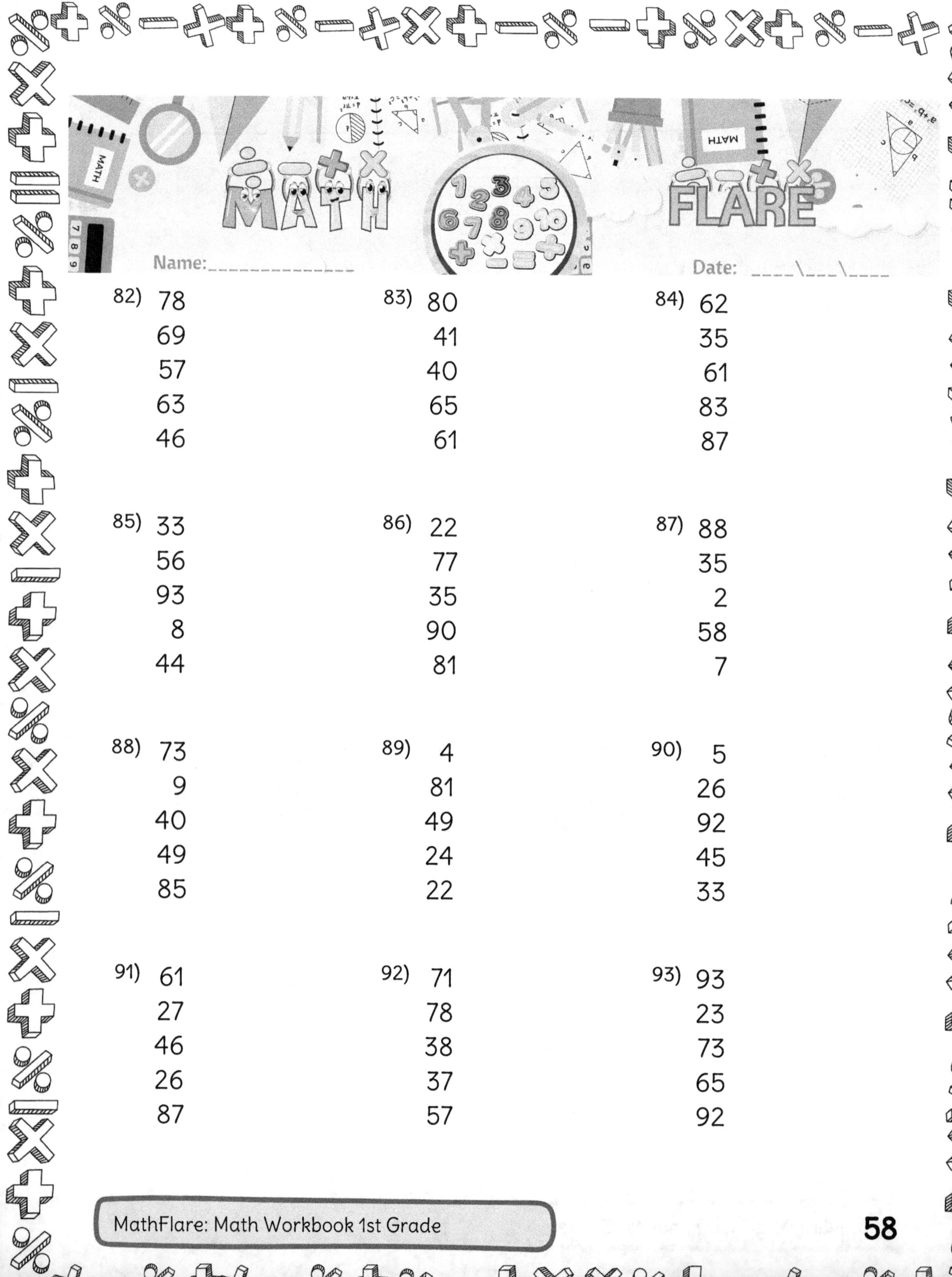

82) 78
     69
     57
     63
     46

83) 80
     41
     40
     65
     61

84) 62
     35
     61
     83
     87

85) 33
     56
     93
      8
     44

86) 22
     77
     35
     90
     81

87) 88
     35
      2
     58
      7

88) 73
      9
     40
     49
     85

89)   4
     81
     49
     24
     22

90)   5
     26
     92
     45
     33

91) 61
     27
     46
     26
     87

92) 71
     78
     38
     37
     57

93) 93
     23
     73
     65
     92

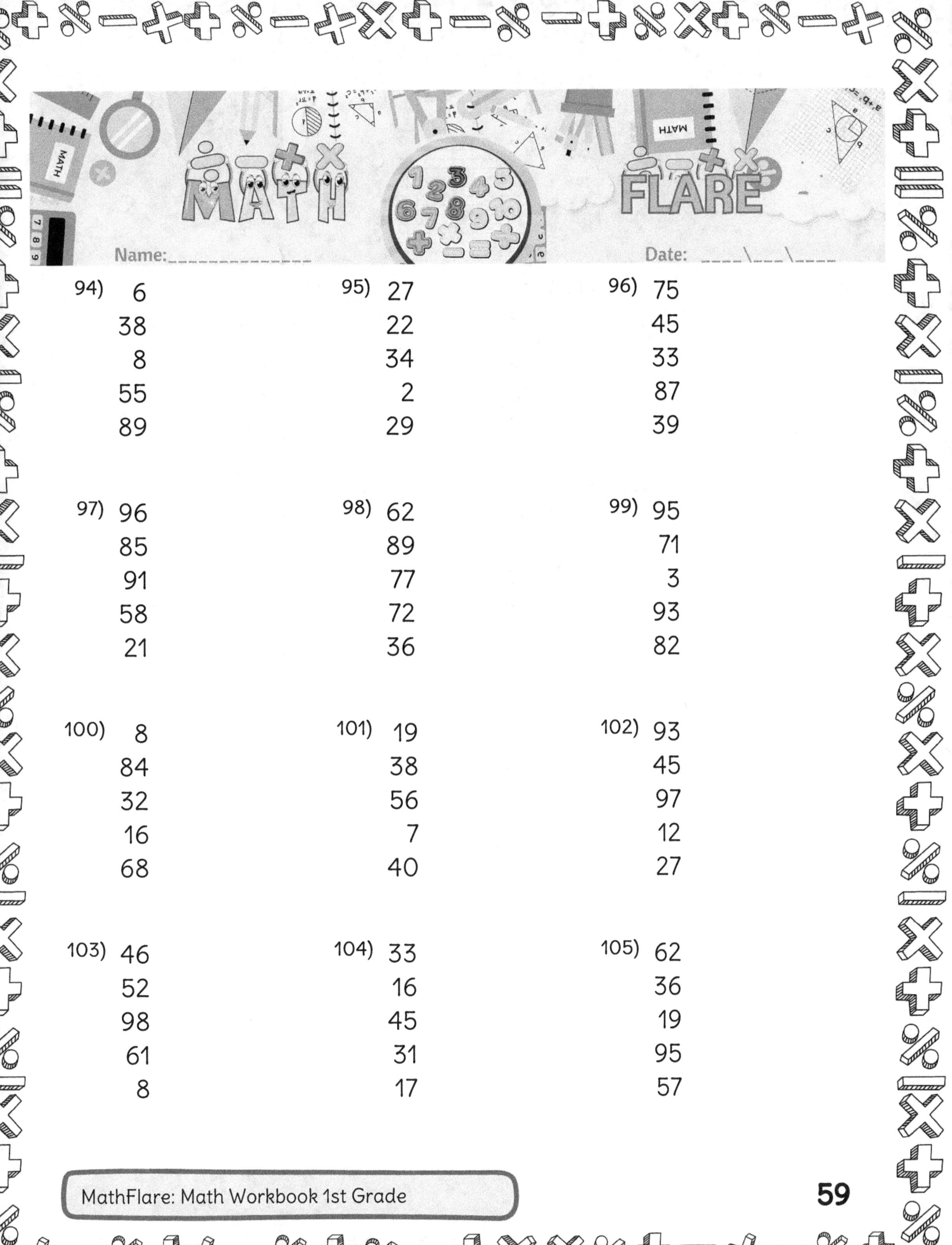

94)
```
  6
 38
  8
 55
 89
```

95)
```
 27
 22
 34
  2
 29
```

96)
```
 75
 45
 33
 87
 39
```

97)
```
 96
 85
 91
 58
 21
```

98)
```
 62
 89
 77
 72
 36
```

99)
```
 95
 71
  3
 93
 82
```

100)
```
  8
 84
 32
 16
 68
```

101)
```
 19
 38
 56
  7
 40
```

102)
```
 93
 45
 97
 12
 27
```

103)
```
 46
 52
 98
 61
  8
```

104)
```
 33
 16
 45
 31
 17
```

105)
```
 62
 36
 19
 95
 57
```

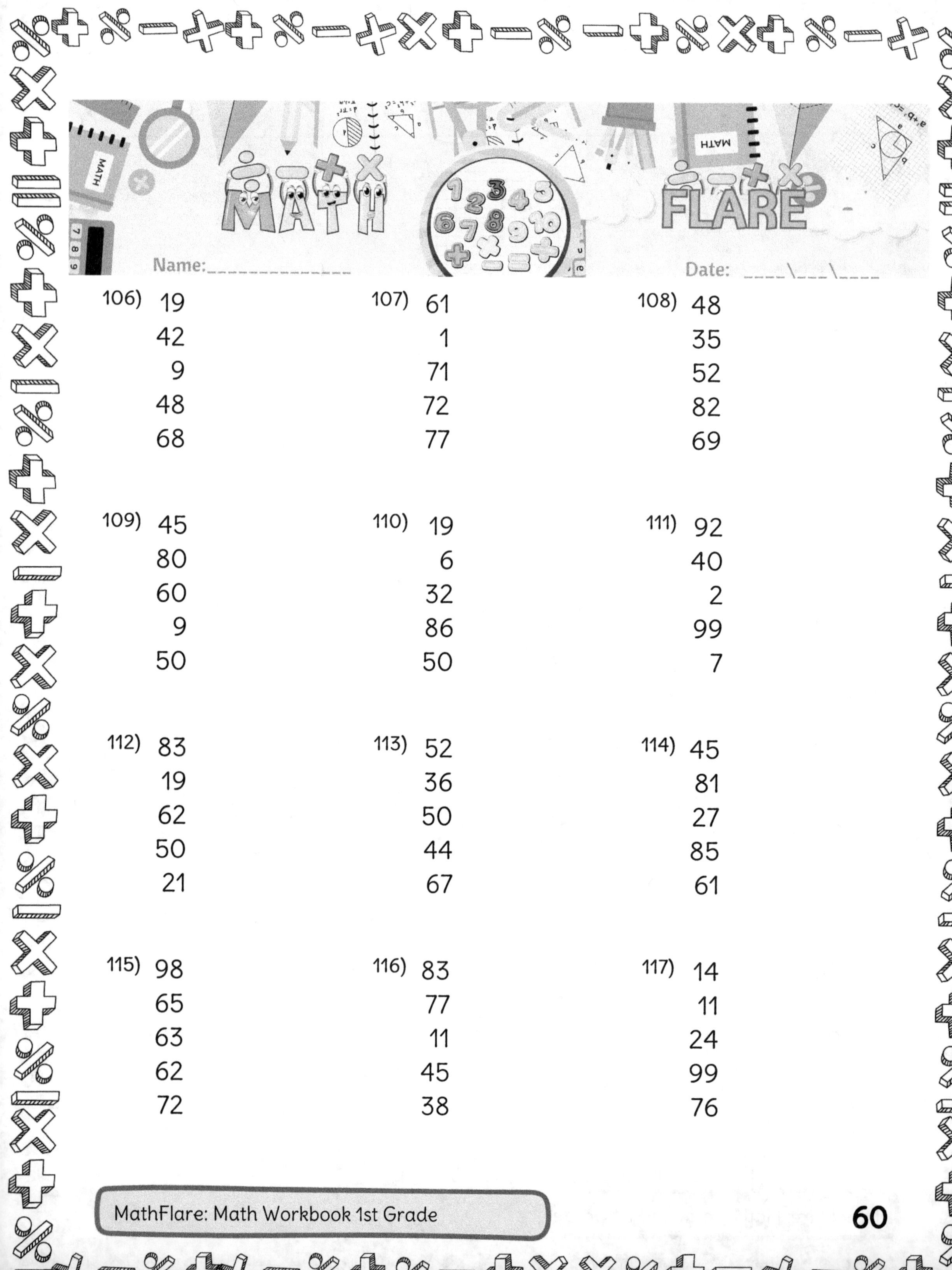

106)	107)	108)
19	61	48
42	1	35
9	71	52
48	72	82
68	77	69

109)	110)	111)
45	19	92
80	6	40
60	32	2
9	86	99
50	50	7

112)	113)	114)
83	52	45
19	36	81
62	50	27
50	44	85
21	67	61

115)	116)	117)
98	83	14
65	77	11
63	11	24
62	45	99
72	38	76

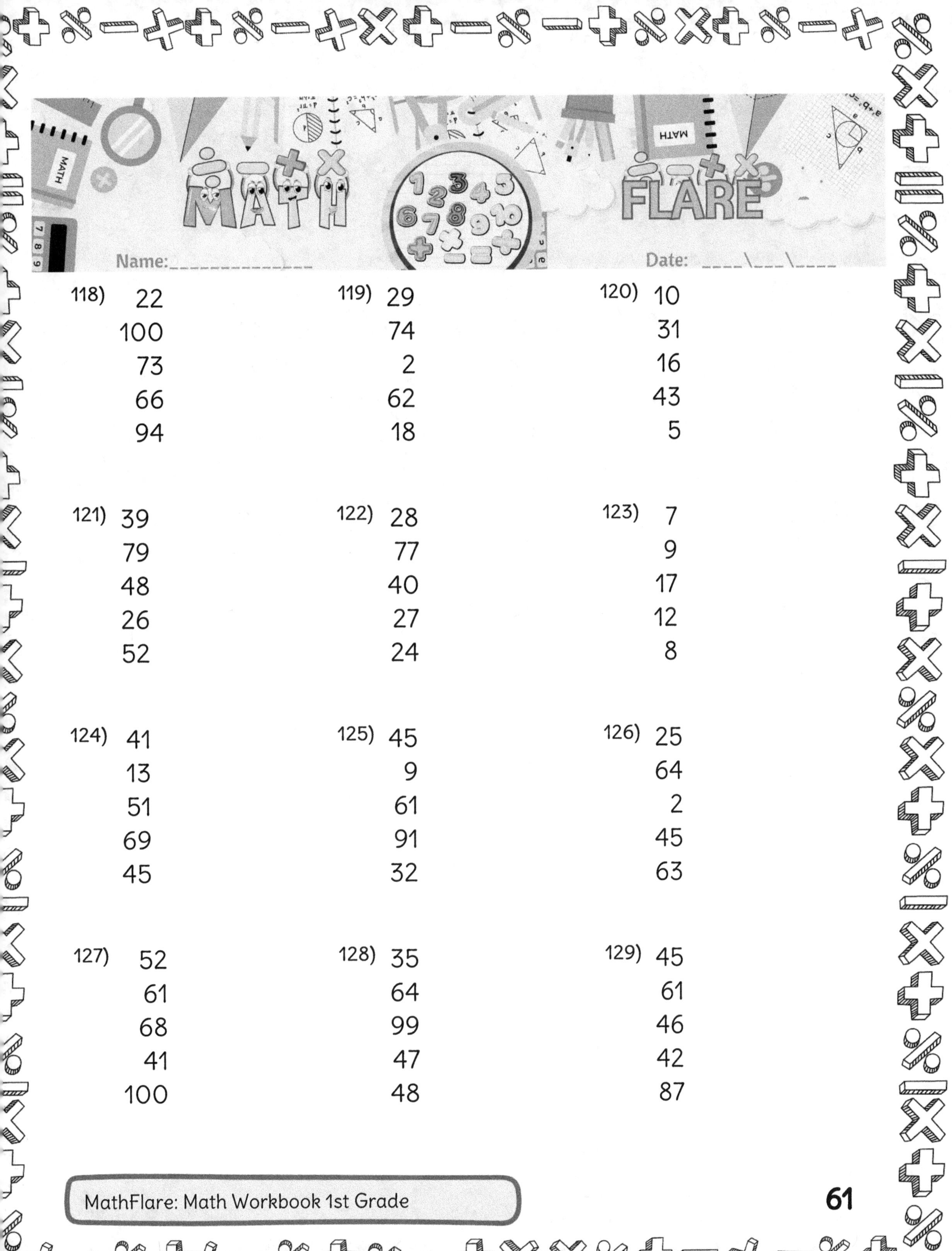

118)
22
100
73
66
94

119)
29
74
2
62
18

120)
10
31
16
43
5

121)
39
79
48
26
52

122)
28
77
40
27
24

123)
7
9
17
12
8

124)
41
13
51
69
45

125)
45
9
61
91
32

126)
25
64
2
45
63

127)
52
61
68
41
100

128)
35
64
99
47
48

129)
45
61
46
42
87

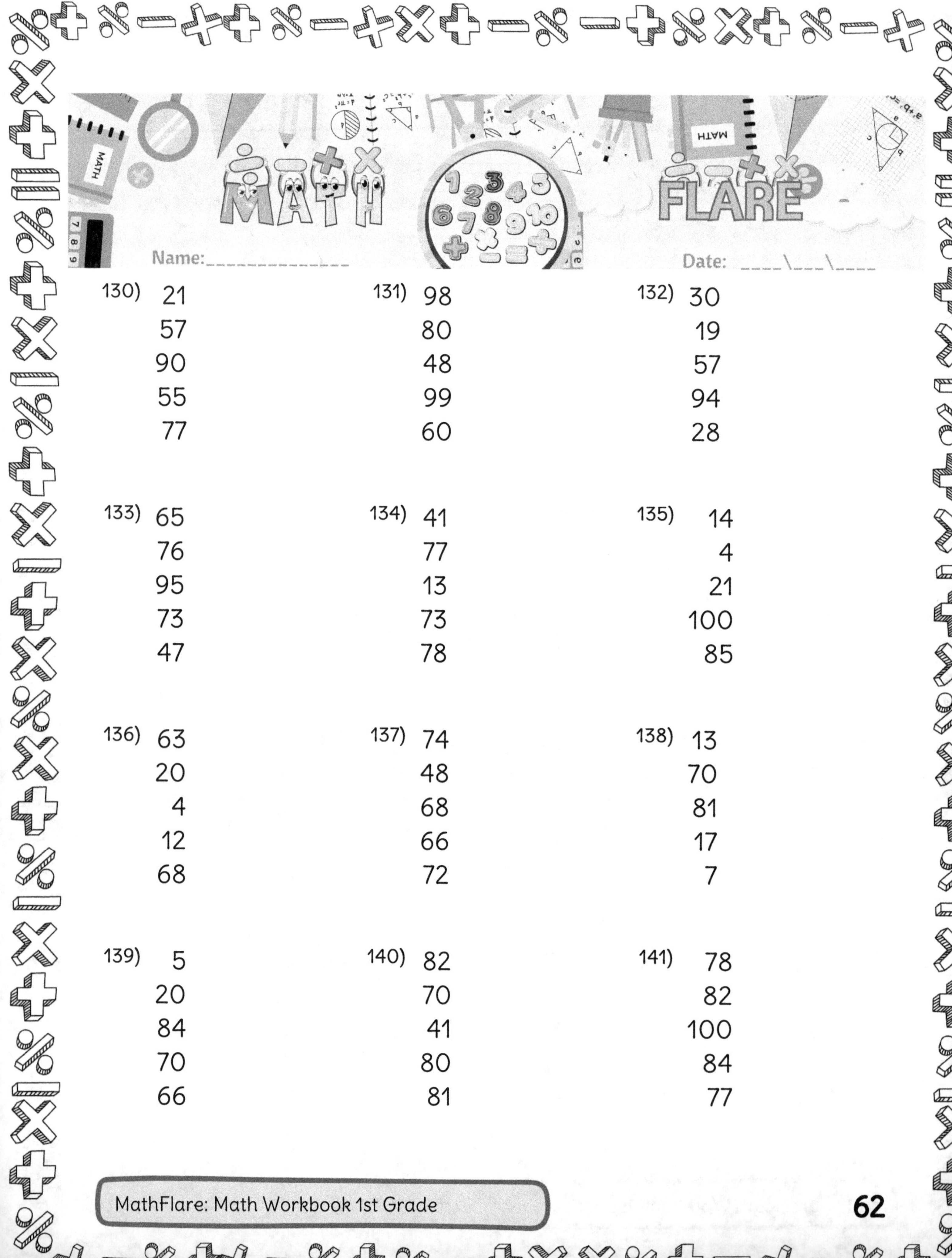

Name:_______________   Date: ____________

130)	131)	132)
21	98	30
57	80	19
90	48	57
55	99	94
77	60	28

133)	134)	135)
65	41	14
76	77	4
95	13	21
73	73	100
47	78	85

136)	137)	138)
63	74	13
20	48	70
4	68	81
12	66	17
68	72	7

139)	140)	141)
5	82	78
20	70	82
84	41	100
70	80	84
66	81	77

142)
28
99
76
68
100

143)
54
83
60
91
28

144)
27
99
1
34
72

145)
96
43
57
72
9

146)
84
37
31
19
82

147)
50
64
33
88
97

148)
67
69
82
96
86

149)
72
5
3
17
54

150)
23
61
93
42
40

151)
83
69
7
8
85

152)
35
25
29
75
93

153)
91
69
58
87
50

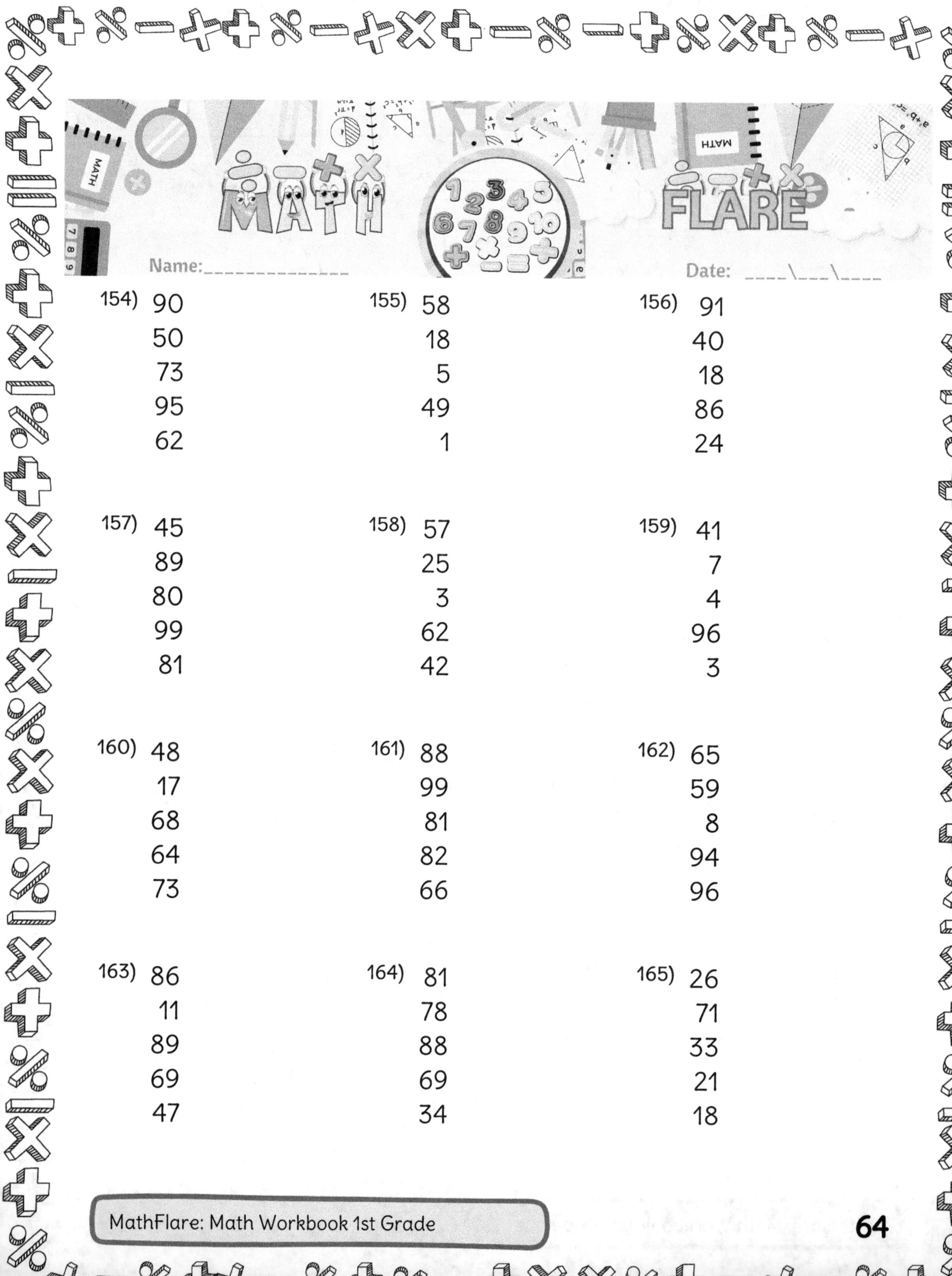

154)
90
50
73
95
62

155)
58
18
5
49
1

156)
91
40
18
86
24

157)
45
89
80
99
81

158)
57
25
3
62
42

159)
41
7
4
96
3

160)
48
17
68
64
73

161)
88
99
81
82
66

162)
65
59
8
94
96

163)
86
11
89
69
47

164)
81
78
88
69
34

165)
26
71
33
21
18

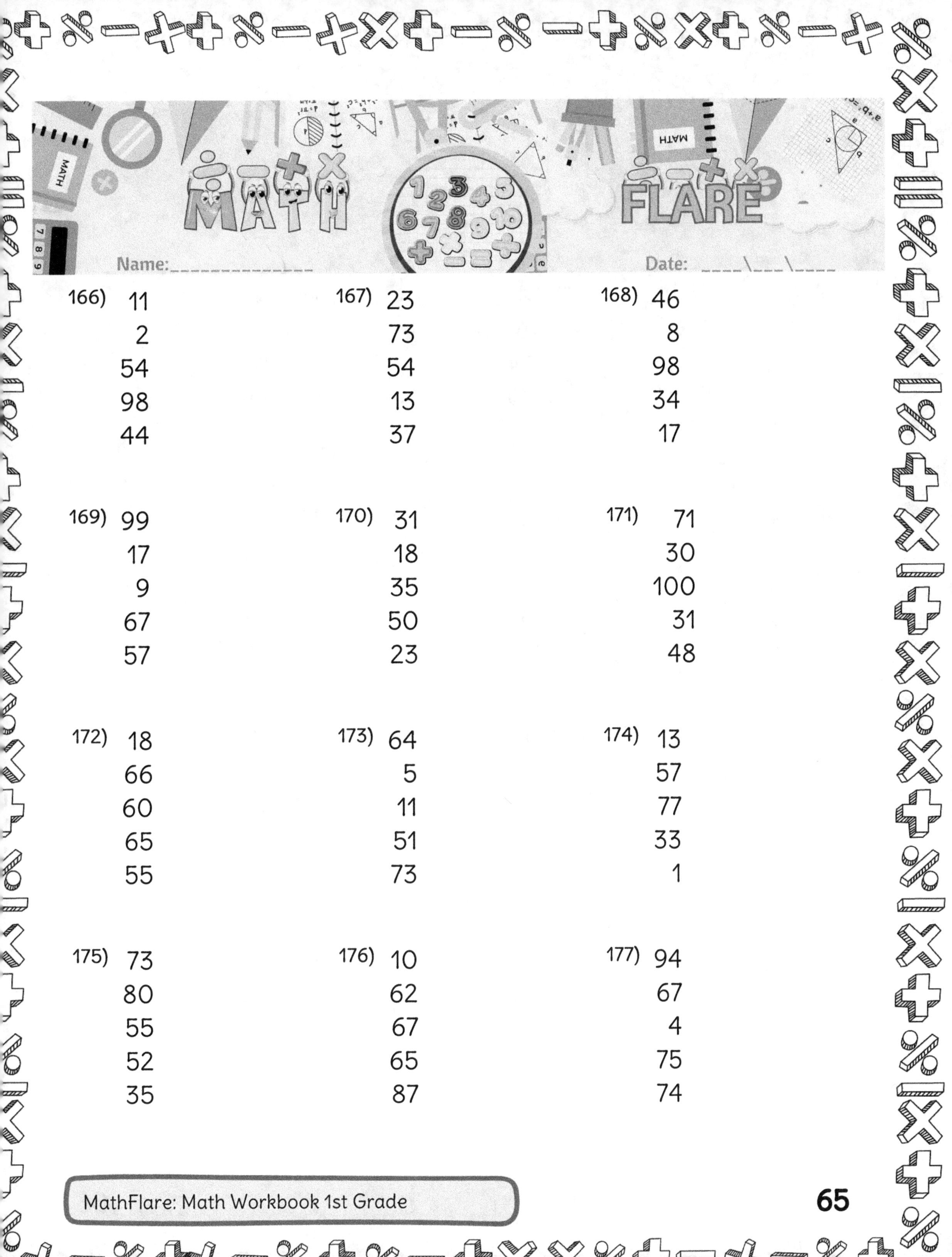

166)	11	167)	23	168)	46
	2		73		8
	54		54		98
	98		13		34
	44		37		17

169)	99	170)	31	171)	71
	17		18		30
	9		35		100
	67		50		31
	57		23		48

172)	18	173)	64	174)	13
	66		5		57
	60		11		77
	65		51		33
	55		73		1

175)	73	176)	10	177)	94
	80		62		67
	55		67		4
	52		65		75
	35		87		74

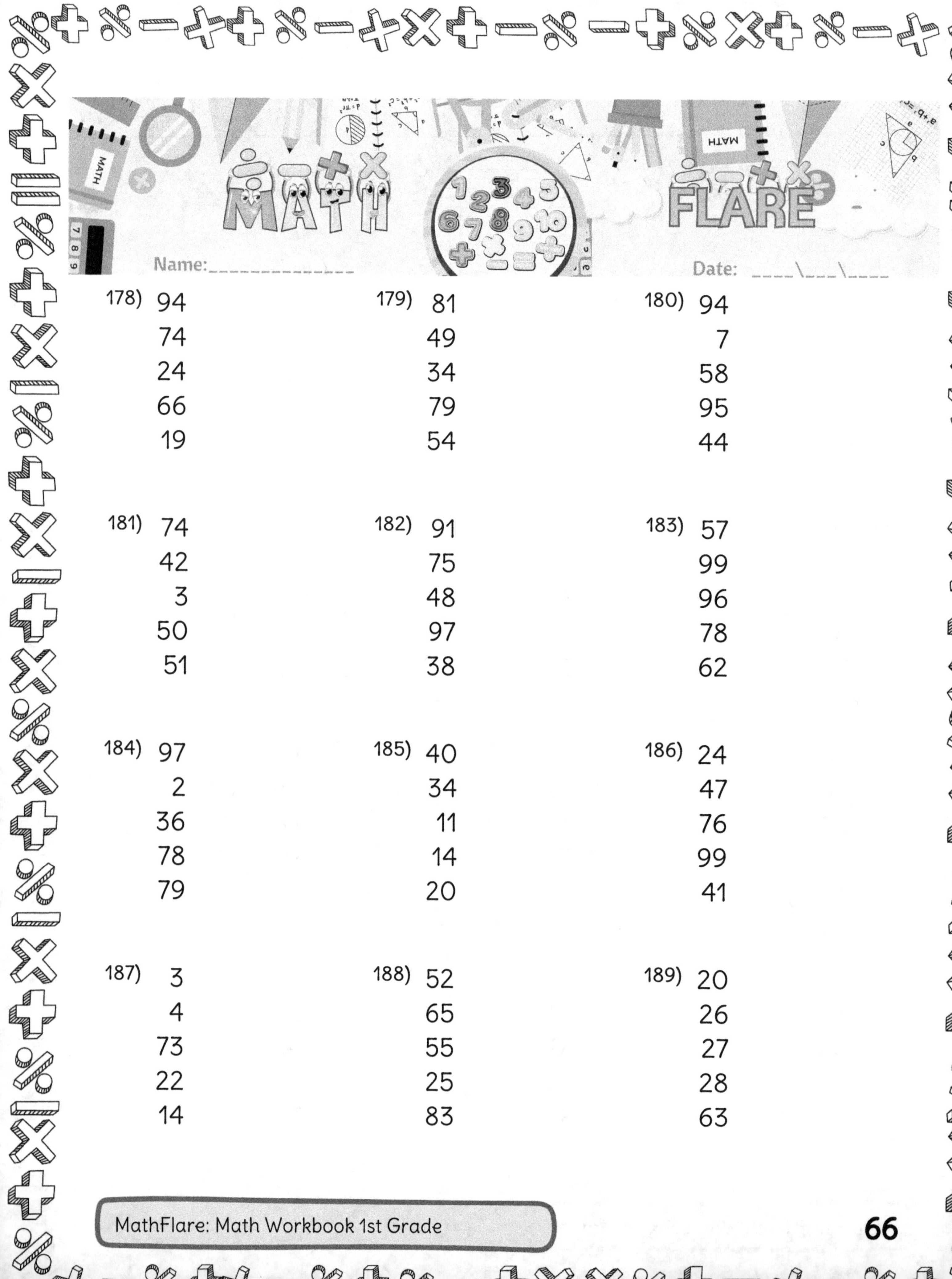

Name:_________________   Date: _______________

178) 94
74
24
66
19

179) 81
49
34
79
54

180) 94
7
58
95
44

181) 74
42
3
50
51

182) 91
75
48
97
38

183) 57
99
96
78
62

184) 97
2
36
78
79

185) 40
34
11
14
20

186) 24
47
76
99
41

187) 3
4
73
22
14

188) 52
65
55
25
83

189) 20
26
27
28
63

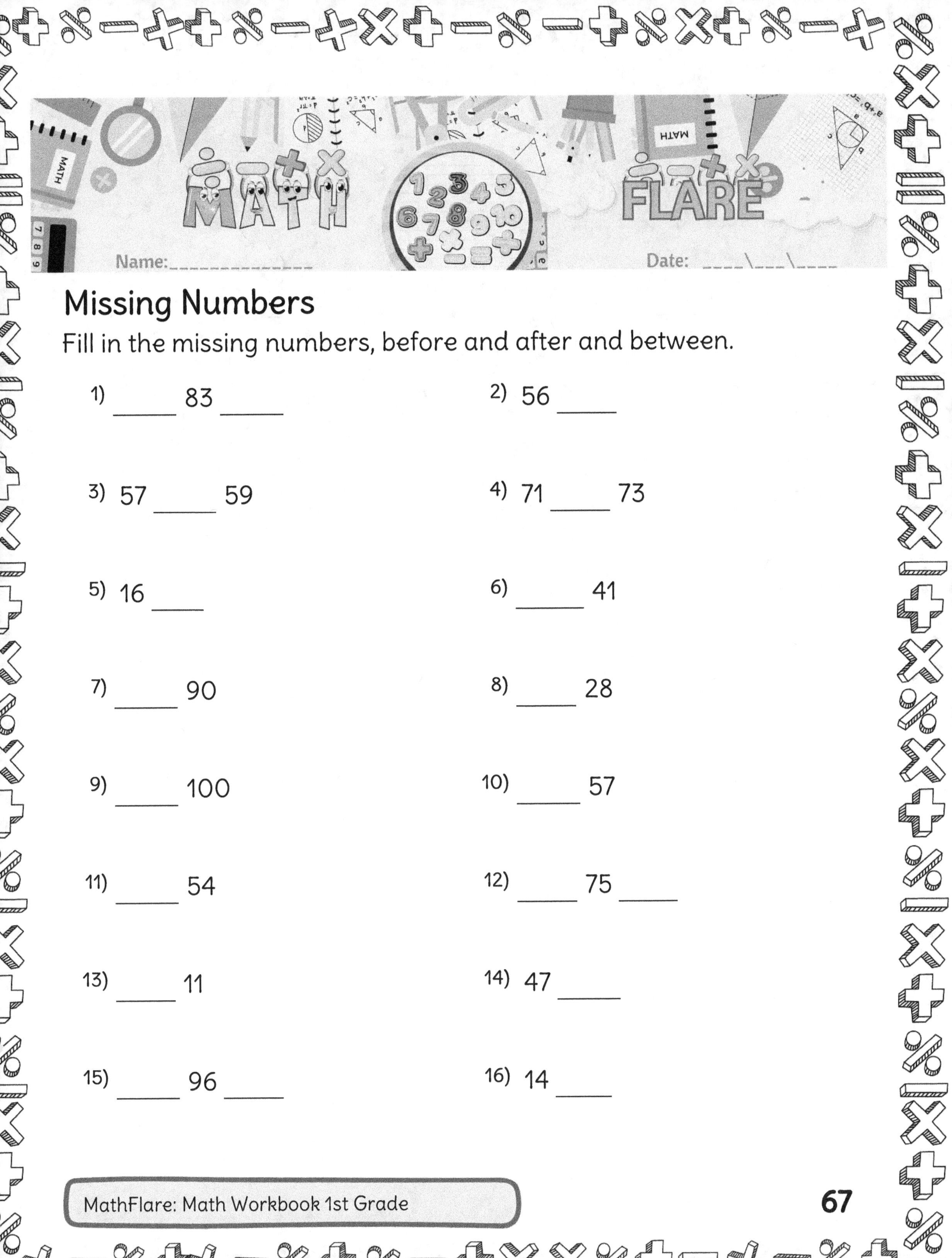

Missing Numbers

Fill in the missing numbers, before and after and between.

1) ____ 83 ____

2) 56 ____

3) 57 ____ 59

4) 71 ____ 73

5) 16 ____

6) ____ 41

7) ____ 90

8) ____ 28

9) ____ 100

10) ____ 57

11) ____ 54

12) ____ 75 ____

13) ____ 11

14) 47 ____

15) ____ 96 ____

16) 14 ____

17) _____ 84 _____   18) _____ 39 _____

19) _____ 92 _____   20) _____ 43

21) 32 _____   22) 58 _____

23) 74 _____   24) _____ 77

25) _____ 99   26) 21 _____ 23

27) _____ 11 _____   28) 80 _____ 82

29) 8 _____   30) _____ 48 _____

31) _____ 87 _____   32) _____ 92

33) _____ 51   34) _____ 93

35) _____ 55

36) ___ 5

37) _____ 70 _____

38) 92 _____ 94

39) _____ 16 _____

40) 37 _____ 39

41) 42 _____ 44

42) 52 _____

43) ___ 3 ___

44) 38 _____

45) _____ 29

46) _____ 72

47) _____ 36

48) 87 _____ 89

49) 90 _____ 92

50) 87 _____

51) 1 ___

52) _____ 69

53) ____ 47

54) ____ 19 ____

55) ____ 99 ____

56) 96 ____

57) ____ 66 ____

58) __ 8

59) ____ 30 ____

60) 19 ____

61) ____ 88 ____

62) ____ 69 ____

63) __ 2 ___

64) ____ 97 ____

65) 51 ____ 53

66) 28 ____

67) ____ 86 ____

68) 44 ____

69) ____ 44

70) ___ 78

71) 91 ____ 93

72) ____ 58 ____

73) 88 ____

74) ____ 96

75) ____ 40 ____

76) ____ 63

77) 86 ____

78) ____ 61

79) 14 ____ 16

80) ____ 57 ____

81) ____ 42

82) 4 ___ 6

83) ____ 85 ____

84) ____ 78 ____

85) ____ 98

86) 69 ____ 71

87) ____ 18

88) 75 ___ 77

89) _____ 76

90) 36 _____

91) _____ 48

92) 89 _____

93) 53 _____

94) 12 _____ 14

95) _____ 39

96) _____ 37

97) 72 _____ 74

98) 76 _____

99) 23 _____

100) _____ 22

101) 66 _____ 68

102) 51 _____

103) _____ 62

104) 53 _____ 55

105) _____ 32 _____

106) 79 _____

107) ____ 14

108) ____ 52 ____

109) ____ 59 ____

110) 16 ____ 18

111) 37 ____

112) ____ 76 ____

113) ____ 28 ____

114) ____ 65 ____

115) 32 ____ 34

116) 97 ____ 99

117) 1 ____ 3

118) ____ 10

119) 71 ____

120) ____ 23 ____

121) 77 ____

122) 17 ____ 19

123) 59 ____ 61

124) ____ 6 ____

125) ____ 62 ____

126) 35 ____

127) 50 ____ 52

128) ___ 4 ___

129) ____ 70

130) 91 ____

131) ____ 38

132) 57 ____

133) 78 ____

134) ____ 90 ____

135) 40 ____ 42

136) ____ 67

137) ____ 86

138) ____ 59

139) 23 ____ 25

140) ____ 20 ____

141) 100 ____ 102

142) ____ 64

143) ____ 45 ____

144) ___ 7 ___

145) 76 ____ 78

146) 19 ____ 21

147) ____ 42 ____

148) ____ 30

149) ____ 79

150) 42 ____

151) 13 ____ 15

152) 93 ____

153) ____ 97

154) ____ 51 ____

155) 29 ____

156) 48 ____

157) ____ 34 ____

158) ____ 55 ____

159) ____ 79 ____

160) ____ 10 ____

161) 63 ____ 65

162) 79 ____ 81

163) 98 ____

164) 33 ____

165) ____ 15 ____

166) 61 ____

167) 56 ____ 58

168) ____ 66

169) ____ 53 ____

170) ____ 89 ____

171) ____ 68

172) ____ 33

173) 44 ____ 46

174) ____ 6

175) 43 ____ 45

176) ____ 31 ____

177) 83 ____ 85

178) 18 ____

179) _____ 26

180) 86 _____ 88

181) 85 _____ 87

182) 52 _____ 54

183) ____ 80 ____

184) ____ 63

185) ____ 85

186) ____ 49 ____

187) 94 ____ 96

188) 96 ____ 98

189) 7 ___ 9

190) 58 ____ 60

191) 73 ____

192) ____ 81 ____

193) 7 ___

194) 18 ____ 20

195) ____ 73 ____

196) 67 ____ 69

Chapter. 02

Addition and Subtraction

Addition

Adding is like putting things together to see how many we have altogether.

For instance, imagine we have 2 colorful blocks. Then, we add 3 more blocks. How many blocks do we have in total?

Let's count them together. 1, 2, 3, 4, 5.

Exactly! We have 5 blocks altogether! We show this with a plus sign (+) like this:

$$2 + 3 = 5.$$

Let's try another one.

If we have 5 pencils and we add four more pencils, how many pencils do we have in total?

Right, we have 9 pencils! We can write it down like this:

$$5 + 4 = 9.$$

Adding is fun! It helps us figure out how many things we have when we put them all together.

Let's solve a problem from the exercises.

$$
\begin{array}{r}
11 \\
+\ \ 3 \\
\hline
14 \\
\end{array}
$$

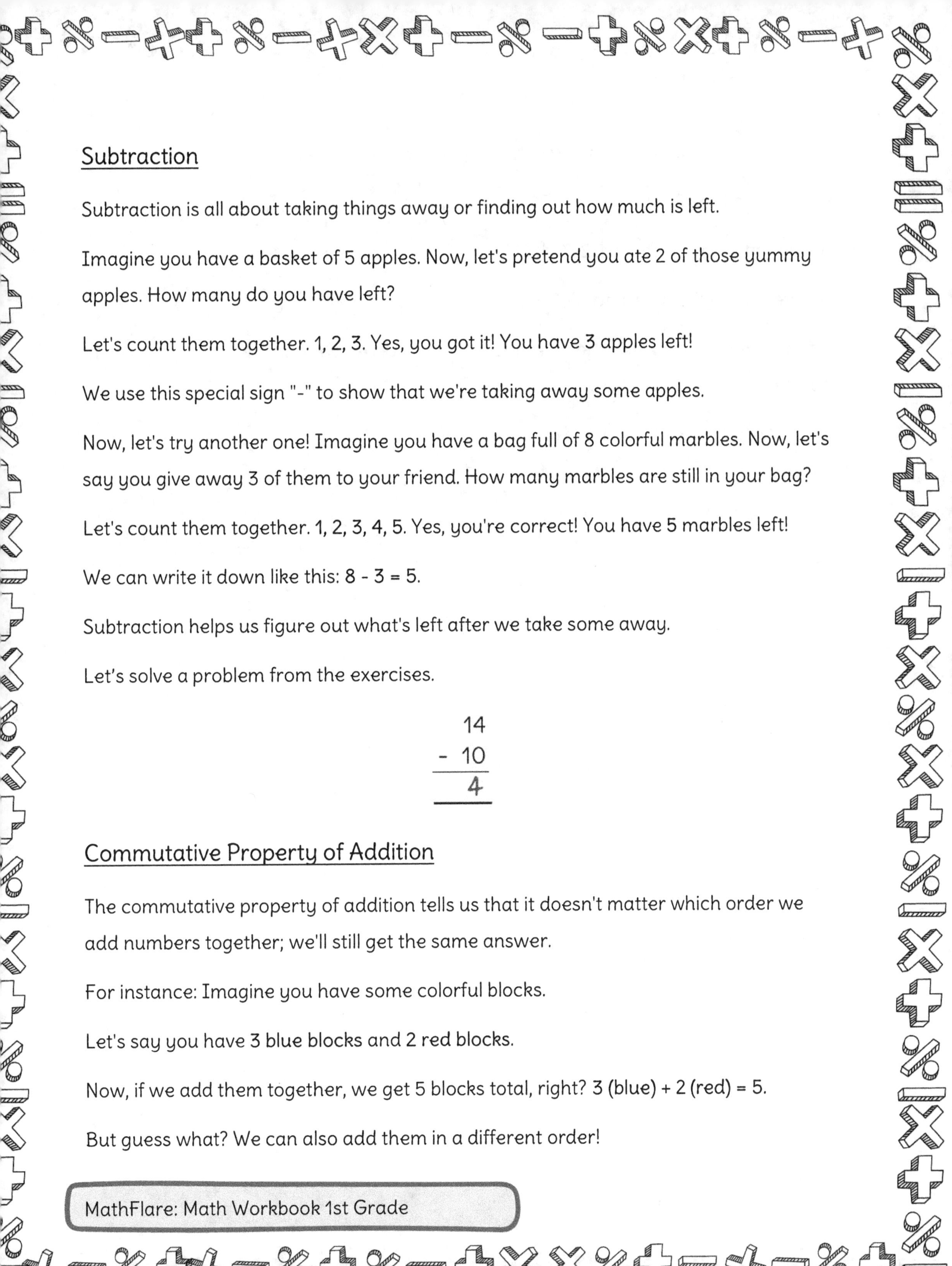

Subtraction

Subtraction is all about taking things away or finding out how much is left.

Imagine you have a basket of 5 apples. Now, let's pretend you ate 2 of those yummy apples. How many do you have left?

Let's count them together. 1, 2, 3. Yes, you got it! You have 3 apples left!

We use this special sign "-" to show that we're taking away some apples.

Now, let's try another one! Imagine you have a bag full of 8 colorful marbles. Now, let's say you give away 3 of them to your friend. How many marbles are still in your bag?

Let's count them together. 1, 2, 3, 4, 5. Yes, you're correct! You have 5 marbles left!

We can write it down like this: 8 - 3 = 5.

Subtraction helps us figure out what's left after we take some away.

Let's solve a problem from the exercises.

$$\begin{array}{r} 14 \\ -\ 10 \\ \hline 4 \end{array}$$

Commutative Property of Addition

The commutative property of addition tells us that it doesn't matter which order we add numbers together; we'll still get the same answer.

For instance: Imagine you have some colorful blocks.

Let's say you have 3 blue blocks and 2 red blocks.

Now, if we add them together, we get 5 blocks total, right? 3 (blue) + 2 (red) = 5.

But guess what? We can also add them in a different order!

Let's try adding the red blocks first, then the blue ones.

So, we have 2 (red) + 3 (blue).

Let's count them together. 1, 2, 3, 4, 5!

Yes, we still get 5 blocks in total!

It doesn't matter if we add the blue blocks first or the red ones first, we still end up with the same number of blocks.

Let's solve a problem from the exercises.

$$2 + \underline{9} = 9 + 2$$

$$\text{or} \quad 11 = 11$$

$$\underline{3} + 8 = 8 + 3$$

$$\text{or} \quad 11 = 11$$

Addition and Subtraction Activities

a. 14 + 1 = _______   E

b. 19 – 13 = _______   H

c. 8 + 13 = _______   A

d. 2 – 2 = _______   J

e. 19 + 17 = _______   C

f. 16 + 18 = _______   I

g. 6 + 15 = _______   F

h. 2 + 14 = _______   B

i. 13 – 13 = _______   G

j. 4 + 20 = _______   D

F = 21
H = 6
A = 21
G = 0
I = 34
B = 16
J = 0
E = 15
C = 36
D = 24

Word Problems

Word problems are like little puzzles that help us use addition in real-life situations.

For instance:

1. Jake has 6 carrots. He gets 2 more carrots. How many carrots does he have now?

To find out how many carrots he has now, we add the number of carrots he started with (6) to the number of carrots he got (2).

So, we add 6 + 2, which equals 8.

Jake now has 8 carrots in total!

Let's solve a problem:

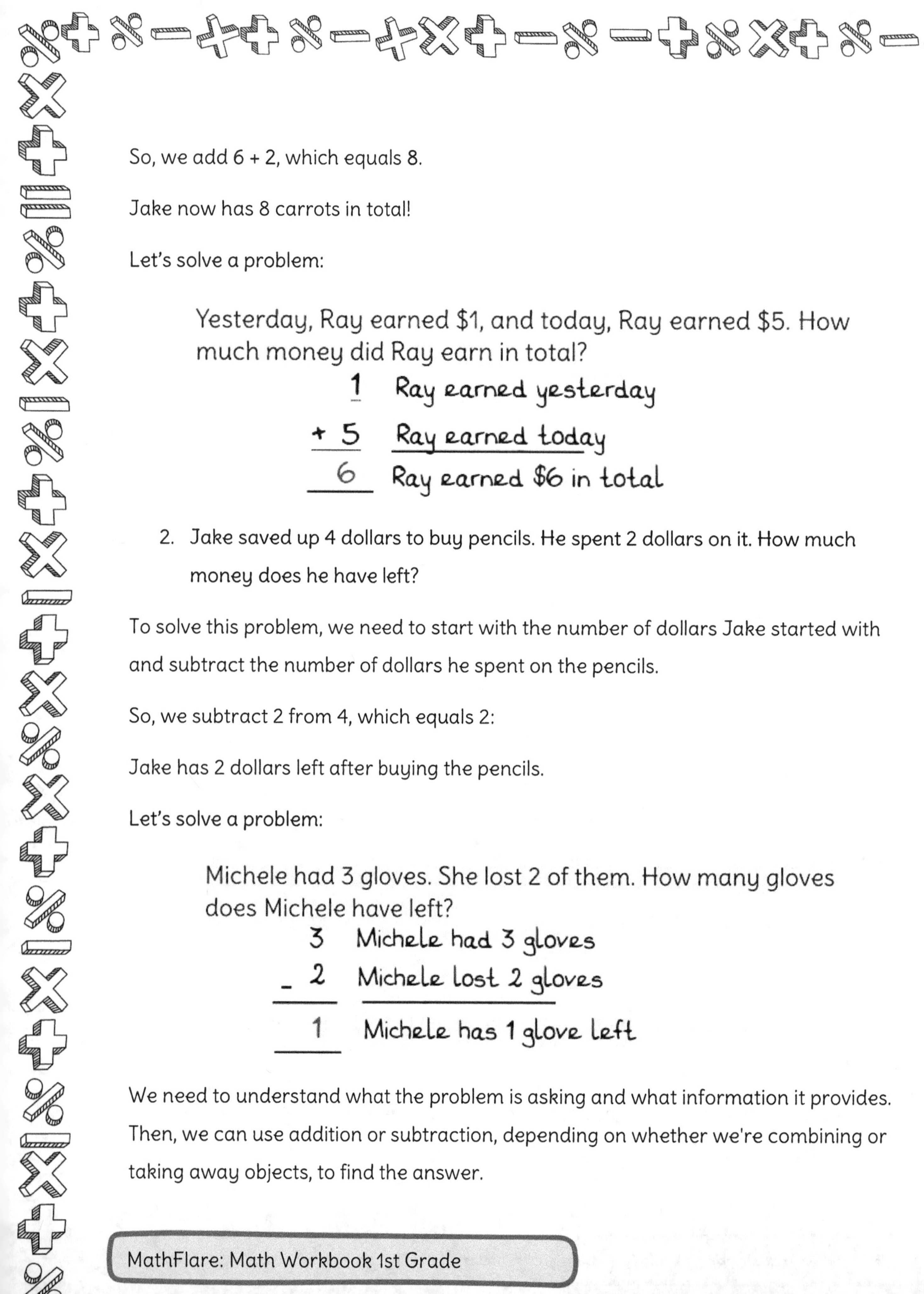

Yesterday, Ray earned $1, and today, Ray earned $5. How much money did Ray earn in total?

$$
\begin{array}{rl}
\underline{1} & \text{Ray earned yesterday} \\
+\ 5 & \underline{\text{Ray earned today}} \\
\hline
6 & \text{Ray earned \$6 in total}
\end{array}
$$

2. Jake saved up 4 dollars to buy pencils. He spent 2 dollars on it. How much money does he have left?

To solve this problem, we need to start with the number of dollars Jake started with and subtract the number of dollars he spent on the pencils.

So, we subtract 2 from 4, which equals 2:

Jake has 2 dollars left after buying the pencils.

Let's solve a problem:

Michele had 3 gloves. She lost 2 of them. How many gloves does Michele have left?

$$
\begin{array}{rl}
3 & \text{Michele had 3 gloves} \\
-\ 2 & \underline{\text{Michele lost 2 gloves}} \\
\hline
1 & \text{Michele has 1 glove left}
\end{array}
$$

We need to understand what the problem is asking and what information it provides. Then, we can use addition or subtraction, depending on whether we're combining or taking away objects, to find the answer.

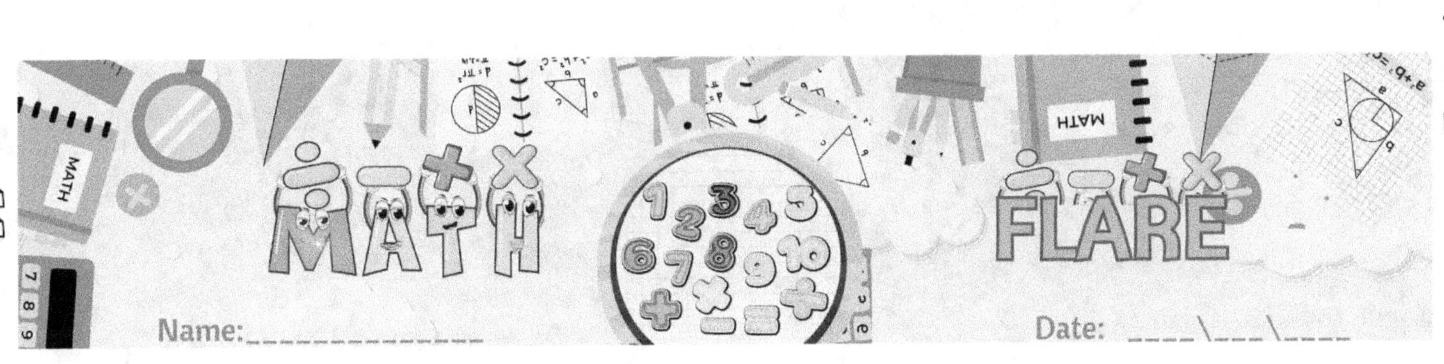

Addition: 1 through 20

Find the Sum.

1) 11
+ 3

2) 8
+ 16

3) 11
+ 7

4) 12
+ 1

5) 19
+ 12

6) 19
+ 18

7) 11
+ 9

8) 17
+ 17

9) 13
+ 5

10) 8
+ 5

11) 17
+ 14

12) 15
+ 3

13) 9
+ 2

14) 12
+ 18

15) 10
+ 16

16) 4
+ 15

17) 19
+ 8

18) 2
+ 19

19) 16
+ 9

20) 7
+ 3

21) 16 + 1	22) 4 + 3	23) 13 + 18	24) 6 + 11	25) 4 + 12
26) 8 + 6	27) 7 + 10	28) 19 + 17	29) 8 + 10	30) 15 + 14
31) 11 + 4	32) 10 + 5	33) 19 + 5	34) 8 + 18	35) 3 + 5
36) 18 + 5	37) 8 + 17	38) 11 + 12	39) 10 + 10	40) 15 + 2
41) 14 + 19	42) 9 + 17	43) 9 + 10	44) 9 + 5	45) 12 + 11

Name: ___________   Date: ___ \ ___ \ ___

46) 2 + 17	47) 8 + 3	48) 10 + 1	49) 14 + 10	50) 19 + 3
51) 4 + 6	52) 10 + 4	53) 9 + 3	54) 2 + 3	55) 7 + 16
56) 15 + 18	57) 20 + 12	58) 15 + 12	59) 16 + 10	60) 16 + 4
61) 7 + 11	62) 4 + 1	63) 17 + 6	64) 19 + 1	65) 11 + 13
66) 17 + 9	67) 9 + 6	68) 10 + 7	69) 18 + 16	70) 4 + 14

Name:____________________ Date: _______________

71) 4 + 18 ———	72) 6 + 3 ———	73) 7 + 20 ———	74) 19 + 19 ———	75) 1 + 8 ———
76) 6 + 16 ———	77) 16 + 17 ———	78) 17 + 15 ———	79) 7 + 2 ———	80) 17 + 12 ———
81) 4 + 10 ———	82) 3 + 10 ———	83) 15 + 1 ———	84) 18 + 4 ———	85) 3 + 9 ———
86) 5 + 17 ———	87) 7 + 18 ———	88) 5 + 2 ———	89) 2 + 12 ———	90) 10 + 2 ———
91) 19 + 2 ———	92) 17 + 2 ———	93) 15 + 16 ———	94) 5 + 20 ———	95) 14 + 8 ———

Name: _________________ Date: ___ / ___ / ___

96) 13 + 1	97) 15 + 19	98) 3 + 14	99) 6 + 2	100) 9 + 11
101) 20 + 6	102) 11 + 14	103) 4 + 16	104) 6 + 12	105) 14 + 9
106) 15 + 11	107) 5 + 19	108) 6 + 6	109) 10 + 19	110) 14 + 12
111) 11 + 19	112) 17 + 10	113) 19 + 11	114) 16 + 14	115) 17 + 3
116) 14 + 4	117) 4 + 5	118) 11 + 5	119) 15 + 4	120) 9 + 1

121) 10 + 11	122) 13 + 17	123) 16 + 12	124) 10 + 8	125) 3 + 13
126) 18 + 19	127) 14 + 15	128) 1 + 14	129) 9 + 18	130) 2 + 16
131) 3 + 4	132) 4 + 7	133) 13 + 11	134) 10 + 6	135) 4 + 19
136) 12 + 5	137) 5 + 11	138) 1 + 3	139) 6 + 5	140) 11 + 1
141) 12 + 12	142) 10 + 18	143) 20 + 8	144) 10 + 3	145) 15 + 15

146) 2 + 13

147) 16 + 8

148) 20 + 13

149) 13 + 10

150) 13 + 4

151) 13 + 2

152) 7 + 4

153) 3 + 18

154) 17 + 16

155) 12 + 8

156) 18 + 18

157) 3 + 2

158) 18 + 20

159) 14 + 2

160) 9 + 12

161) 20 + 3

162) 10 + 15

163) 5 + 3

164) 5 + 13

165) 7 + 12

166) 20 + 19

167) 5 + 15

168) 5 + 6

169) 11 + 2

170) 9 + 8

171)   11
   + 10

172)   19
   + 4

173)   7
   + 17

174)   17
   + 1

175)   13
   + 8

176)   7
   + 14

177)   6
   + 9

178)   18
   + 14

179)   12
   + 20

180)   13
   + 16

181)   5
   + 4

182)   3
   + 17

183)   6
   + 13

184)   9
   + 7

185)   3
   + 19

186)   12
   + 13

187)   9
   + 13

188)   14
   + 14

189)   2
   + 2

190)   2
   + 14

191)   18
   + 2

192)   5
   + 9

193)   8
   + 19

194)   15
   + 8

Subtraction: 1 through 20

Find the Difference.

1) 14 − 10	2) 12 − 6	3) 8 − 6	4) 20 − 9	5) 18 − 13
6) 2 − 2	7) 19 − 8	8) 16 − 13	9) 4 − 1	10) 17 − 7
11) 6 − 6	12) 13 − 11	13) 10 − 2	14) 14 − 2	15) 19 − 18
16) 11 − 10	17) 2 − 1	18) 14 − 7	19) 9 − 7	20) 19 − 7

21) 10 − 9 = ___

22) 12 − 5 = ___

23) 5 − 3 = ___

24) 16 − 11 = ___

25) 10 − 4 = ___

26) 9 − 6 = ___

27) 16 − 9 = ___

28) 19 − 15 = ___

29) 20 − 19 = ___

30) 20 − 1 = ___

31) 17 − 3 = ___

32) 16 − 6 = ___

33) 3 − 2 = ___

34) 20 − 11 = ___

35) 19 − 6 = ___

36) 7 − 5 = ___

37) 18 − 3 = ___

38) 7 − 3 = ___

39) 9 − 3 = ___

40) 14 − 3 = ___

41) 7 − 6 = ___

42) 16 − 10 = ___

43) 15 − 1 = ___

44) 8 − 4 = ___

45) 1 − 1 = ___

46) 15 − 13 ―――	47) 19 − 17 ―――	48) 13 − 9 ―――	49) 12 − 8 ―――	50) 14 − 6 ―――
51) 13 − 13 ―――	52) 9 − 8 ―――	53) 16 − 15 ―――	54) 18 − 15 ―――	55) 12 − 12 ―――
56) 13 − 4 ―――	57) 7 − 1 ―――	58) 19 − 11 ―――	59) 19 − 16 ―――	60) 3 − 3 ―――
61) 14 − 12 ―――	62) 16 − 3 ―――	63) 6 − 3 ―――	64) 8 − 5 ―――	65) 15 − 8 ―――
66) 15 − 6 ―――	67) 15 − 14 ―――	68) 11 − 3 ―――	69) 18 − 6 ―――	70) 15 − 2 ―――

Name: _______________________   Date: ___ / ___ / ___

71)	72)	73)	74)	75)
19 − 1	12 − 7	12 − 1	15 − 11	5 − 2

76)	77)	78)	79)	80)
10 − 6	16 − 14	18 − 9	18 − 10	13 − 6

81)	82)	83)	84)	85)
18 − 5	16 − 5	14 − 4	11 − 5	17 − 2

86)	87)	88)	89)	90)
18 − 2	11 − 4	3 − 1	17 − 13	9 − 9

91)	92)	93)	94)	95)
16 − 4	4 − 3	8 − 1	10 − 10	17 − 8

Name: ___________   Date: ___ \ ___ \ ___

96) 18 − 11	97) 12 − 2	98) 17 − 14	99) 5 − 4	100) 14 − 8
101) 6 − 2	102) 6 − 4	103) 19 − 5	104) 15 − 3	105) 4 − 2
106) 18 − 7	107) 8 − 7	108) 17 − 11	109) 11 − 2	110) 7 − 4
111) 15 − 4	112) 10 − 5	113) 11 − 7	114) 14 − 13	115) 6 − 5
116) 8 − 3	117) 9 − 4	118) 14 − 11	119) 10 − 8	120) 20 − 17

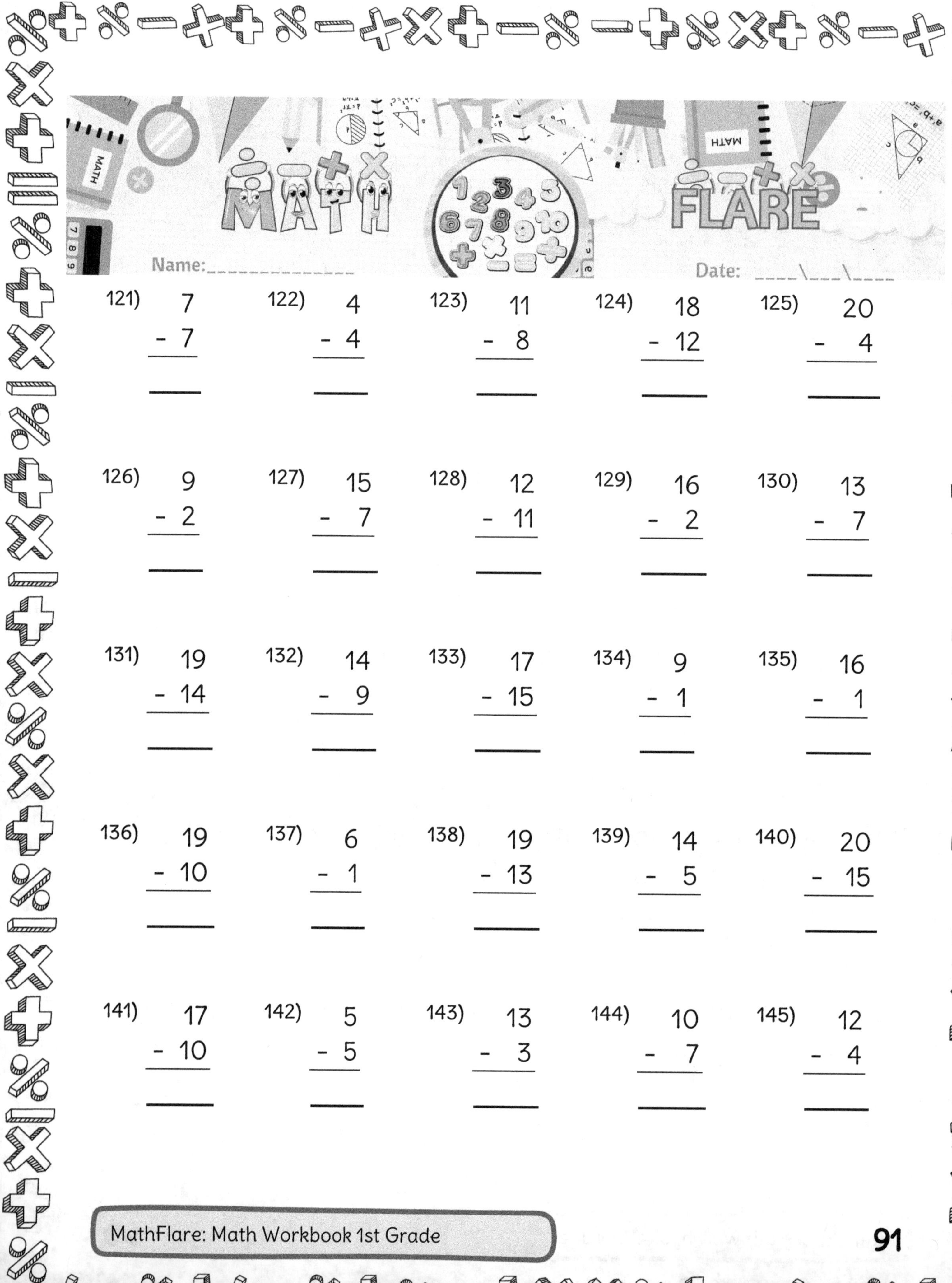

Name:______________________   Date: _______________

| 121) 7
− 7 | 122) 4
− 4 | 123) 11
− 8 | 124) 18
− 12 | 125) 20
− 4 |

| 126) 9
− 2 | 127) 15
− 7 | 128) 12
− 11 | 129) 16
− 2 | 130) 13
− 7 |

| 131) 19
− 14 | 132) 14
− 9 | 133) 17
− 15 | 134) 9
− 1 | 135) 16
− 1 |

| 136) 19
− 10 | 137) 6
− 1 | 138) 19
− 13 | 139) 14
− 5 | 140) 20
− 15 |

| 141) 17
− 10 | 142) 5
− 5 | 143) 13
− 3 | 144) 10
− 7 | 145) 12
− 4 |

Name:_________________________   Date:_____ _____ _____

146) 17 − 4	147) 16 − 12	148) 11 − 9	149) 16 − 7	150) 15 − 5
151) 13 − 10	152) 12 − 9	153) 19 − 2	154) 11 − 6	155) 12 − 3
156) 8 − 2	157) 5 − 1	158) 18 − 4	159) 16 − 8	160) 19 − 9
161) 15 − 10	162) 10 − 3	163) 7 − 2	164) 18 − 14	165) 9 − 5
166) 13 − 2	167) 13 − 5	168) 13 − 12	169) 20 − 13	170) 15 − 9

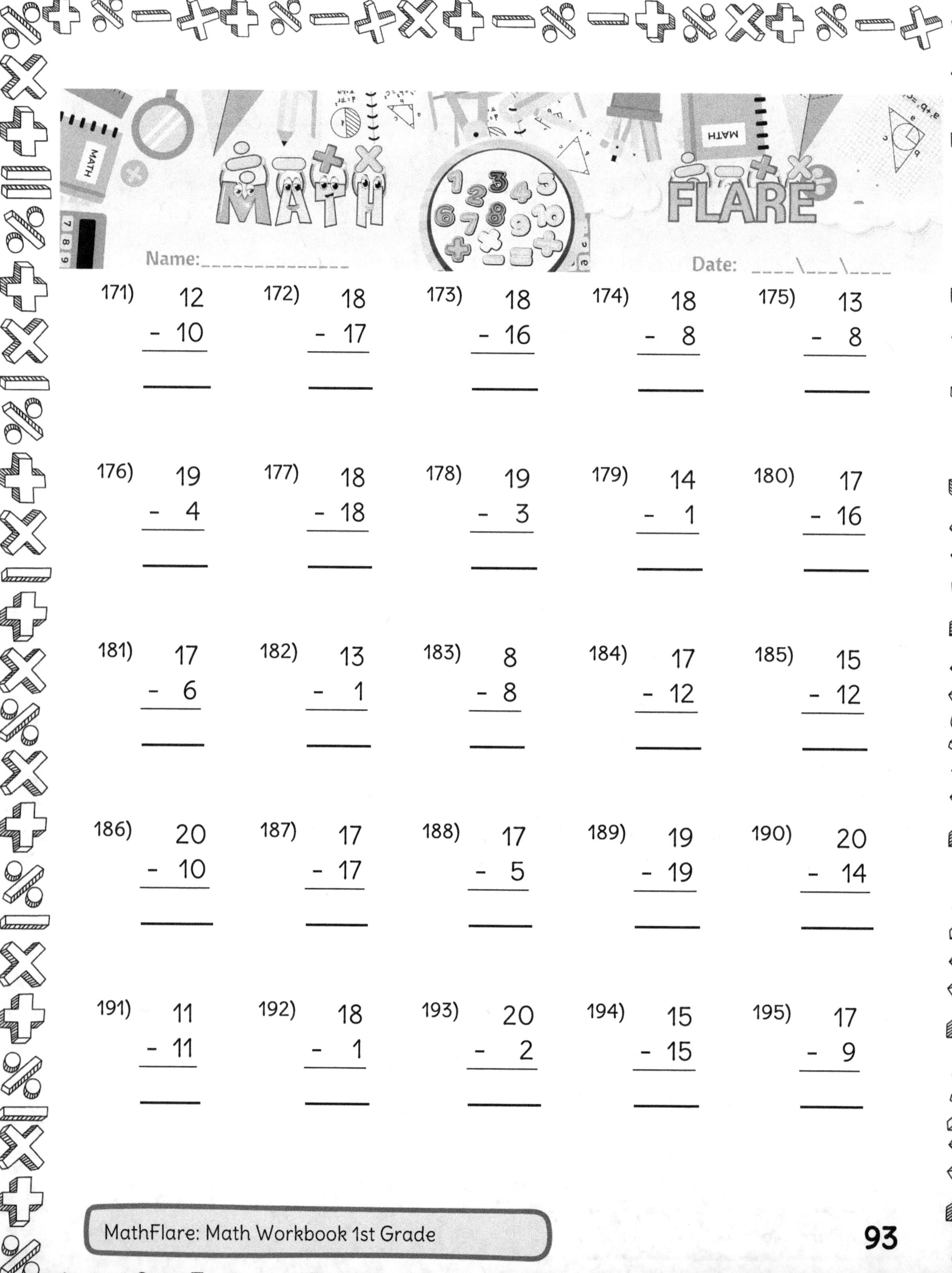

171) 12 − 10	172) 18 − 17	173) 18 − 16	174) 18 − 8	175) 13 − 8
176) 19 − 4	177) 18 − 18	178) 19 − 3	179) 14 − 1	180) 17 − 16
181) 17 − 6	182) 13 − 1	183) 8 − 8	184) 17 − 12	185) 15 − 12
186) 20 − 10	187) 17 − 17	188) 17 − 5	189) 19 − 19	190) 20 − 14
191) 11 − 11	192) 18 − 1	193) 20 − 2	194) 15 − 15	195) 17 − 9

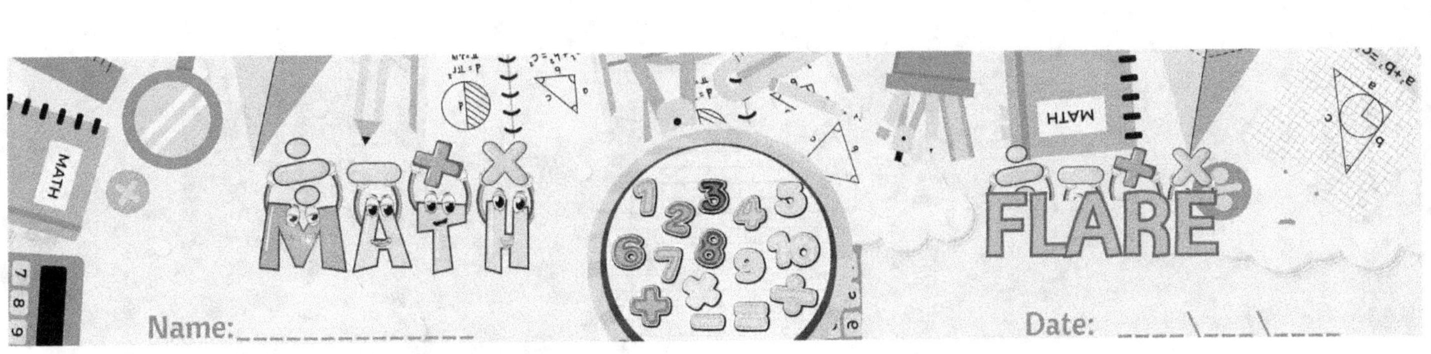

Commutative Property

Use the commutative property to fill the missing values.

1) 2 + __ = 9 + 2

2) __ + 8 = 8 + 3

3) 2 + 8 = 8 + __

4) 8 + __ = 4 + 8

5) __ + 1 = 1 + 10

6) 1 + 5 = 5 + __

7) 2 + 5 = __ + 2

8) __ + 7 = 7 + 2

9) __ + 3 = 3 + 4

10) __ + 8 = 8 + 10

11) 9 + __ = 6 + 9

12) 3 + 7 = 7 + __

13) 7 + 9 = __ + 7

14) 2 + __ = 3 + 2

15) 10 + 5 = 5 + __

16) 5 + __ = 7 + 5

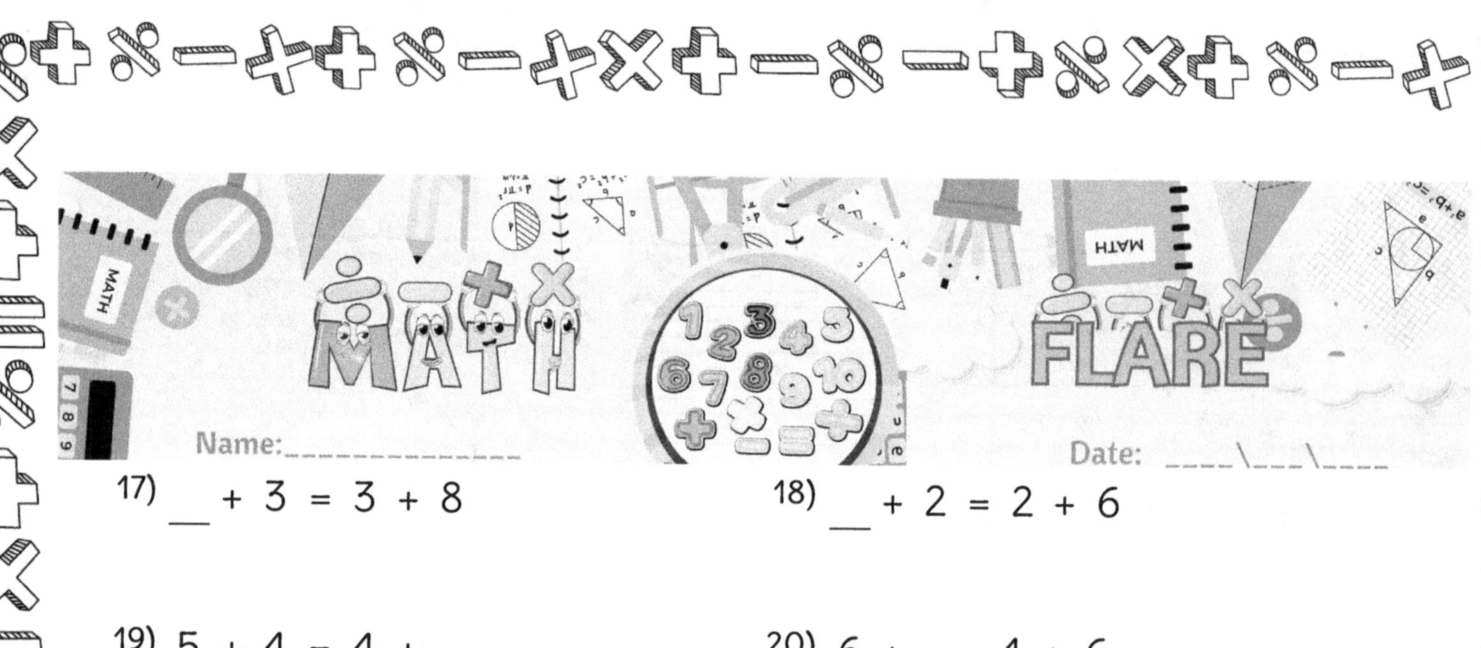

17) __ + 3 = 3 + 8

18) __ + 2 = 2 + 6

19) 5 + 4 = 4 + __

20) 6 + __ = 1 + 6

21) 5 + __ = 3 + 5

22) __ + 1 = 1 + 5

23) 1 + __ = 2 + 1

24) 9 + 5 = 5 + __

25) 6 + __ = 5 + 6

26) __ + 4 = 4 + 7

27) __ + 9 = 9 + 3

28) 3 + __ = 10 + 3

29) 7 + 2 = __ + 7

30) 8 + 2 = 2 + __

31) 2 + __ = 1 + 2

32) 6 + 9 = __ + 6

33) 6 + __ = 3 + 6

34) 2 + 6 = 6 + __

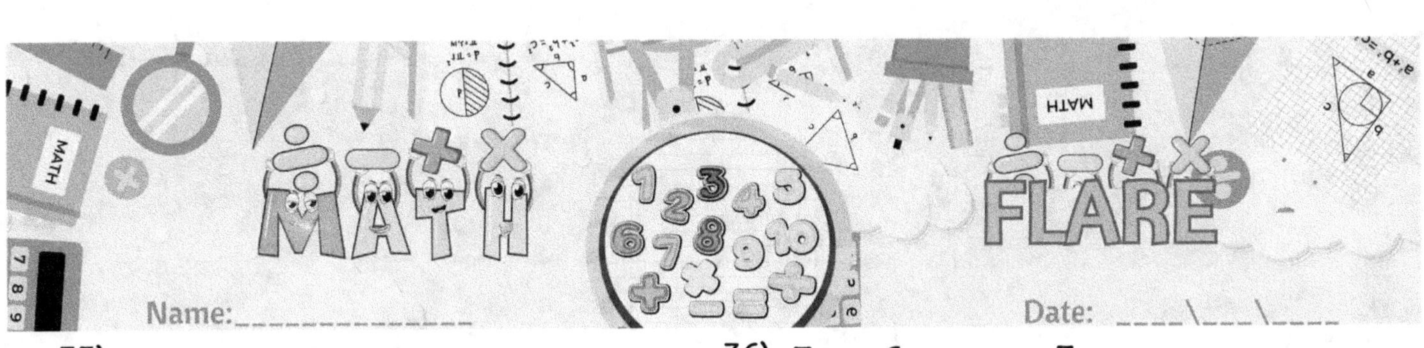

35) 4 + __ = 7 + 4

36) 3 + 6 = __ + 3

37) 1 + __ = 8 + 1

38) 1 + 10 = ___ + 1

39) 4 + 6 = __ + 4

40) 3 + 2 = 2 + __

41) 4 + 9 = 9 + __

42) 3 + 5 = 5 + __

43) 5 + 8 = 8 + __

44) 9 + 10 = 10 + __

45) 5 + 9 = 9 + __

46) __ + 4 = 4 + 2

47) 10 + 6 = 6 + ___

48) __ + 8 = 8 + 4

49) __ + 5 = 5 + 7

50) __ + 7 = 7 + 6

51) 7 + __ = 3 + 7

52) 5 + 2 = 2 + __

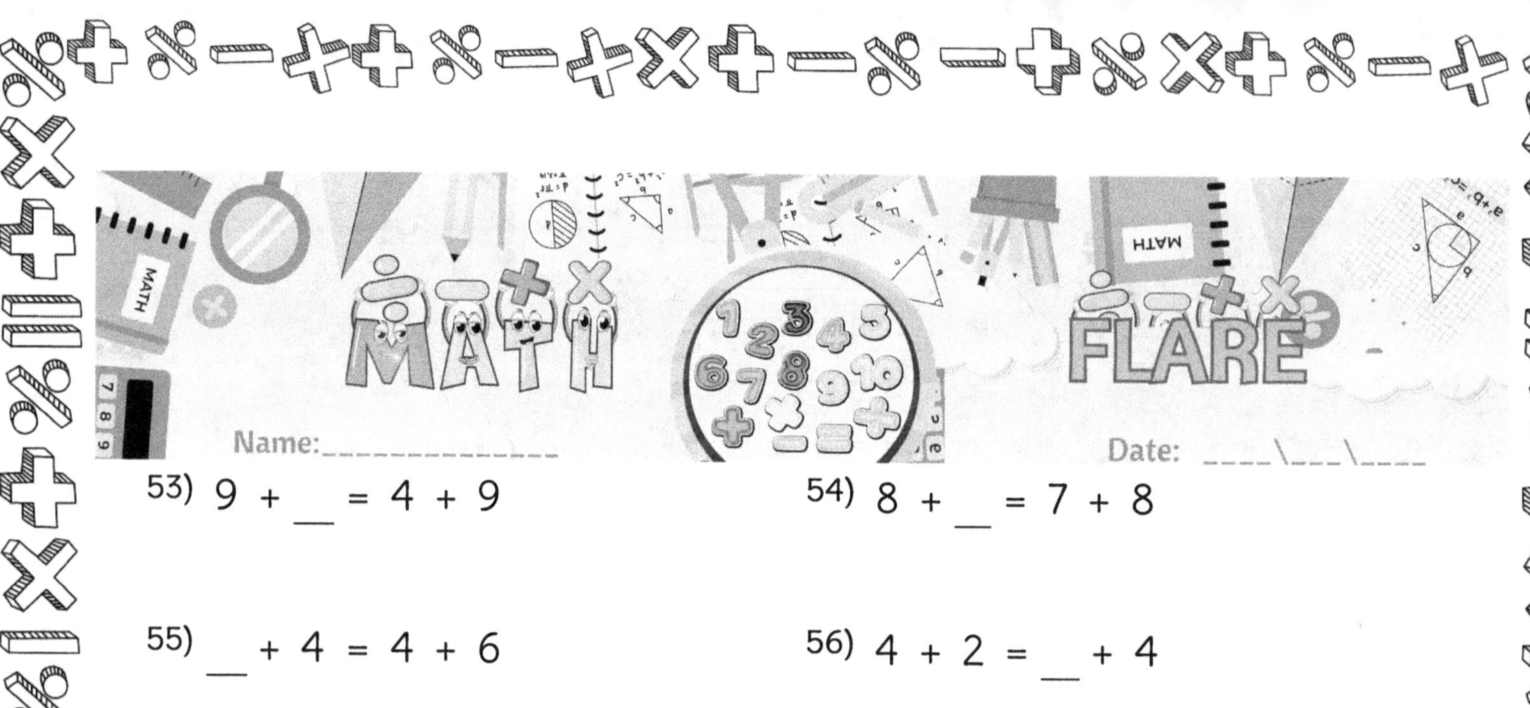

53) 9 + __ = 4 + 9

54) 8 + __ = 7 + 8

55) __ + 4 = 4 + 6

56) 4 + 2 = __ + 4

57) 6 + 10 = 10 + __

58) __ + 8 = 8 + 7

59) 8 + __ = 9 + 8

60) __ + 3 = 3 + 9

61) 8 + 5 = 5 + __

62) 4 + __ = 1 + 4

63) 10 + 2 = 2 + __

64) __ + 9 = 9 + 1

65) 1 + __ = 6 + 1

66) 10 + __ = 4 + 10

67) 10 + __ = 7 + 10

68) 1 + 3 = 3 + __

69) 3 + 1 = 1 + __

70) 10 + __ = 3 + 10

71) 7 + __ = 6 + 7

72) __ + 4 = 4 + 3

73) __ + 5 = 5 + 4

74) 7 + 10 = __ + 7

75) 5 + __ = 10 + 5

76) 10 + __ = 9 + 10

77) __ + 6 = 6 + 8

78) 1 + 4 = 4 + __

79) __ + 8 = 8 + 9

80) __ + 2 = 2 + 9

81) __ + 6 = 6 + 5

82) 4 + 10 = __ + 4

83) 9 + __ = 1 + 9

84) __ + 7 = 7 + 9

85) __ + 8 = 8 + 6

86) __ + 10 = 10 + 8

87) 1 + 7 = 7 + __

88) 7 + __ = 1 + 7

Addition-Subtraction Activities

1)

a. 14 + 1 = _______ •	• F = 21
b. 19 – 13 = _______ •	• H = 6
c. 8 + 13 = _______ •	• A = 21
d. 2 – 2 = _______ •	• G = 0
e. 19 + 17 = _______ •	• I = 34
f. 16 + 18 = _______ •	• B = 16
g. 6 + 15 = _______ •	• J = 0
h. 2 + 14 = _______ •	• E = 15
i. 13 – 13 = _______ •	• C = 36
j. 4 + 20 = _______ •	• D = 24

2)

a. 4 + 7 = _________ •

b. 19 – 1 = _______ •

c. 9 + 3 = _______ •

d. 5 – 5 = _______ •

e. 11 – 11 = ______ •

f. 17 – 16 = ______ •

g. 8 – 4 = _______ •

h. 4 + 12 = ______ •

i. 11 + 17 = ______ •

j. 5 – 3 = _______ •

• G = 2

• B = 0

• D = 1

• I = 4

• C = 18

• H = 16

• F = 28

• E = 11

• J = 12

• A = 0

Name:______________   Date: ____________

3)

a. 4 − 2 = _______   •

b. 18 + 6 = _______   •

c. 14 + 9 = _______   •

d. 5 + 10 = _______   •

e. 8 − 2 = _______   •

f. 3 − 1 = _______   •

g. 13 + 15 = _______   •

h. 14 + 8 = _______   •

i. 5 + 18 = _______   •

j. 13 − 7 = _______   •

• G = 22

• J = 2

• E = 6

• D = 23

• H = 6

• F = 28

• A = 24

• I = 23

• C = 15

• B = 2

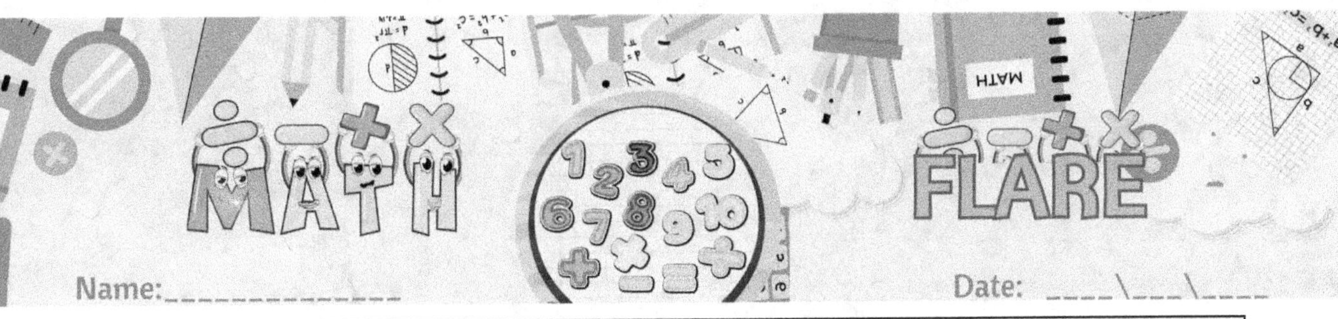

Name:________________   Date: ____________

4)

a. 20 + 14 = _______   •   • B = 34

b. 6 + 3 = _______   •   • E = 6

c. 19 + 5 = _______   •   • D = 27

d. 5 + 5 = _______   •   • F = 9

e. 15 + 18 = _______   •   • C = 24

f. 16 + 11 = _______   •   • H = 9

g. 10 - 4 = _______   •   • G = 33

h. 12 + 6 = _______   •   • I = 2

i. 2 + 7 = _______   •   • A = 18

j. 3 - 1 = _______   •   • J = 10

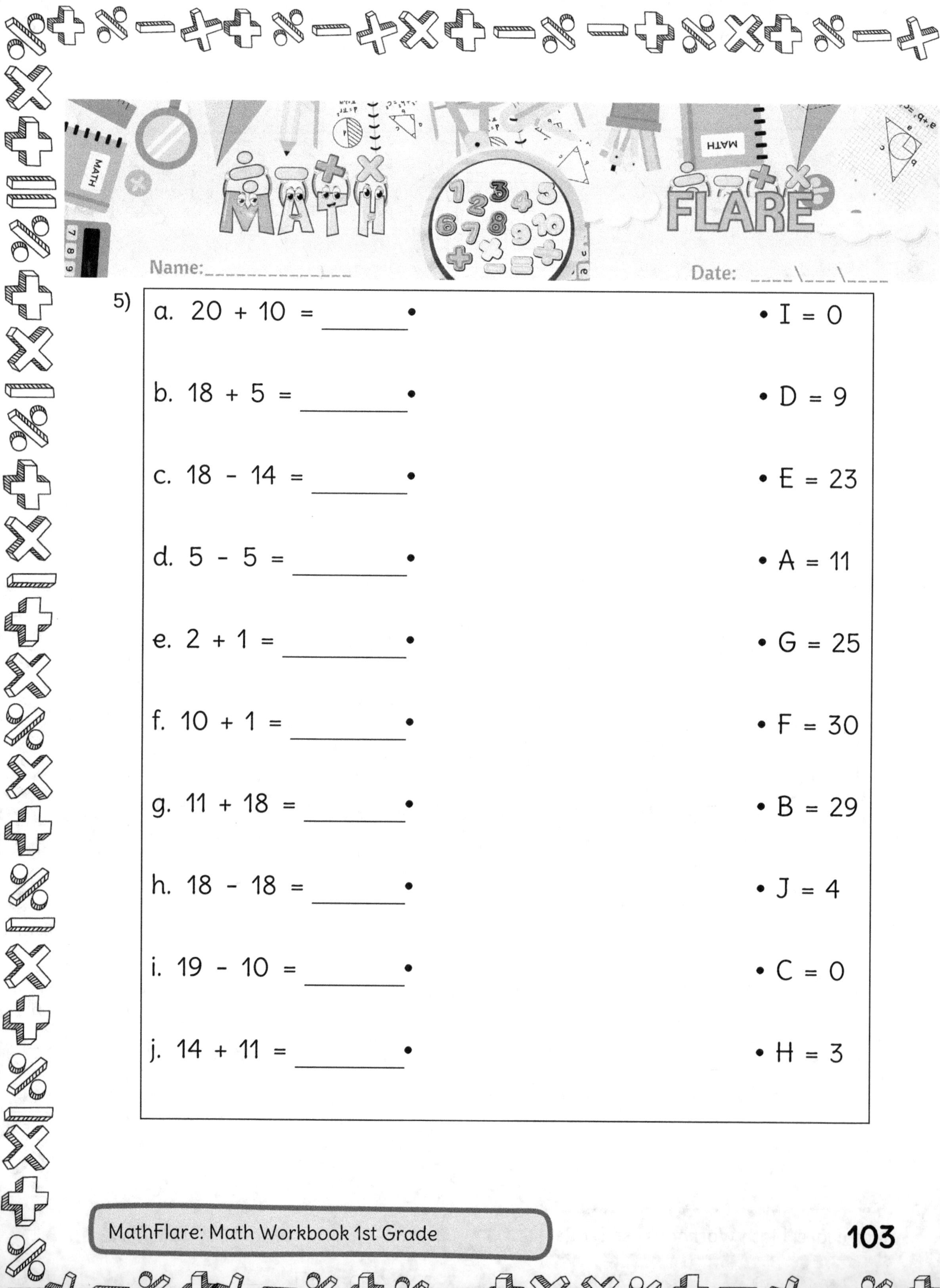

5)

a. 20 + 10 = ________ •

b. 18 + 5 = ________ •

c. 18 − 14 = ________ •

d. 5 − 5 = ________ •

e. 2 + 1 = ________ •

f. 10 + 1 = ________ •

g. 11 + 18 = ________ •

h. 18 − 18 = ________ •

i. 19 − 10 = ________ •

j. 14 + 11 = ________ •

• I = 0

• D = 9

• E = 23

• A = 11

• G = 25

• F = 30

• B = 29

• J = 4

• C = 0

• H = 3

Addition Word Problems

1) Yesterday, Raelynn earned $1, and today, Raelynn earned $5. How much money did Raelynn earn in total?

2) Gabriel made 6 cookies and Emily made 4 cookies. How many cookies were made in total?

3) Miles had 7 dollars and earned 5 more dollars. How much money does Miles have now?

4) Charlotte wrote 9 pages of her book yesterday and 9 pages today. How many pages did she write in total?

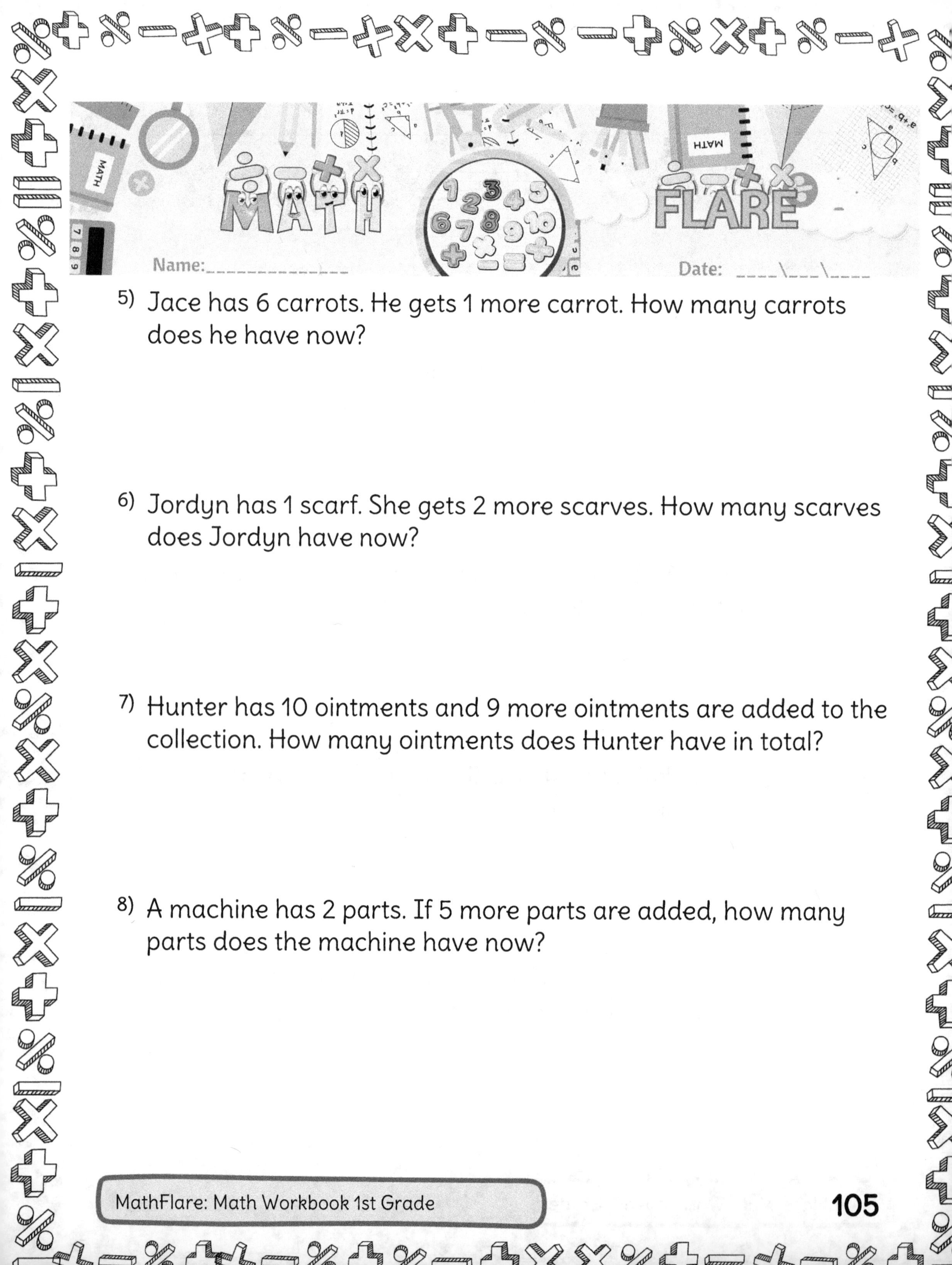

5) Jace has 6 carrots. He gets 1 more carrot. How many carrots does he have now?

6) Jordyn has 1 scarf. She gets 2 more scarves. How many scarves does Jordyn have now?

7) Hunter has 10 ointments and 9 more ointments are added to the collection. How many ointments does Hunter have in total?

8) A machine has 2 parts. If 5 more parts are added, how many parts does the machine have now?

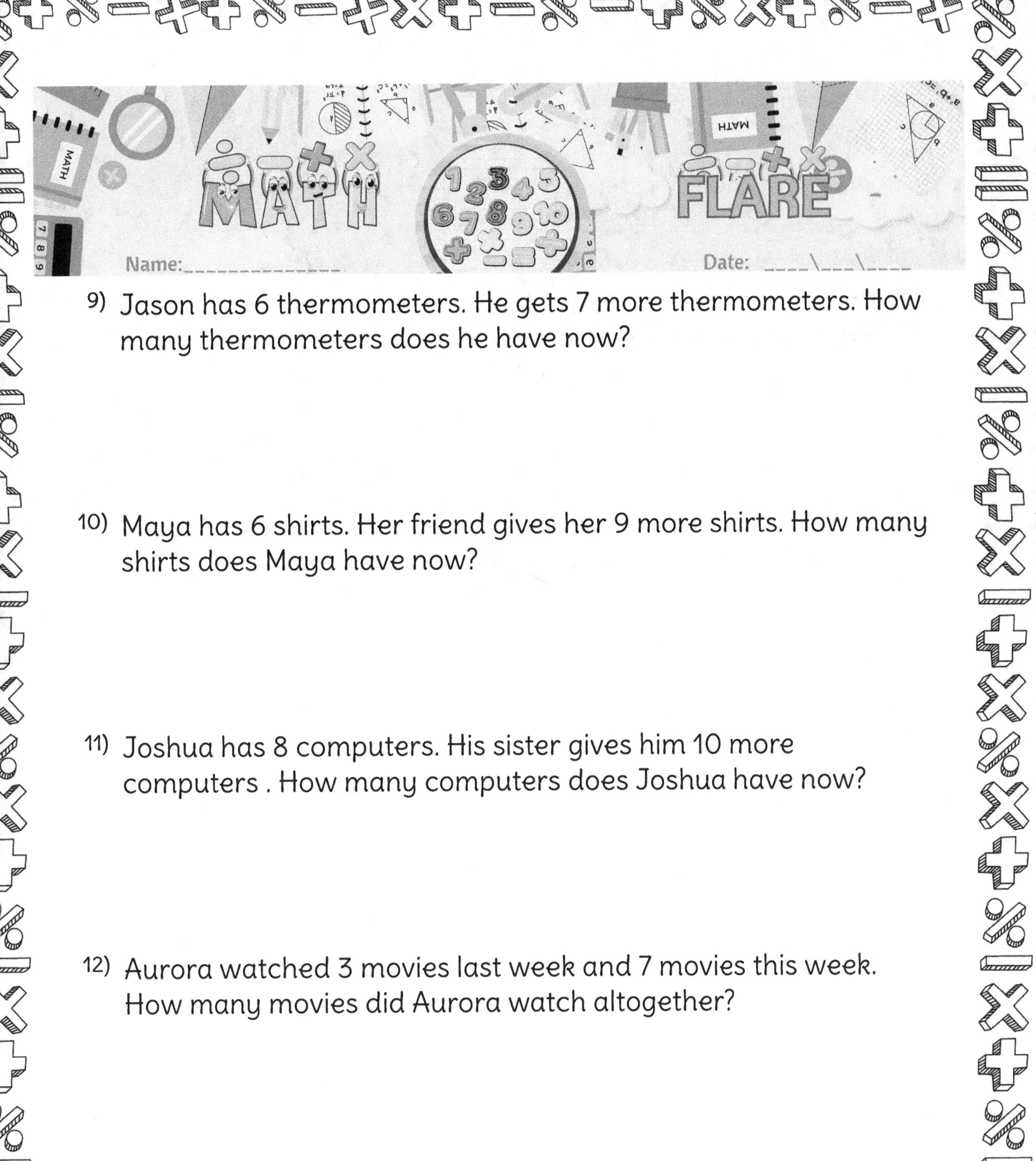

9) Jason has 6 thermometers. He gets 7 more thermometers. How many thermometers does he have now?

10) Maya has 6 shirts. Her friend gives her 9 more shirts. How many shirts does Maya have now?

11) Joshua has 8 computers. His sister gives him 10 more computers . How many computers does Joshua have now?

12) Aurora watched 3 movies last week and 7 movies this week. How many movies did Aurora watch altogether?

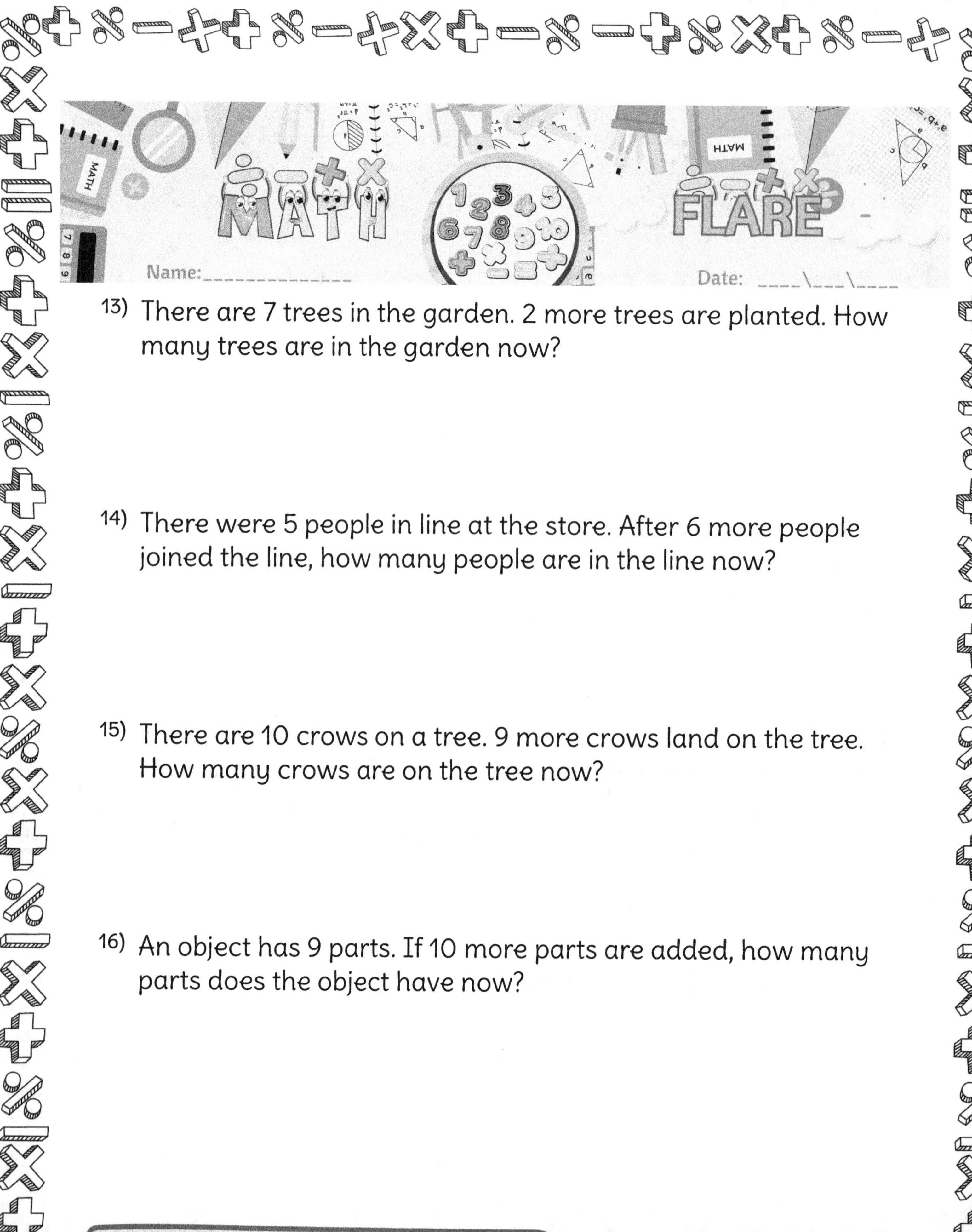

13) There are 7 trees in the garden. 2 more trees are planted. How many trees are in the garden now?

14) There were 5 people in line at the store. After 6 more people joined the line, how many people are in the line now?

15) There are 10 crows on a tree. 9 more crows land on the tree. How many crows are on the tree now?

16) An object has 9 parts. If 10 more parts are added, how many parts does the object have now?

17) Luke drove 9 miles in the morning and 2 miles in the evening. How many miles did Luke drive in total?

18) Eva bought 8 flowers and later bought 3 flowers. How many flowers does Eva have now?

19) Kai bought 7 pencils and 8 pens. How many writing instruments did Kai buy in total?

20) Nathan has 1 phone. He finds 6 more phones. How many phones does he have now?

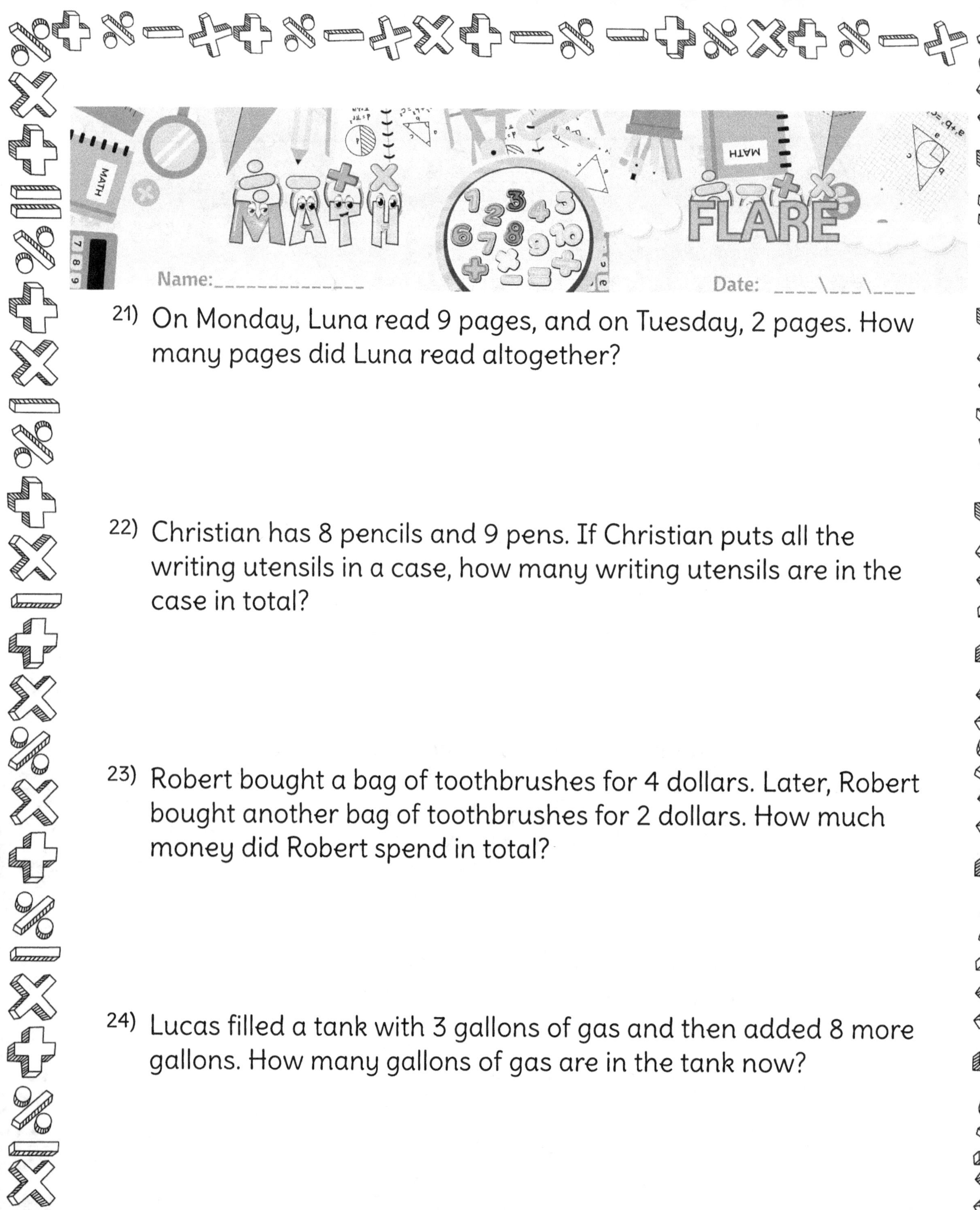

21) On Monday, Luna read 9 pages, and on Tuesday, 2 pages. How many pages did Luna read altogether?

22) Christian has 8 pencils and 9 pens. If Christian puts all the writing utensils in a case, how many writing utensils are in the case in total?

23) Robert bought a bag of toothbrushes for 4 dollars. Later, Robert bought another bag of toothbrushes for 2 dollars. How much money did Robert spend in total?

24) Lucas filled a tank with 3 gallons of gas and then added 8 more gallons. How many gallons of gas are in the tank now?

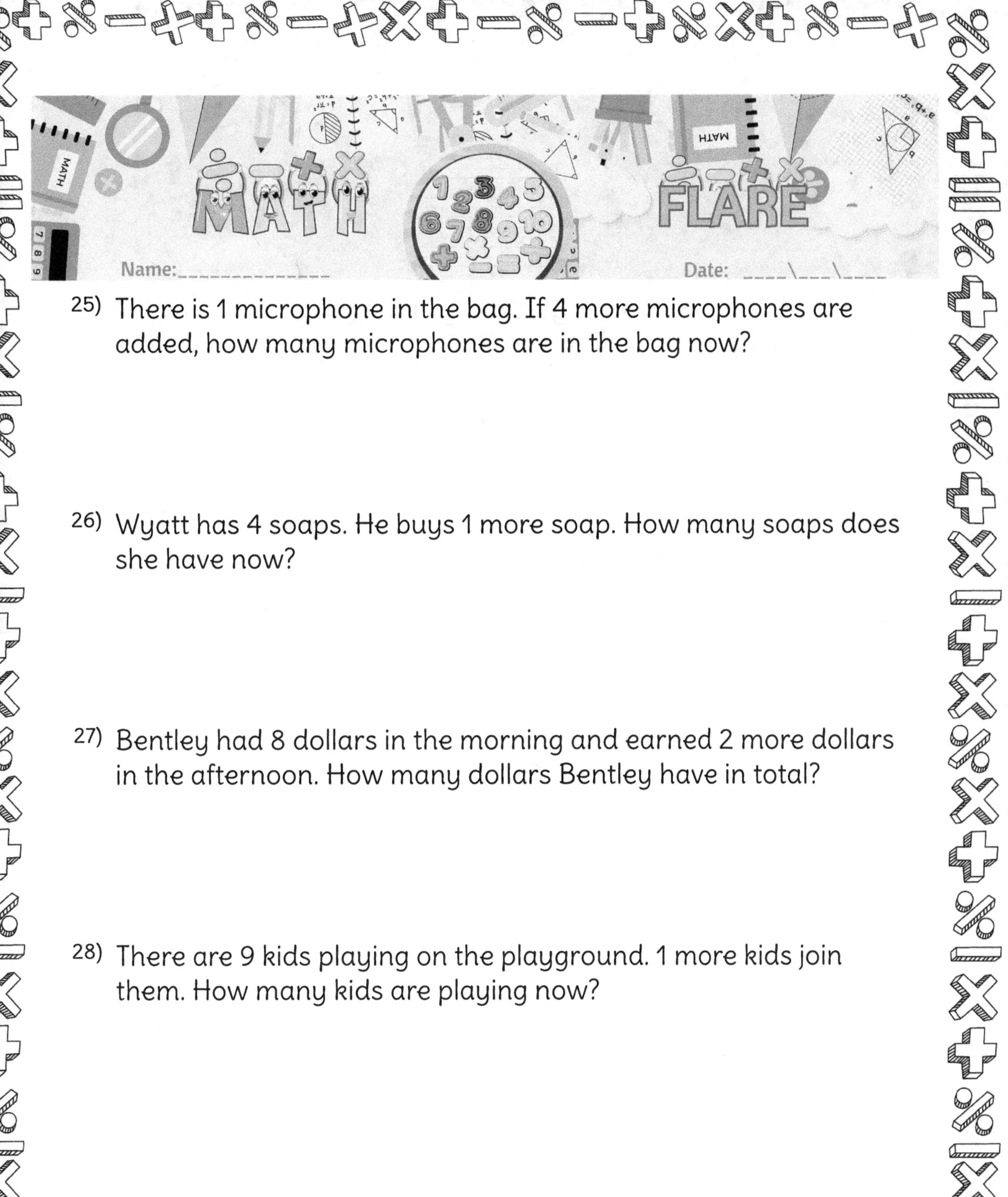

25) There is 1 microphone in the bag. If 4 more microphones are added, how many microphones are in the bag now?

26) Wyatt has 4 soaps. He buys 1 more soap. How many soaps does she have now?

27) Bentley had 8 dollars in the morning and earned 2 more dollars in the afternoon. How many dollars Bentley have in total?

28) There are 9 kids playing on the playground. 1 more kids join them. How many kids are playing now?

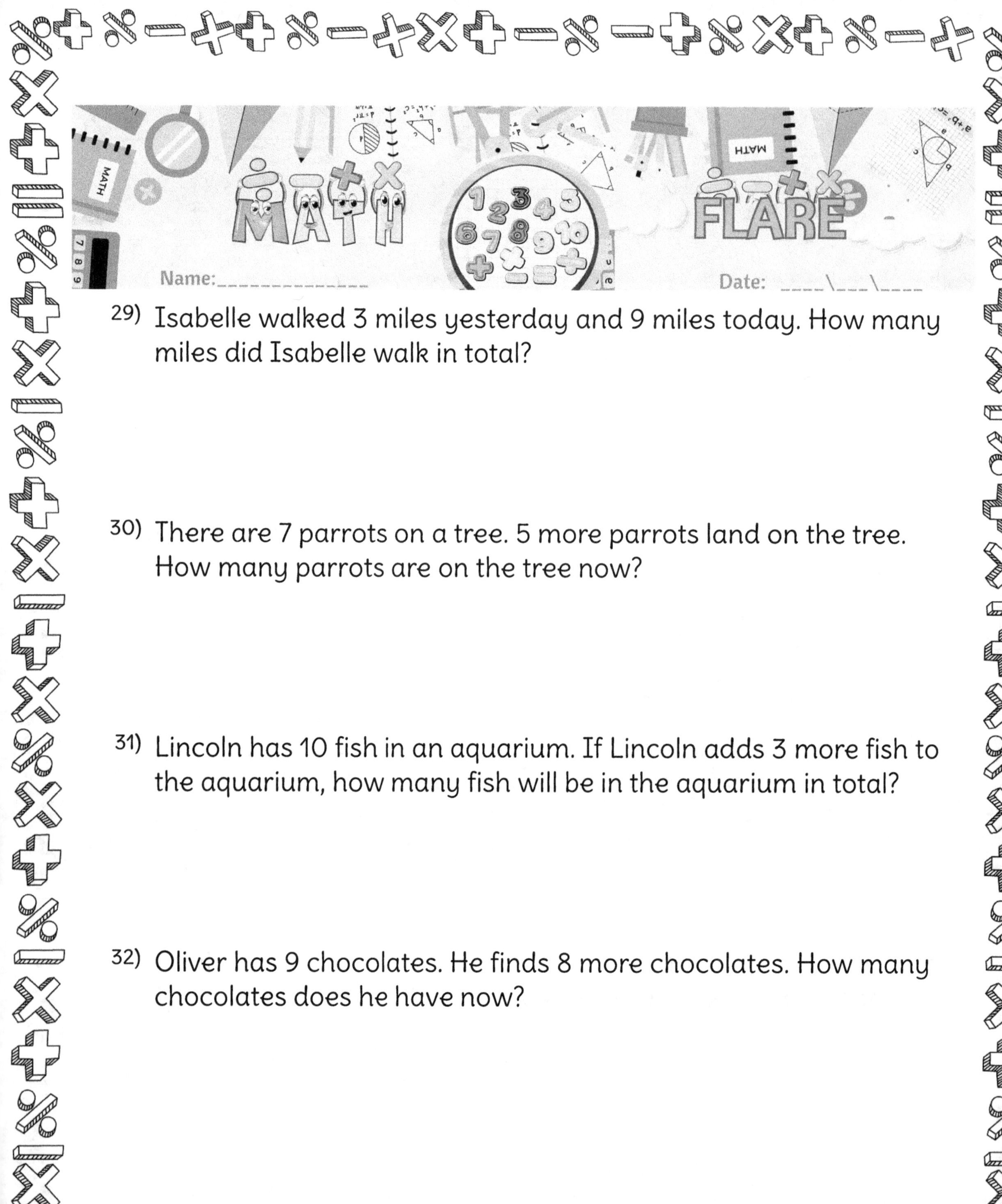

29) Isabelle walked 3 miles yesterday and 9 miles today. How many miles did Isabelle walk in total?

30) There are 7 parrots on a tree. 5 more parrots land on the tree. How many parrots are on the tree now?

31) Lincoln has 10 fish in an aquarium. If Lincoln adds 3 more fish to the aquarium, how many fish will be in the aquarium in total?

32) Oliver has 9 chocolates. He finds 8 more chocolates. How many chocolates does he have now?

33) There are 3 sticks in the room. 1 more stick is brought in. How many sticks are in the room now?

34) There are 4 vitamins on the shelf. Violet puts 9 more vitamins on the shelf. How many vitamins are there on the shelf now?

35) Owen baked 1 cookies and 10 cupcakes. How many desserts did Owen bake in total?

36) Layla has 8 bananas. She buys 9 more bananas at the store. How many bananas does Layla have now?

Subtraction Word Problems

1) Michele has 3 gloves. She lost 2 of them. How many gloves does Michele have left?

2) Knives costs 9 dollars. If you paid $8. How much change will you get back?

3) Mark had 1 spoon. He gave 1 spoon to Deborah. How many spoons does Mark have left?

4) There are 7 dogs in a park. If 7 leave, how many dogs are left in the park?

5) Donald is 10 years old and Paul is 10 years old. What is the difference in their ages?

6) Susan bought compasses for 9 dollars. She later returned some compasses and received a refund of 7 dollars. How much money did she end up spending on compasses?

7) A box had 3 chocolates. Marcie ate 3 chocolates. How many chocolates are left in the box?

8) If gauzes costs 4 dollars and you have 4 dollars, how much more money do you need to buy it?

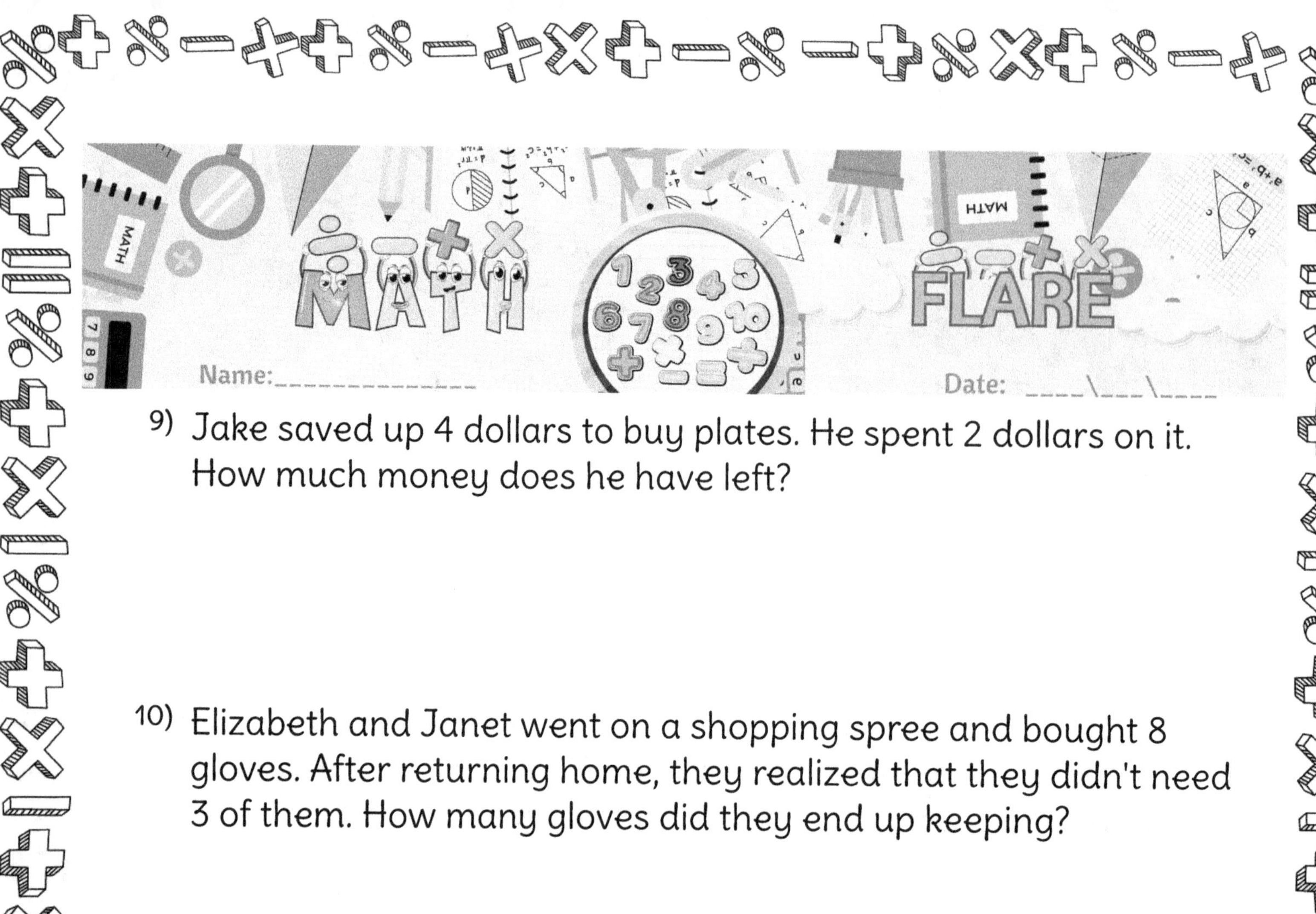

9) Jake saved up 4 dollars to buy plates. He spent 2 dollars on it. How much money does he have left?

10) Elizabeth and Janet went on a shopping spree and bought 8 gloves. After returning home, they realized that they didn't need 3 of them. How many gloves did they end up keeping?

11) Betty and Sandra went shopping for ointments. They had 9 dollars to spend but 4 dollars ended up being spent. How much money do they have left?

12) A box of forks weighs 6 pounds. If you remove 5 pounds from it, how much does it weigh now?

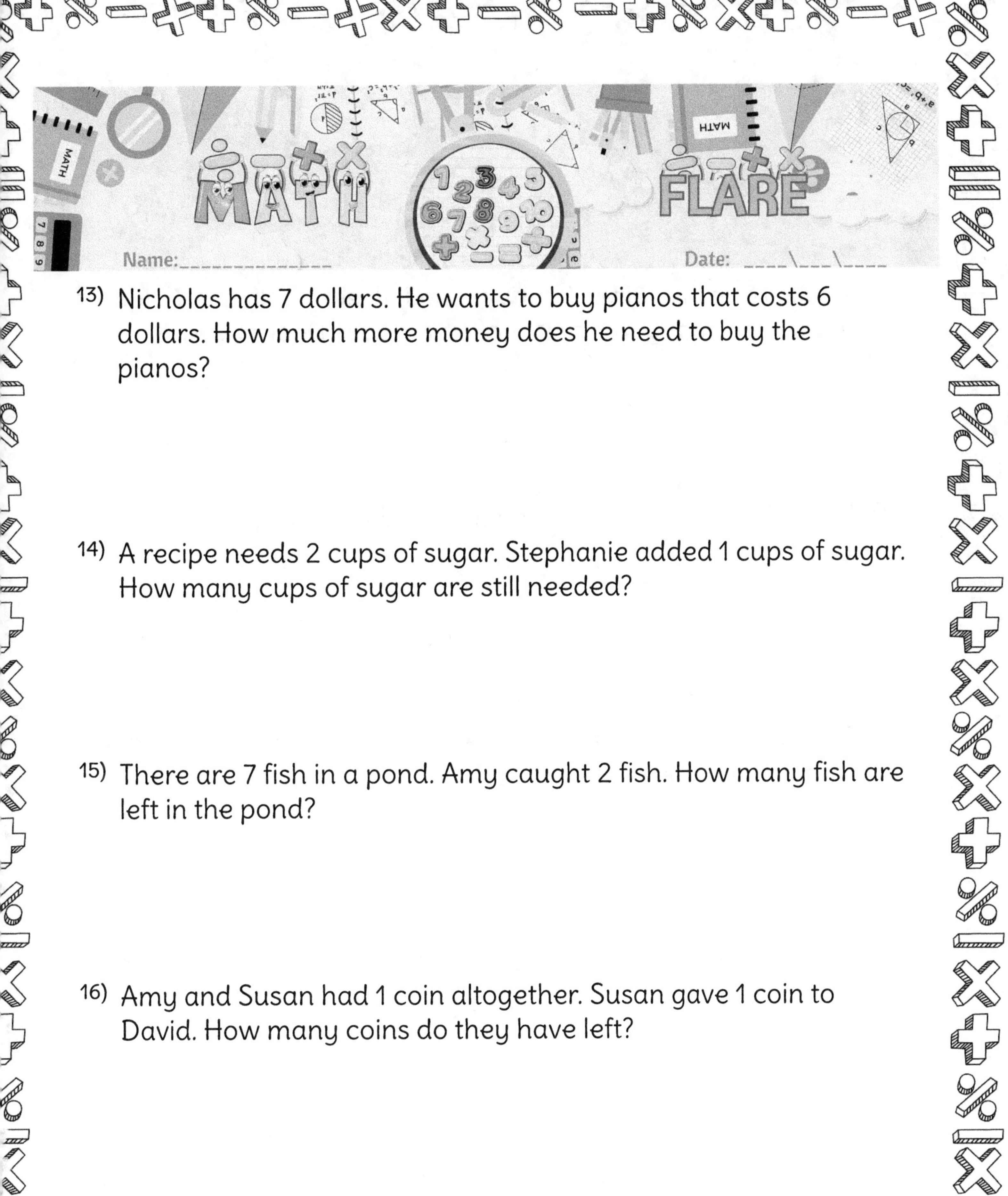

Name:_________________ Date: _______________

13) Nicholas has 7 dollars. He wants to buy pianos that costs 6 dollars. How much more money does he need to buy the pianos?

14) A recipe needs 2 cups of sugar. Stephanie added 1 cups of sugar. How many cups of sugar are still needed?

15) There are 7 fish in a pond. Amy caught 2 fish. How many fish are left in the pond?

16) Amy and Susan had 1 coin altogether. Susan gave 1 coin to David. How many coins do they have left?

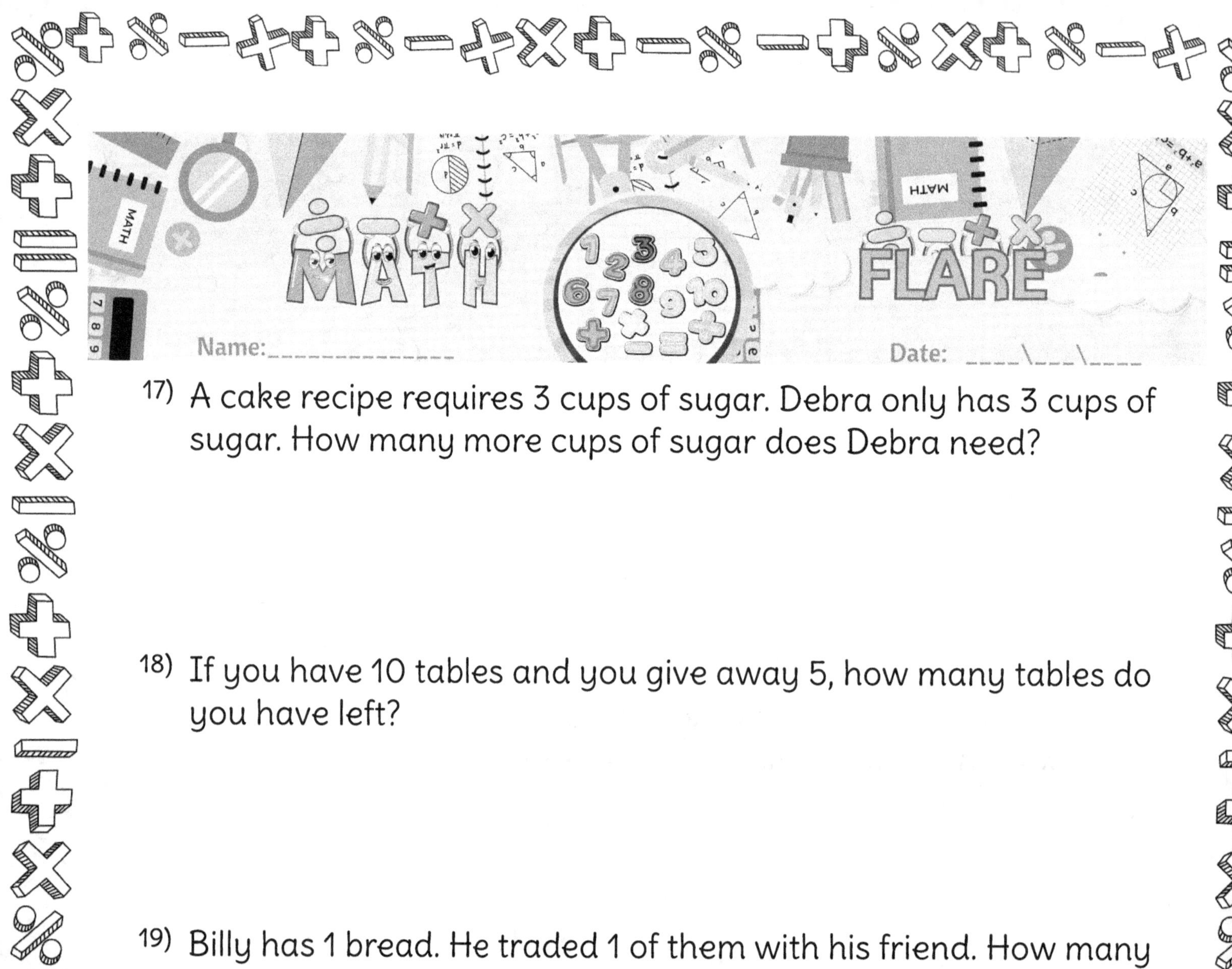

17) A cake recipe requires 3 cups of sugar. Debra only has 3 cups of sugar. How many more cups of sugar does Debra need?

18) If you have 10 tables and you give away 5, how many tables do you have left?

19) Billy has 1 bread. He traded 1 of them with his friend. How many breads does Billy have now?

20) Headphones originally cost 5 dollars, but it is now on sale for 3 dollars. How much money can you save by buying it on sale?

21) A pack of gum had 5 pieces. Jessica took 5 pieces of gum. How many pieces of gum are left in the pack?

22) Karen bought cameras for 8 dollars. She received 7 dollars in change. How much did cameras cost?

23) There are 6 watches. 4 watches are blue and the rest are red. How many red watches are in the box?

24) A lotions costs $3 and a pen costs $2. How much more expensive is the lotions than the pen?

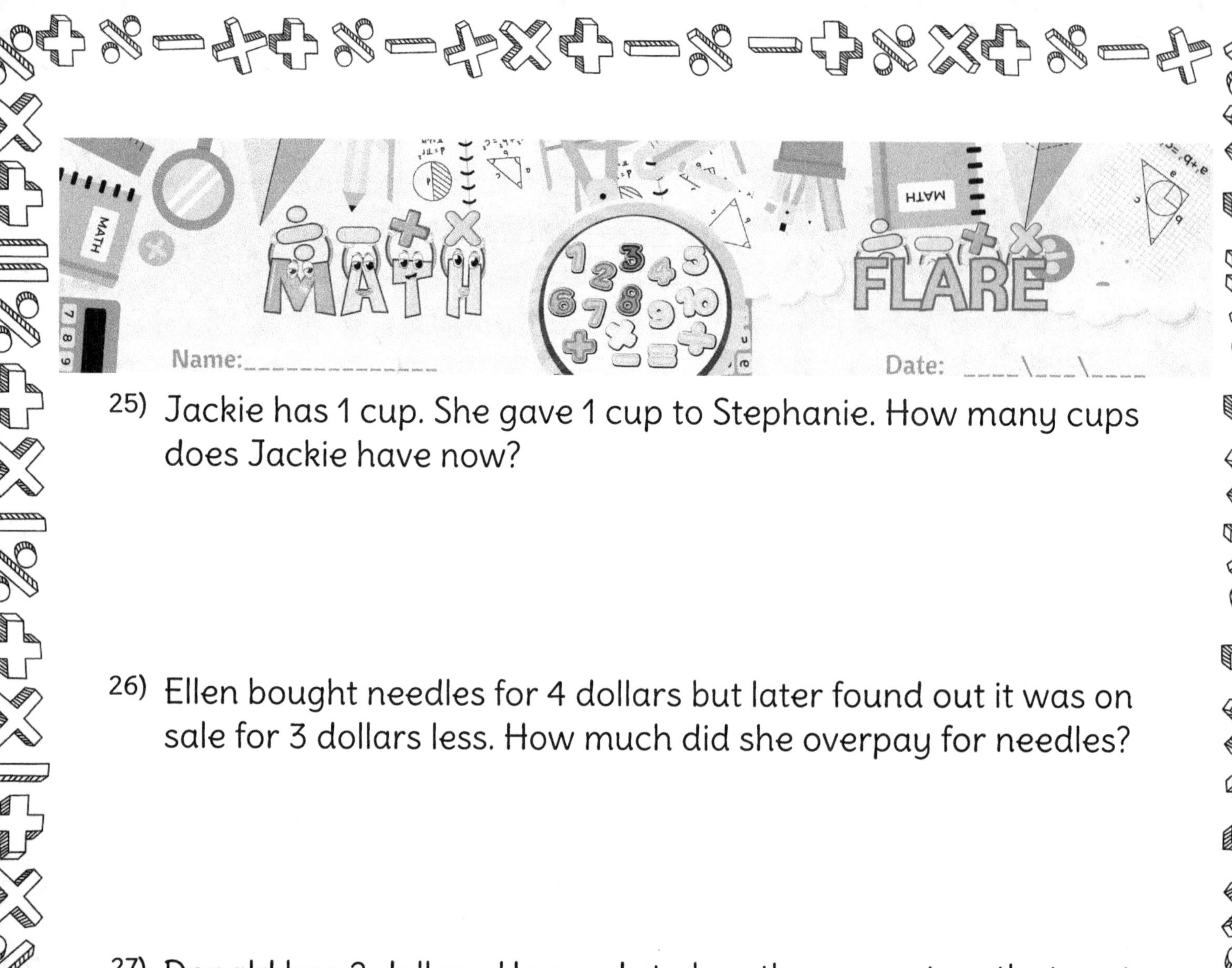

25) Jackie has 1 cup. She gave 1 cup to Stephanie. How many cups does Jackie have now?

26) Ellen bought needles for 4 dollars but later found out it was on sale for 3 dollars less. How much did she overpay for needles?

27) Donald has 2 dollars. He needs to buy thermometers that costs 8 dollars. How much money will he have left after buying the thermometers?

28) A small bag of chips has 5 chips in it. David ate 4 chips. How many chips are left in the bag?

29) A pizza has 4 slices. Sarah ate 3 slices. How many slices of pizza are left?

30) Nicholas has 10 shirts in his collection. He sold 3 of them at a sale. How many shirts does he have left in his collection?

31) Brian had 2 dollars. He spent 2 dollars on a radios. How much money does Brian have left?

32) Audrey wants to buy flosses, which costs 2 dollars. She has 1 dollars and plans to save the rest. How much more money does she need to save to buy flosses?

33) Jennifer had 6 dollars. She spent 2 dollars on shoes. How much money does Jennifer have left?

34) Stephanie has 4 apples in her collection. She gave 4 of them to her friend. How many apples does Stephanie have now?

35) Karen has 2 dollars. She wants to buy folders, which costs 4 dollars. How much more money does she need to buy it?

36) There are 6 cars in a parking lot. John took 2 cars out of the lot. How many cars are still in the lot?

37) There are 9 bats in a bag. Deborah took 1 bat out of the bag. How many bats are still in the bag?

38) There are 10 fish in a tank. If 2 leave, how many fish are left in the tank?

39) Brian has 5 red rocks and 5 green rocks. How many more red rocks does Brian have than green rocks?

40) There is 1 turtles in a pond. If 1 leave, how many turtles are left in the pond?

Chapter. 03

Place Value and Expanded Notations

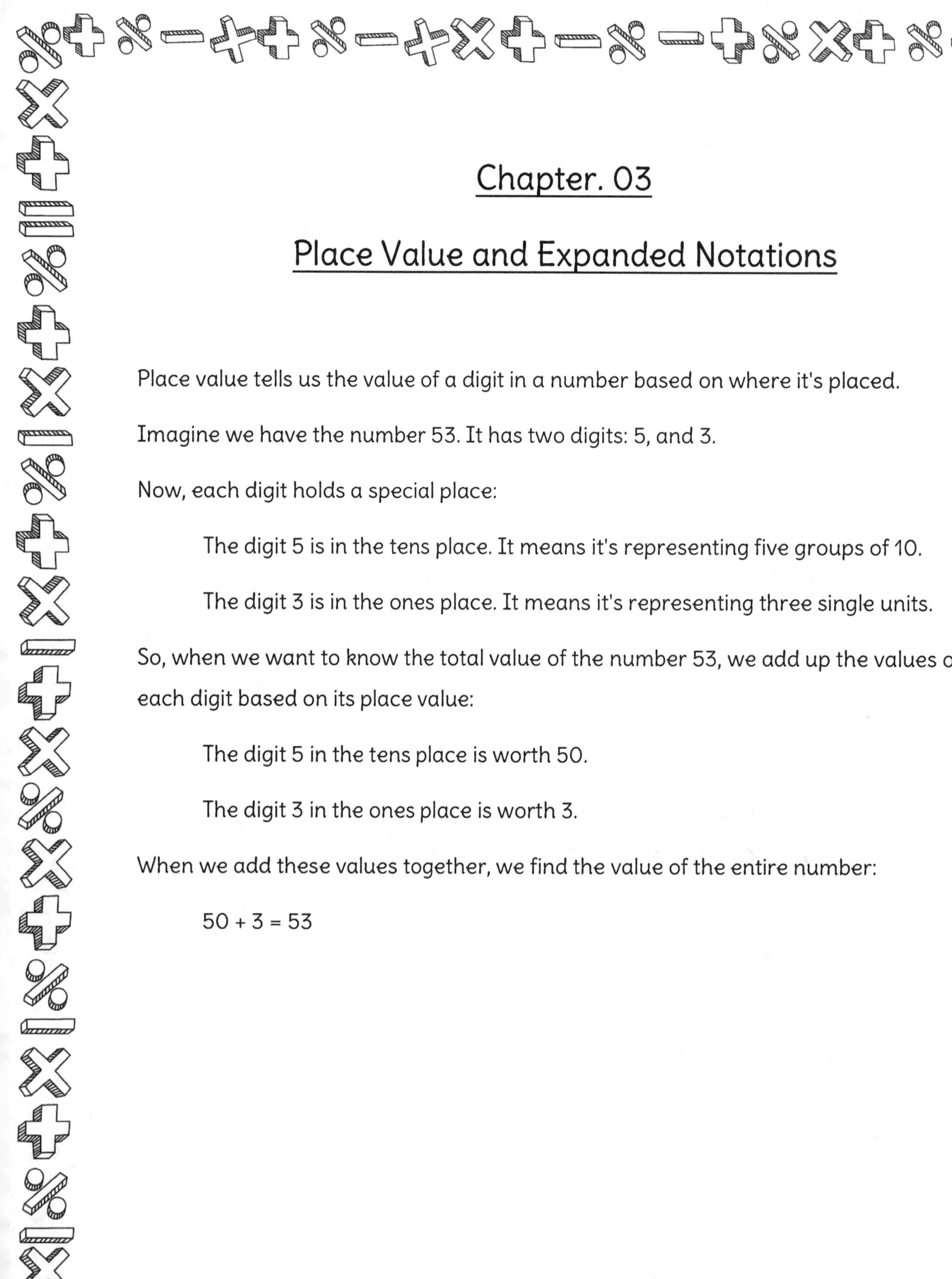

Place value tells us the value of a digit in a number based on where it's placed.

Imagine we have the number 53. It has two digits: 5, and 3.

Now, each digit holds a special place:

The digit 5 is in the tens place. It means it's representing five groups of 10.

The digit 3 is in the ones place. It means it's representing three single units.

So, when we want to know the total value of the number 53, we add up the values of each digit based on its place value:

The digit 5 in the tens place is worth 50.

The digit 3 in the ones place is worth 3.

When we add these values together, we find the value of the entire number:

50 + 3 = 53

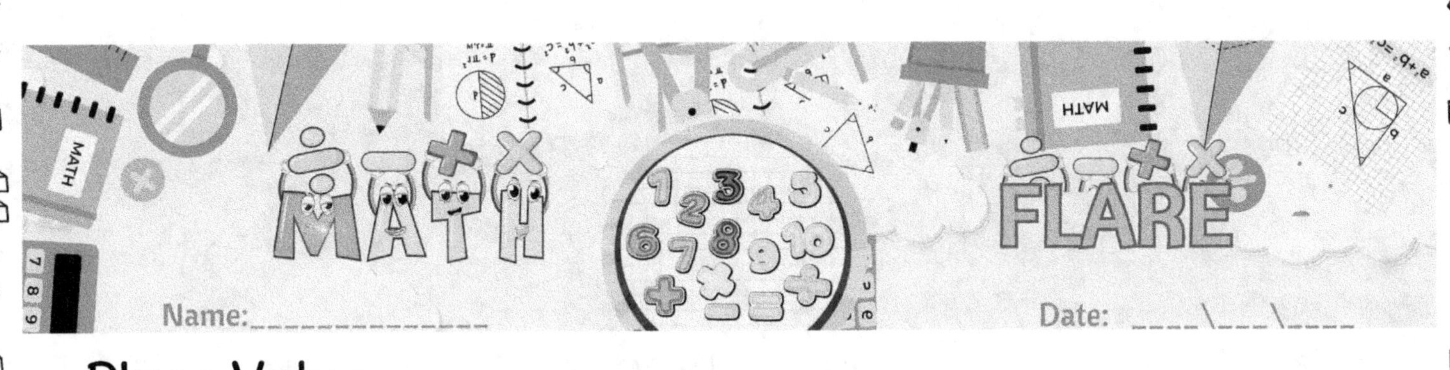

Place Value

Determine the place value of the underlined digit.

1) 2<u>4</u> = ___________________

2) <u>1</u>7 = ___________________

3) <u>6</u>2 = ___________________

4) 9<u>3</u> = ___________________

5) <u>5</u>6 = ___________________

6) <u>4</u> = ___________________

7) <u>3</u> = ___________________

8) 1<u>9</u> = ___________________

9) <u>4</u>0 = ___________________

10) <u>7</u> = ___________________

11) <u>2</u>3 = ___________________

12) 5<u>2</u> = ___________________

13) 4<u>9</u> = ___________________

14) 8<u>9</u> = ___________________

15) <u>6</u>5 = ___________________

16) <u>7</u>4 = ___________________

17) 31 = _______________________

18) 70 = _______________________

19) 78 = _______________________

20) 73 = _______________________

21) 61 = _______________________

22) 68 = _______________________

23) 55 = _______________________

24) 34 = _______________________

25) 14 = _______________________

26) 29 = _______________________

27) 39 = _______________________

28) 99 = _______________________

29) 83 = _______________________

30) 37 = _______________________

31) 97 = _______________________

32) 98 = _______________________

33) 71 = _______________________

34) 41 = _______________________

35) <u>7</u>7 = _______________

36) <u>8</u>2 = _______________

37) <u>1</u>0 = _______________

38) <u>5</u>3 = _______________

39) 7<u>6</u> = _______________

40) 5<u>9</u> = _______________

41) 2<u>8</u> = _______________

42) <u>7</u>9 = _______________

43) <u>2</u> = _______________

44) 5<u>1</u> = _______________

45) <u>9</u>4 = _______________

46) 5<u>4</u> = _______________

47) <u>6</u>9 = _______________

48) <u>9</u>0 = _______________

49) <u>9</u> = _______________

50) <u>8</u>6 = _______________

51) 4<u>2</u> = _______________

52) <u>7</u>5 = _______________

53) 7<u>2</u> = _______________

54) <u>8</u> = _______________

55) <u>8</u>4 = _______________

56) 4<u>8</u> = _______________

57) <u>5</u> = _______________

58) 6<u>3</u> = _______________

59) 8<u>8</u> = _______________

60) 8<u>5</u> = _______________

61) 4<u>6</u> = _______________

62) <u>8</u>1 = _______________

63) <u>4</u>4 = _______________

64) 3<u>0</u> = _______________

65) <u>3</u>5 = _______________

66) <u>6</u>6 = _______________

67) 6<u>7</u> = _______________

68) <u>1</u>8 = _______________

69) 1<u>5</u> = _______________

70) 3<u>8</u> = _______________

71) <u>8</u>0 = _______________

72) 5<u>7</u> = _______________

73) 2<u>7</u> = _______________

74) 9<u>6</u> = _______________

75) 3<u>3</u> = _______________

76) <u>2</u>5 = _______________

77) 9<u>5</u> = _______________

78) <u>5</u>0 = _______________

79) 4<u>3</u> = _______________

80) 2<u>6</u> = _______________

81) <u>3</u>6 = _______________

82) <u>4</u>5 = _______________

83) <u>8</u>7 = _______________

84) 2<u>1</u> = _______________

85) 2<u>0</u> = _______________

86) 22 = _______________

87) 12 = _______________

88) <u>6</u> = _______________

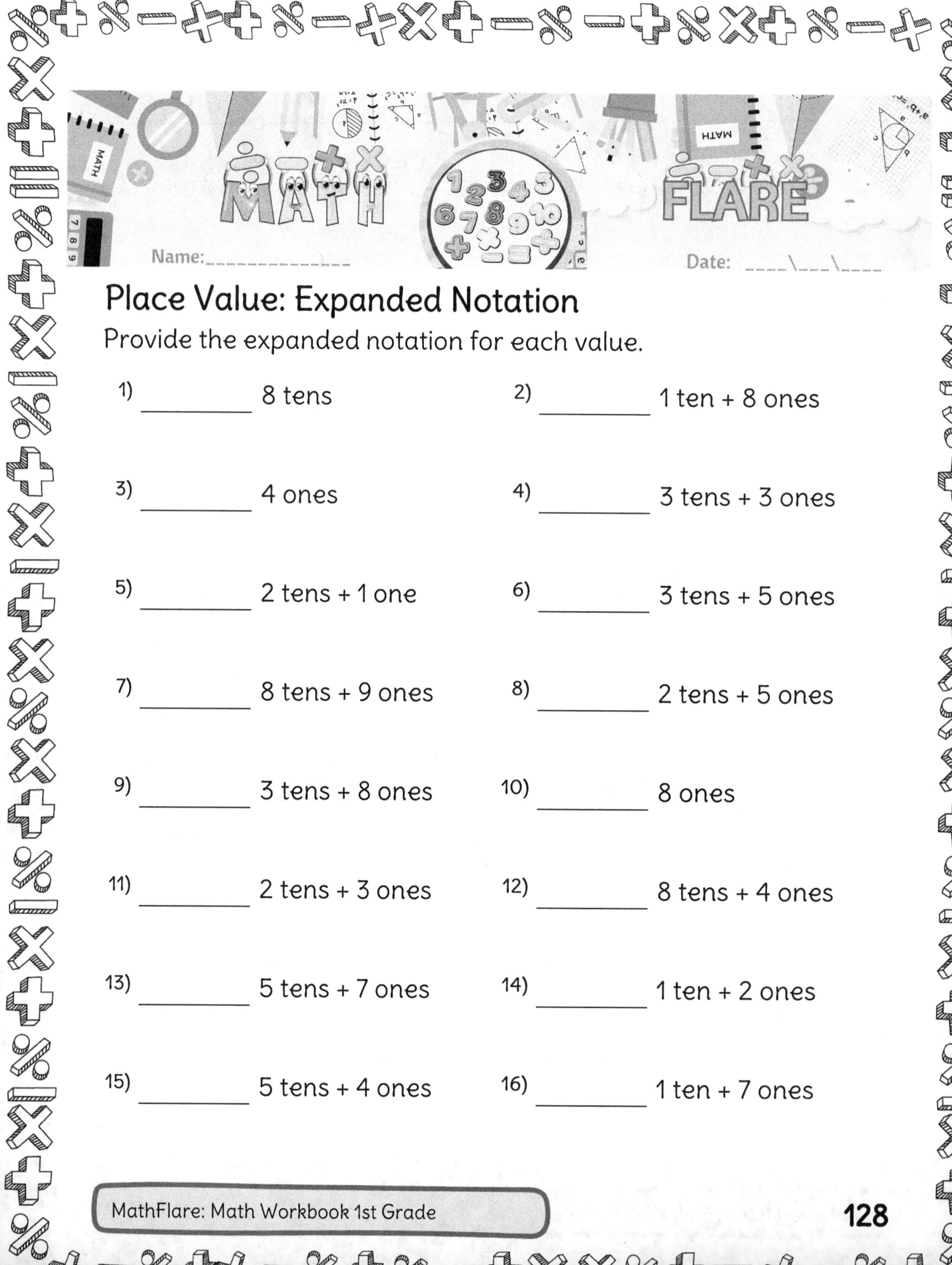

Place Value: Expanded Notation

Provide the expanded notation for each value.

1) __________ 8 tens

2) __________ 1 ten + 8 ones

3) __________ 4 ones

4) __________ 3 tens + 3 ones

5) __________ 2 tens + 1 one

6) __________ 3 tens + 5 ones

7) __________ 8 tens + 9 ones

8) __________ 2 tens + 5 ones

9) __________ 3 tens + 8 ones

10) __________ 8 ones

11) __________ 2 tens + 3 ones

12) __________ 8 tens + 4 ones

13) __________ 5 tens + 7 ones

14) __________ 1 ten + 2 ones

15) __________ 5 tens + 4 ones

16) __________ 1 ten + 7 ones

Name:________________   Date: ____________

17) __________ 1 ten + 9 ones

18) __________ 5 tens + 3 ones

19) __________ 4 tens + 1 one

20) __________ 2 ones

21) __________ 3 ones

22) __________ 9 ones

23) __________ 6 tens

24) __________ 6 tens + 6 ones

25) __________ 7 tens + 2 ones

26) __________ 9 tens + 6 ones

27) __________ 8 tens + 3 ones

28) __________ 8 tens + 5 ones

29) __________ 6 tens + 8 ones

30) __________ 5 tens + 1 one

31) __________ 8 tens + 6 ones

32) __________ 6 tens + 3 ones

33) __________ 1 one

34) __________ 4 tens + 9 ones

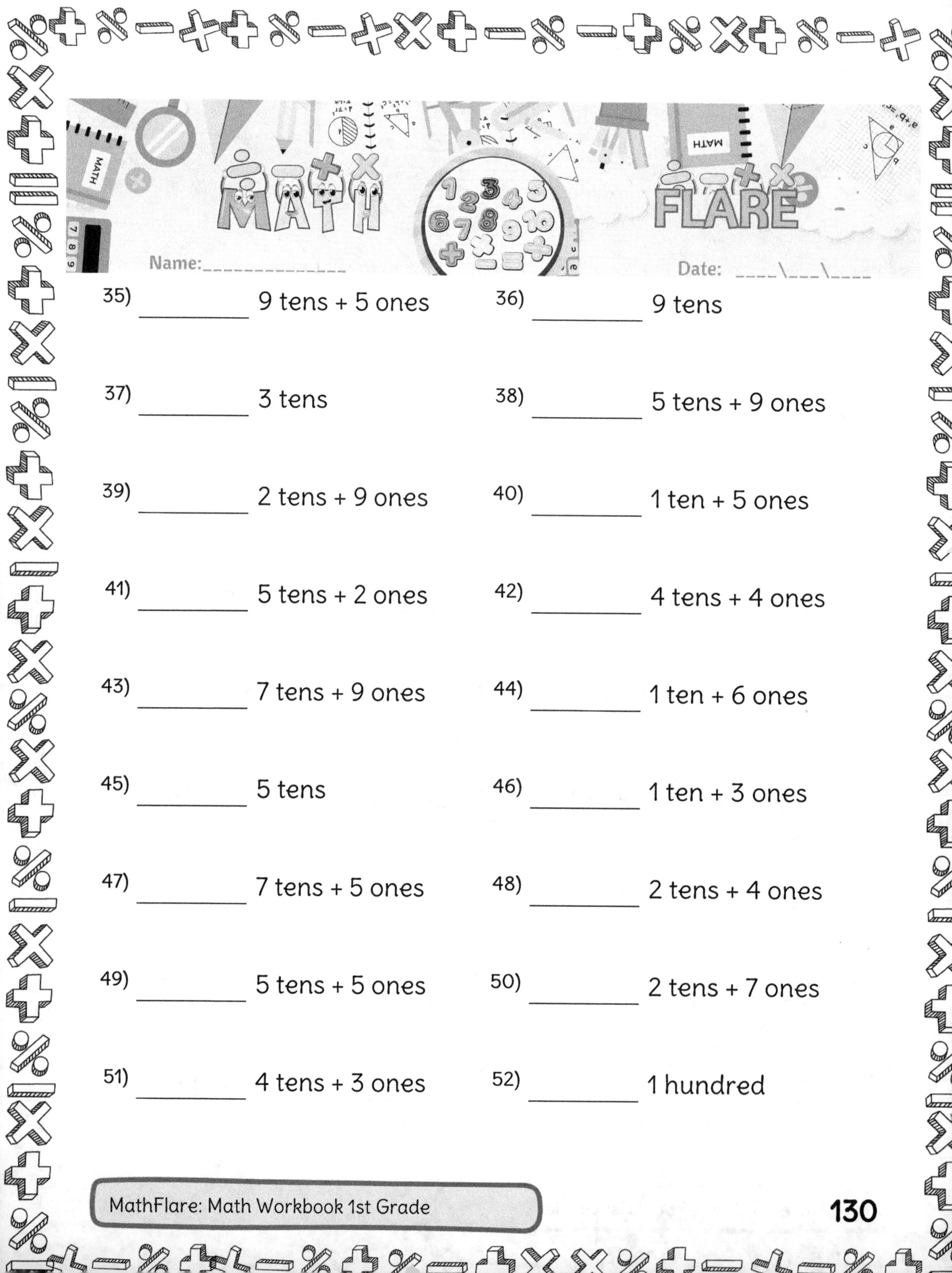

35) __________ 9 tens + 5 ones

36) __________ 9 tens

37) __________ 3 tens

38) __________ 5 tens + 9 ones

39) __________ 2 tens + 9 ones

40) __________ 1 ten + 5 ones

41) __________ 5 tens + 2 ones

42) __________ 4 tens + 4 ones

43) __________ 7 tens + 9 ones

44) __________ 1 ten + 6 ones

45) __________ 5 tens

46) __________ 1 ten + 3 ones

47) __________ 7 tens + 5 ones

48) __________ 2 tens + 4 ones

49) __________ 5 tens + 5 ones

50) __________ 2 tens + 7 ones

51) __________ 4 tens + 3 ones

52) __________ 1 hundred

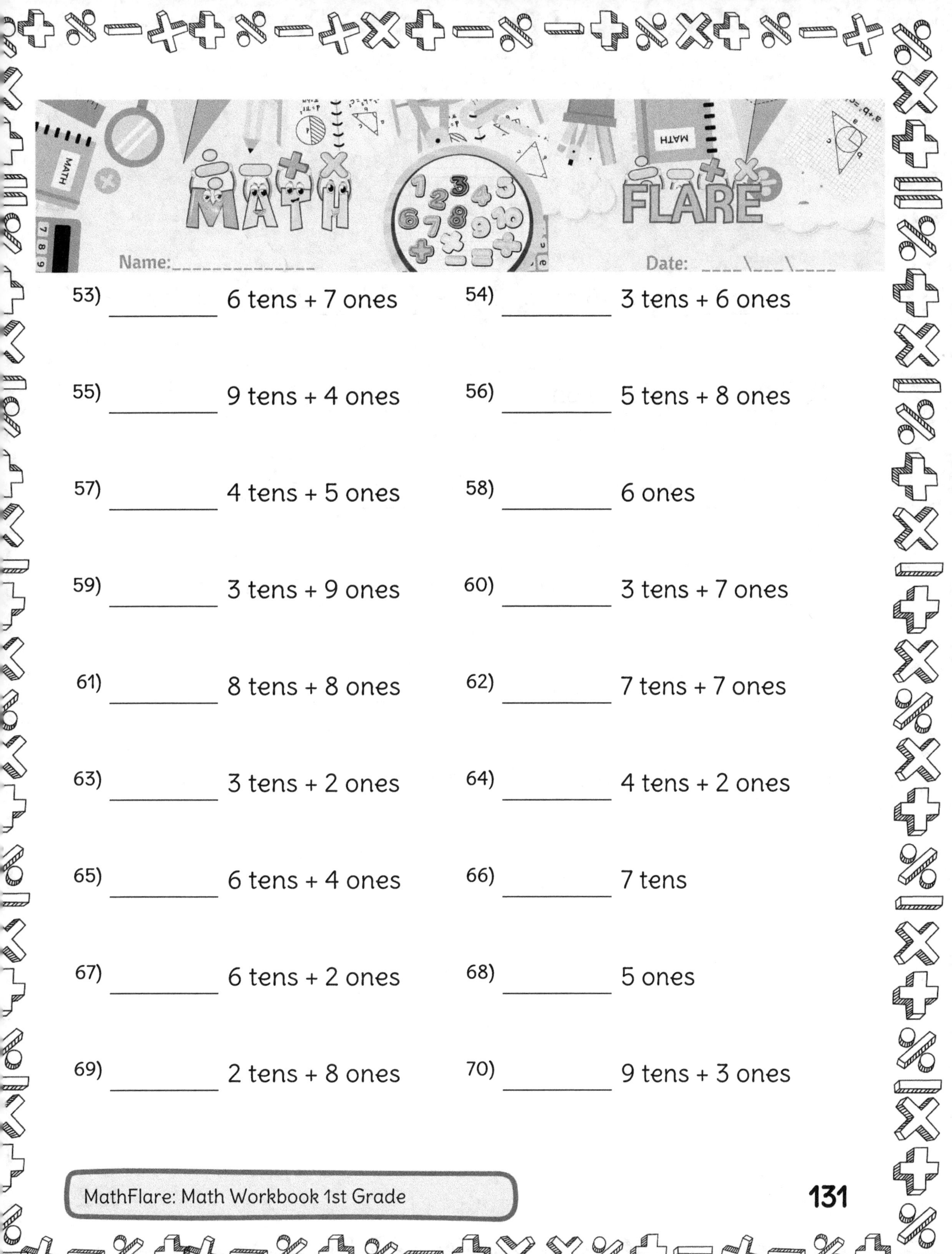

53) _________ 6 tens + 7 ones

54) _________ 3 tens + 6 ones

55) _________ 9 tens + 4 ones

56) _________ 5 tens + 8 ones

57) _________ 4 tens + 5 ones

58) _________ 6 ones

59) _________ 3 tens + 9 ones

60) _________ 3 tens + 7 ones

61) _________ 8 tens + 8 ones

62) _________ 7 tens + 7 ones

63) _________ 3 tens + 2 ones

64) _________ 4 tens + 2 ones

65) _________ 6 tens + 4 ones

66) _________ 7 tens

67) _________ 6 tens + 2 ones

68) _________ 5 ones

69) _________ 2 tens + 8 ones

70) _________ 9 tens + 3 ones

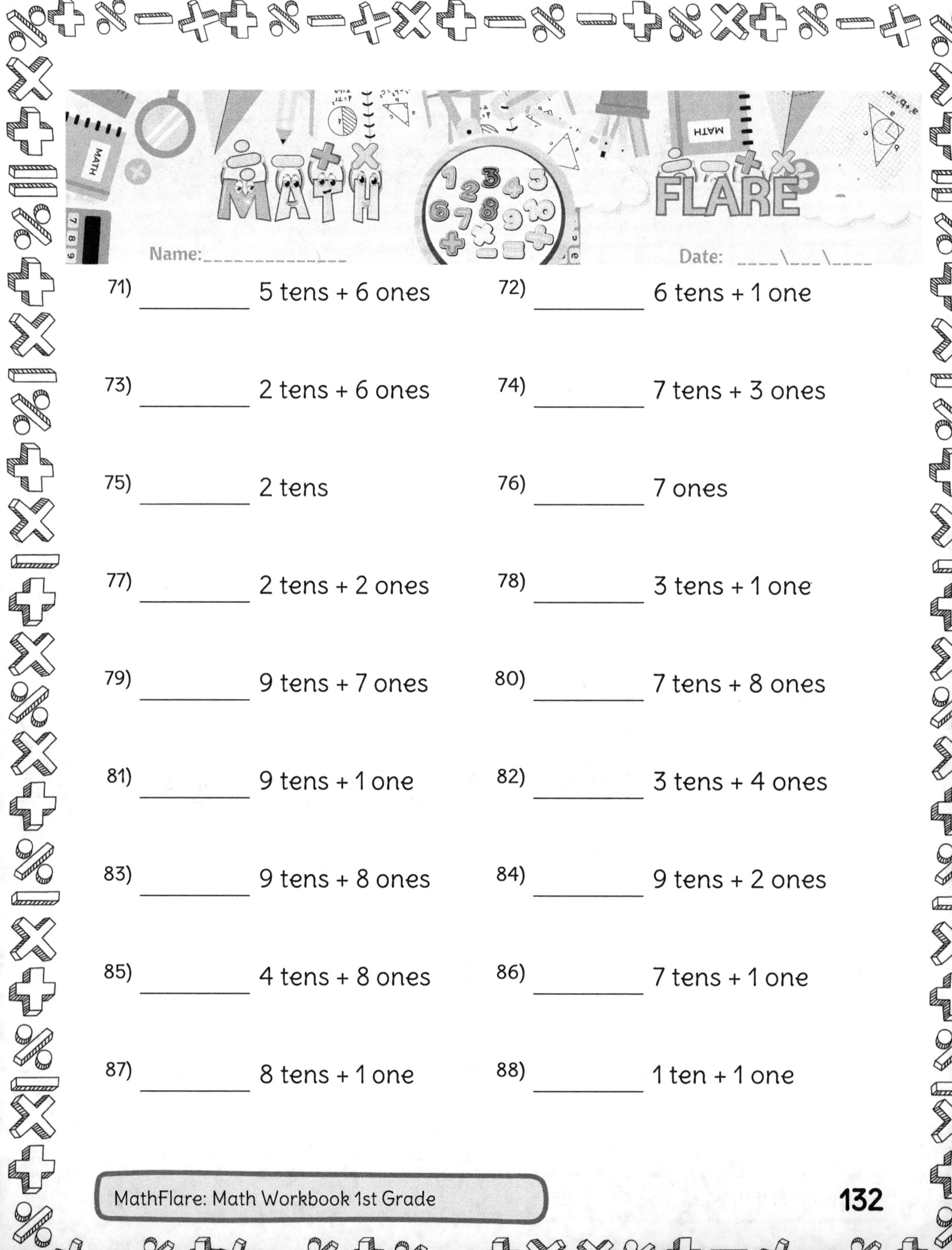

71) __________ 5 tens + 6 ones

72) __________ 6 tens + 1 one

73) __________ 2 tens + 6 ones

74) __________ 7 tens + 3 ones

75) __________ 2 tens

76) __________ 7 ones

77) __________ 2 tens + 2 ones

78) __________ 3 tens + 1 one

79) __________ 9 tens + 7 ones

80) __________ 7 tens + 8 ones

81) __________ 9 tens + 1 one

82) __________ 3 tens + 4 ones

83) __________ 9 tens + 8 ones

84) __________ 9 tens + 2 ones

85) __________ 4 tens + 8 ones

86) __________ 7 tens + 1 one

87) __________ 8 tens + 1 one

88) __________ 1 ten + 1 one

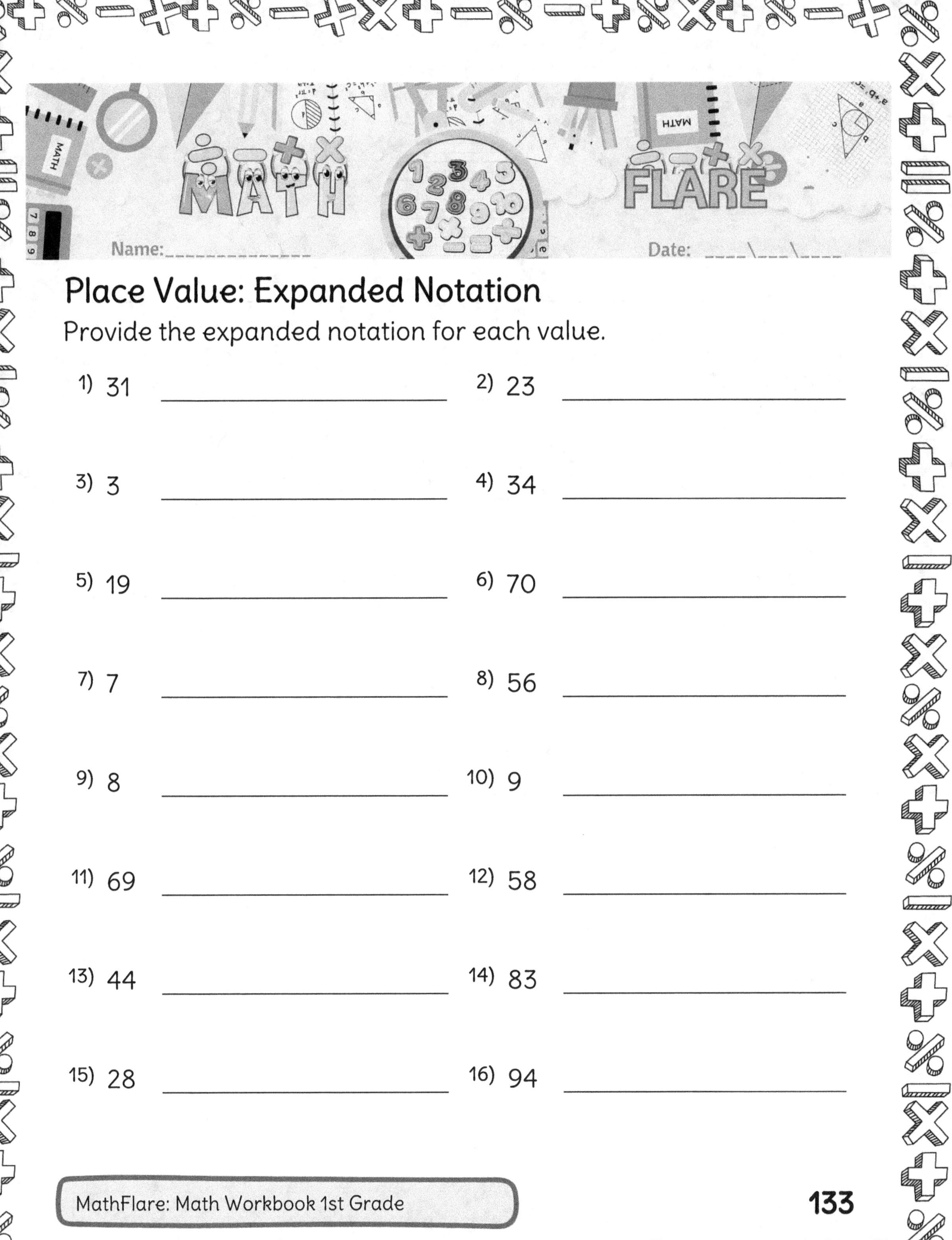

Place Value: Expanded Notation

Provide the expanded notation for each value.

1) 31 _______________

2) 23 _______________

3) 3 _______________

4) 34 _______________

5) 19 _______________

6) 70 _______________

7) 7 _______________

8) 56 _______________

9) 8 _______________

10) 9 _______________

11) 69 _______________

12) 58 _______________

13) 44 _______________

14) 83 _______________

15) 28 _______________

16) 94 _______________

Name:____________________   Date: ____________

17) 71

18) 45

19) 90

20) 27

21) 22

22) 100

23) 24

24) 76

25) 55

26) 35

27) 95

28) 5

29) 14

30) 16

31) 40

32) 11

33) 96

34) 42

Name: __________ Date: _________

35) 38 _______________

36) 82 _______________

37) 67 _______________

38) 99 _______________

39) 15 _______________

40) 46 _______________

41) 65 _______________

42) 61 _______________

43) 12 _______________

44) 29 _______________

45) 84 _______________

46) 80 _______________

47) 51 _______________

48) 74 _______________

49) 52 _______________

50) 30 _______________

51) 54 _______________

52) 20 _______________

53) 33 _______________________

54) 60 _______________________

55) 32 _______________________

56) 18 _______________________

57) 53 _______________________

58) 26 _______________________

59) 89 _______________________

60) 91 _______________________

61) 49 _______________________

62) 2 _______________________

63) 1 _______________________

64) 17 _______________________

65) 68 _______________________

66) 86 _______________________

67) 85 _______________________

68) 37 _______________________

69) 13 _______________________

70) 6 _______________________

71) 62 _______________

72) 57 _______________

73) 43 _______________

74) 64 _______________

75) 63 _______________

76) 77 _______________

77) 41 _______________

78) 97 _______________

79) 36 _______________

80) 79 _______________

81) 73 _______________

82) 93 _______________

83) 47 _______________

84) 92 _______________

85) 25 _______________

86) 39 _______________

87) 48 _______________

88) 88 _______________

Telling Time: Hours and Minutes

1)

6:00

2)

3)

3:00

4)

5)

6)

11:00

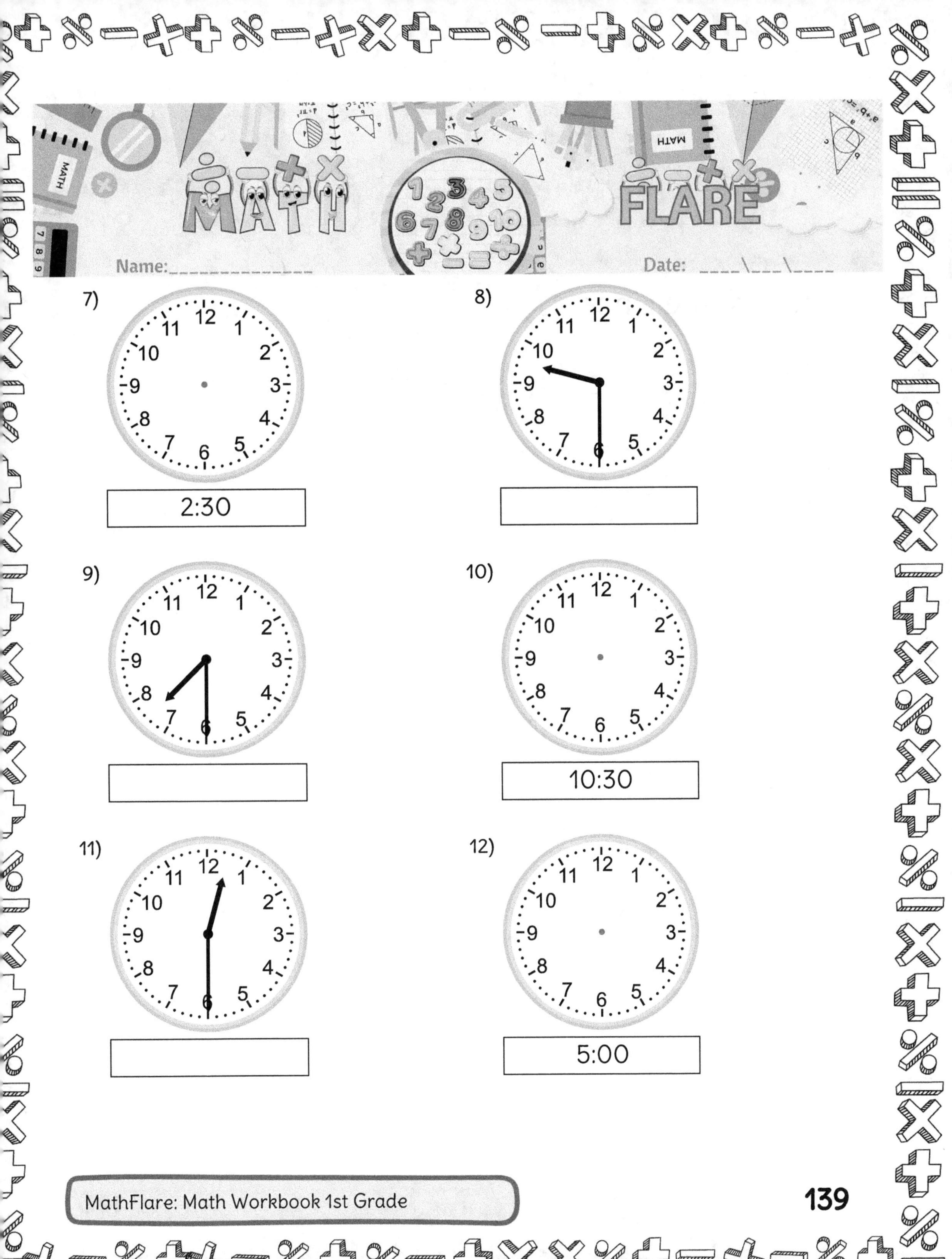

7)

2:30

8)

9)

10)

10:30

11)

12)

5:00

Measure the Lines

1)

2)

3)

4)

5)

6)

7)

8)

____

9)

____

10)

____

11)

____

12)

____

13)

____

14)

____

15)

____

16)

____

17)

____

18)

____

19)

____

20)

____

21)

____

22)

____

23)

____

Measure the Rectangles

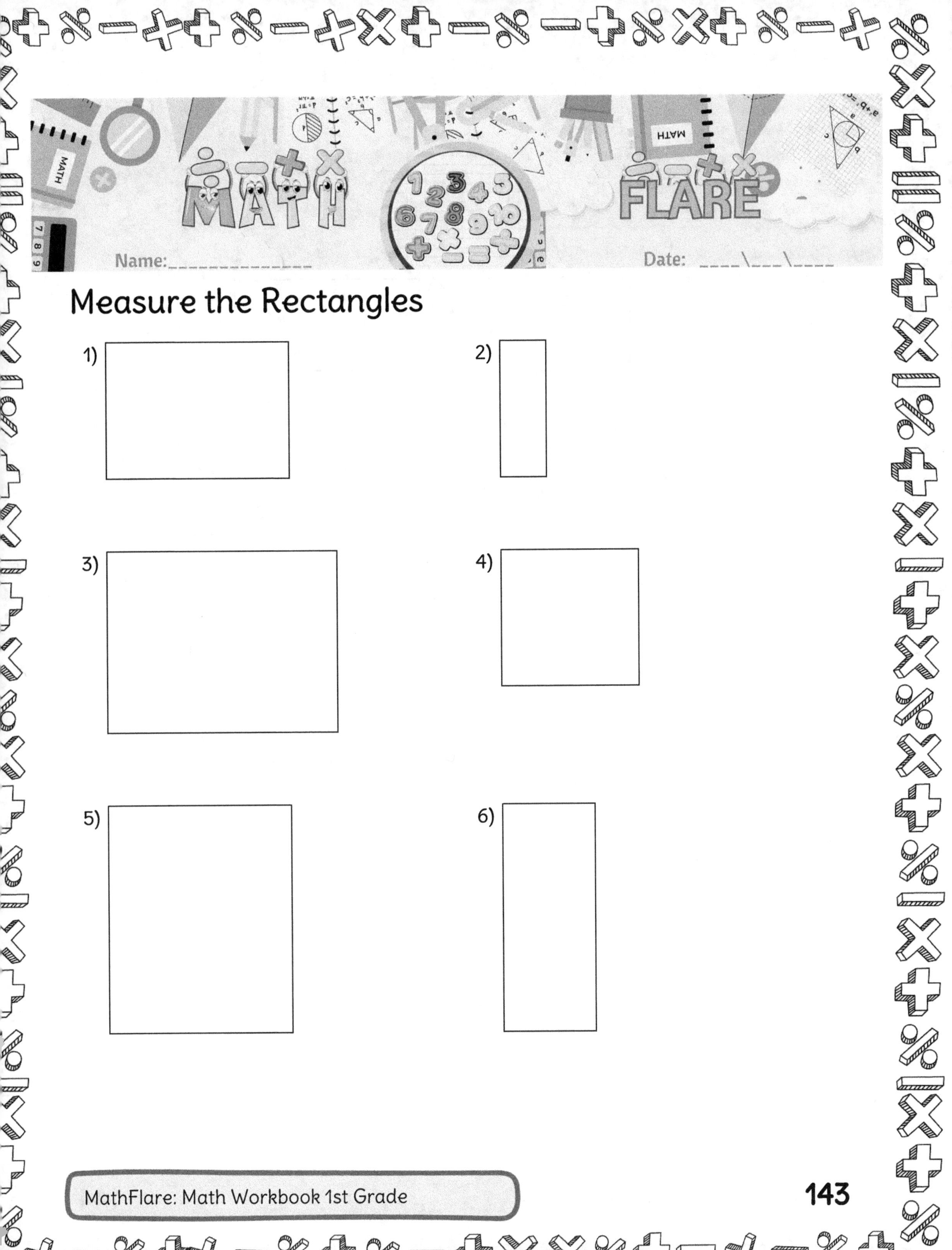

1)

2)

3)

4)

5)

6)

MATH FLARE
Name:
Date:
7)
8)
9)
10)
11)
12)

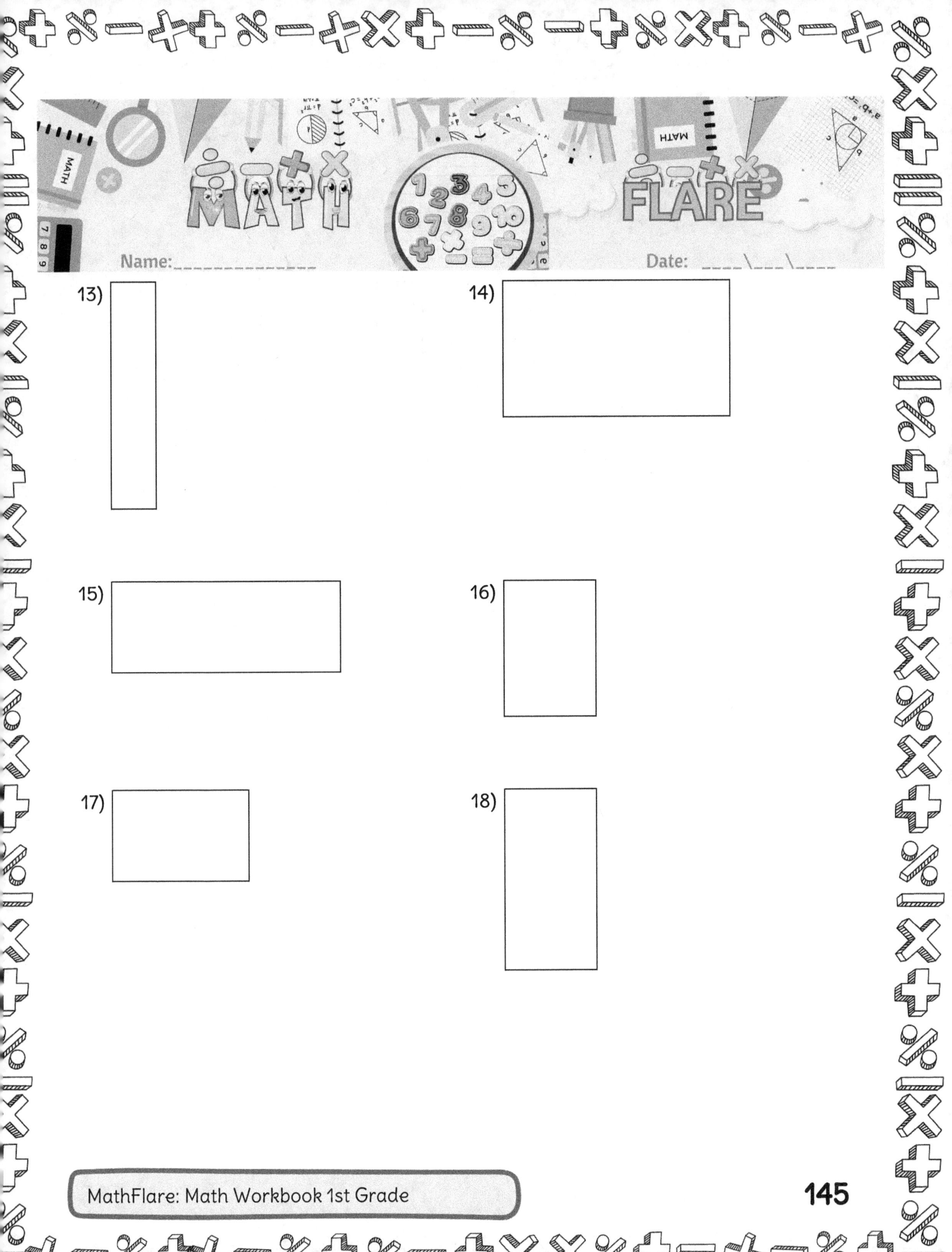

13)

14)

15)

16)

17)

18)

19)

20)

21)

22)

23)

24)

ANSWERS

Page 1:   Skip Counting: Ascending

1.

Count by 1 from 1 to 100

1	2	3	4	5	6	7	8	9	10
11	12	13	14	15	16	17	18	19	20
21	22	23	24	25	26	27	28	29	30
31	32	33	34	35	36	37	38	39	40
41	42	43	44	45	46	47	48	49	50
51	52	53	54	55	56	57	58	59	60
61	62	63	64	65	66	67	68	69	70
71	72	73	74	75	76	77	78	79	80
81	82	83	84	85	86	87	88	89	90
91	92	93	94	95	96	97	98	99	100

Page 2:   Skip Counting: Ascending

1.

Count by 1 from 1 to 100

1	2	3	4	5	6	7	8	9	10
11	12	13	14	15	16	17	18	19	20
21	22	23	24	25	26	27	28	29	30
31	32	33	34	35	36	37	38	39	40
41	42	43	44	45	46	47	48	49	50
51	52	53	54	55	56	57	58	59	60
61	62	63	64	65	66	67	68	69	70
71	72	73	74	75	76	77	78	79	80
81	82	83	84	85	86	87	88	89	90
91	92	93	94	95	96	97	98	99	100

2.

Count by 1 from 1 to 100

1	2	3	4	5	6	7	8	9	10
11	12	13	14	15	16	17	18	19	20
21	22	23	24	25	26	27	28	29	30
31	32	33	34	35	36	37	38	39	40
41	42	43	44	45	46	47	48	49	50
51	52	53	54	55	56	57	58	59	60
61	62	63	64	65	66	67	68	69	70
71	72	73	74	75	76	77	78	79	80
81	82	83	84	85	86	87	88	89	90
91	92	93	94	95	96	97	98	99	100

Page 4:   Skip Counting: Ascending

1.

Count by 1 from 1 to 100

1	2	3	4	5	6	7	8	9	10
11	12	13	14	15	16	17	18	19	20
21	22	23	24	25	26	27	28	29	30
31	32	33	34	35	36	37	38	39	40
41	42	43	44	45	46	47	48	49	50
51	52	53	54	55	56	57	58	59	60
61	62	63	64	65	66	67	68	69	70
71	72	73	74	75	76	77	78	79	80
81	82	83	84	85	86	87	88	89	90
91	92	93	94	95	96	97	98	99	100

Page 5:   Count Up

1.

97	98	99	100	101	102	103	104	105	106

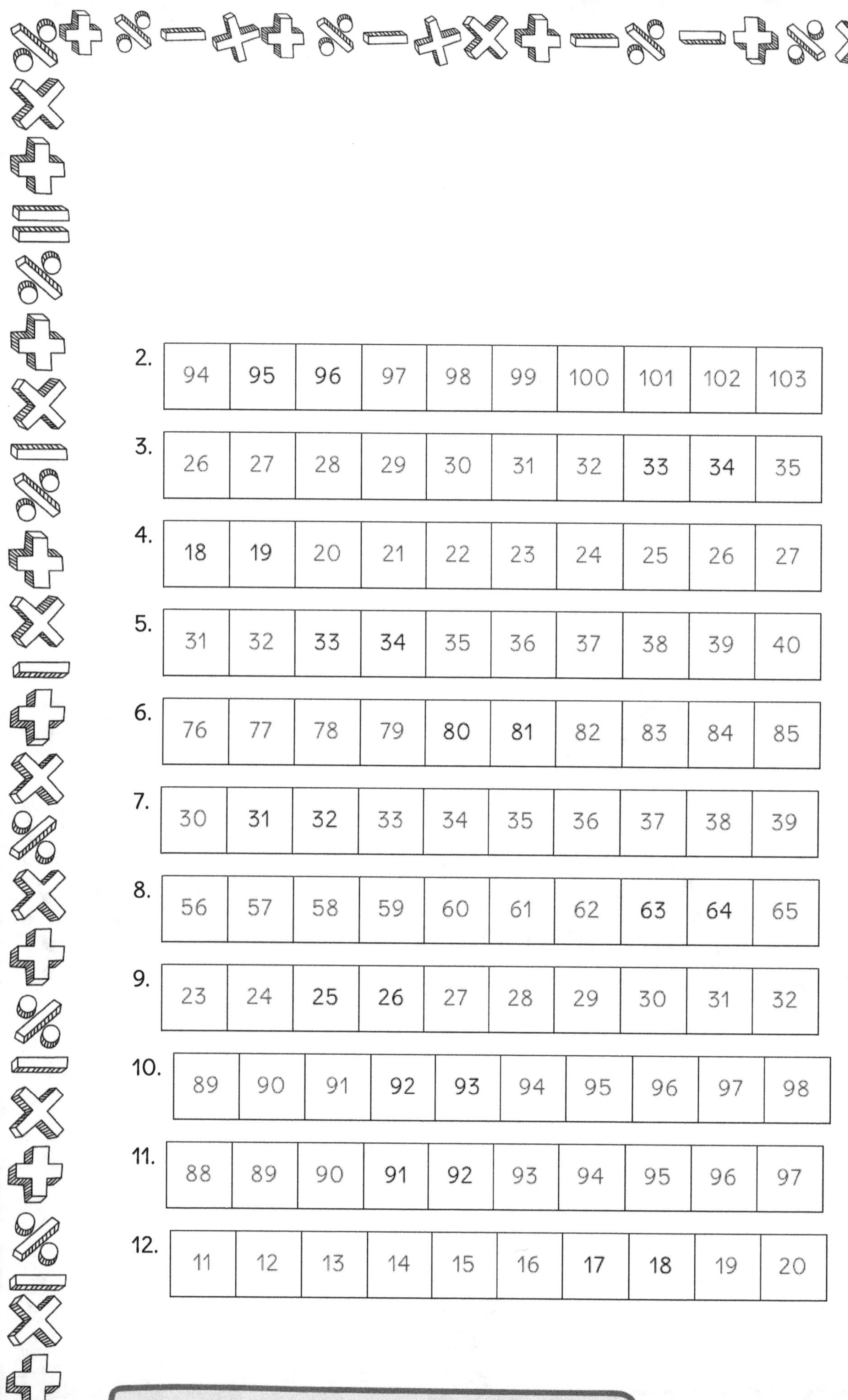

| 2. | 94 | 95 | 96 | 97 | 98 | 99 | 100 | 101 | 102 | 103 |

| 3. | 26 | 27 | 28 | 29 | 30 | 31 | 32 | 33 | 34 | 35 |

| 4. | 18 | 19 | 20 | 21 | 22 | 23 | 24 | 25 | 26 | 27 |

| 5. | 31 | 32 | 33 | 34 | 35 | 36 | 37 | 38 | 39 | 40 |

| 6. | 76 | 77 | 78 | 79 | 80 | 81 | 82 | 83 | 84 | 85 |

| 7. | 30 | 31 | 32 | 33 | 34 | 35 | 36 | 37 | 38 | 39 |

| 8. | 56 | 57 | 58 | 59 | 60 | 61 | 62 | 63 | 64 | 65 |

| 9. | 23 | 24 | 25 | 26 | 27 | 28 | 29 | 30 | 31 | 32 |

| 10. | 89 | 90 | 91 | 92 | 93 | 94 | 95 | 96 | 97 | 98 |

| 11. | 88 | 89 | 90 | 91 | 92 | 93 | 94 | 95 | 96 | 97 |

| 12. | 11 | 12 | 13 | 14 | 15 | 16 | 17 | 18 | 19 | 20 |

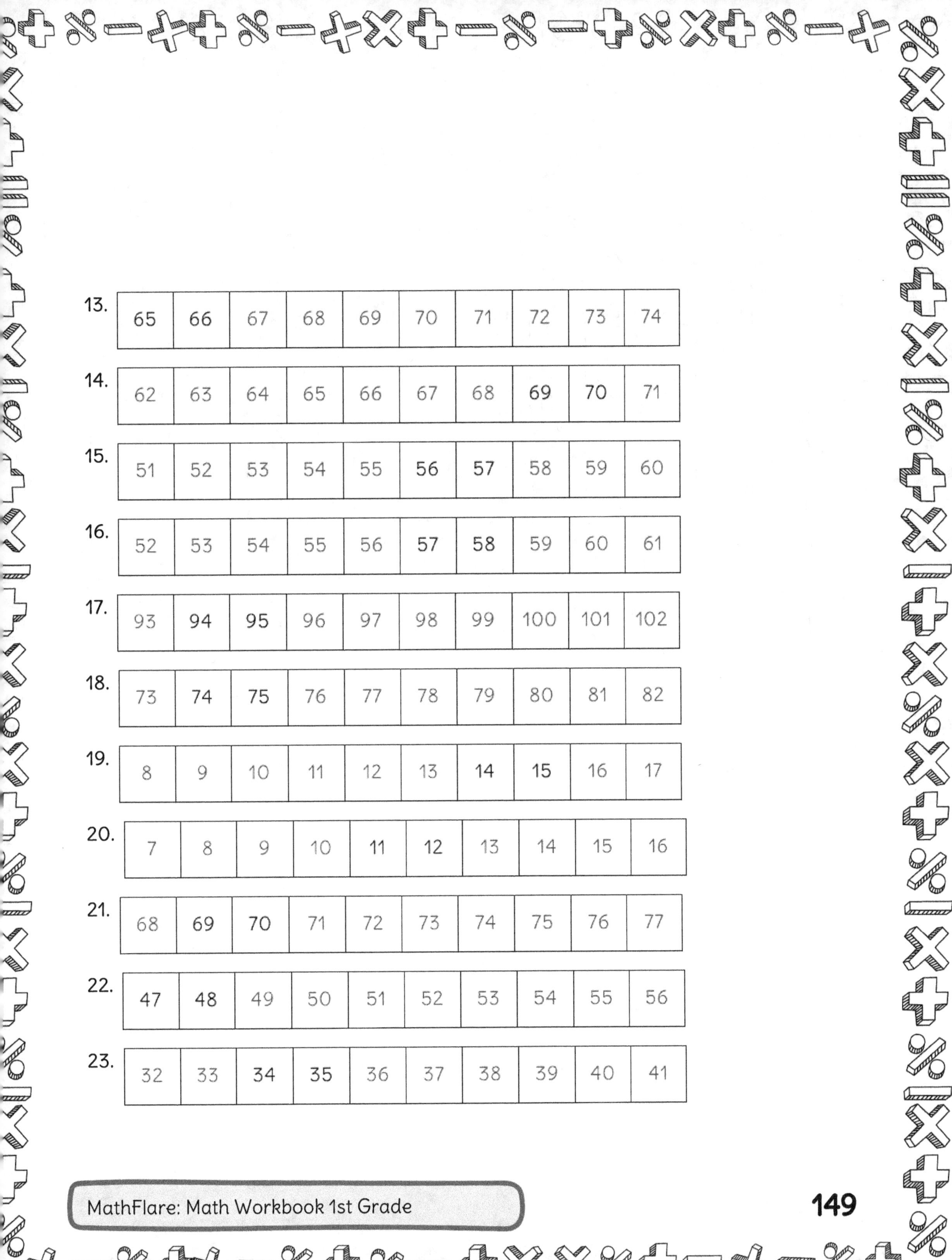

13.

| 65 | 66 | 67 | 68 | 69 | 70 | 71 | 72 | 73 | 74 |

14.

| 62 | 63 | 64 | 65 | 66 | 67 | 68 | 69 | 70 | 71 |

15.

| 51 | 52 | 53 | 54 | 55 | 56 | 57 | 58 | 59 | 60 |

16.

| 52 | 53 | 54 | 55 | 56 | 57 | 58 | 59 | 60 | 61 |

17.

| 93 | 94 | 95 | 96 | 97 | 98 | 99 | 100 | 101 | 102 |

18.

| 73 | 74 | 75 | 76 | 77 | 78 | 79 | 80 | 81 | 82 |

19.

| 8 | 9 | 10 | 11 | 12 | 13 | 14 | 15 | 16 | 17 |

20.

| 7 | 8 | 9 | 10 | 11 | 12 | 13 | 14 | 15 | 16 |

21.

| 68 | 69 | 70 | 71 | 72 | 73 | 74 | 75 | 76 | 77 |

22.

| 47 | 48 | 49 | 50 | 51 | 52 | 53 | 54 | 55 | 56 |

23.

| 32 | 33 | 34 | 35 | 36 | 37 | 38 | 39 | 40 | 41 |

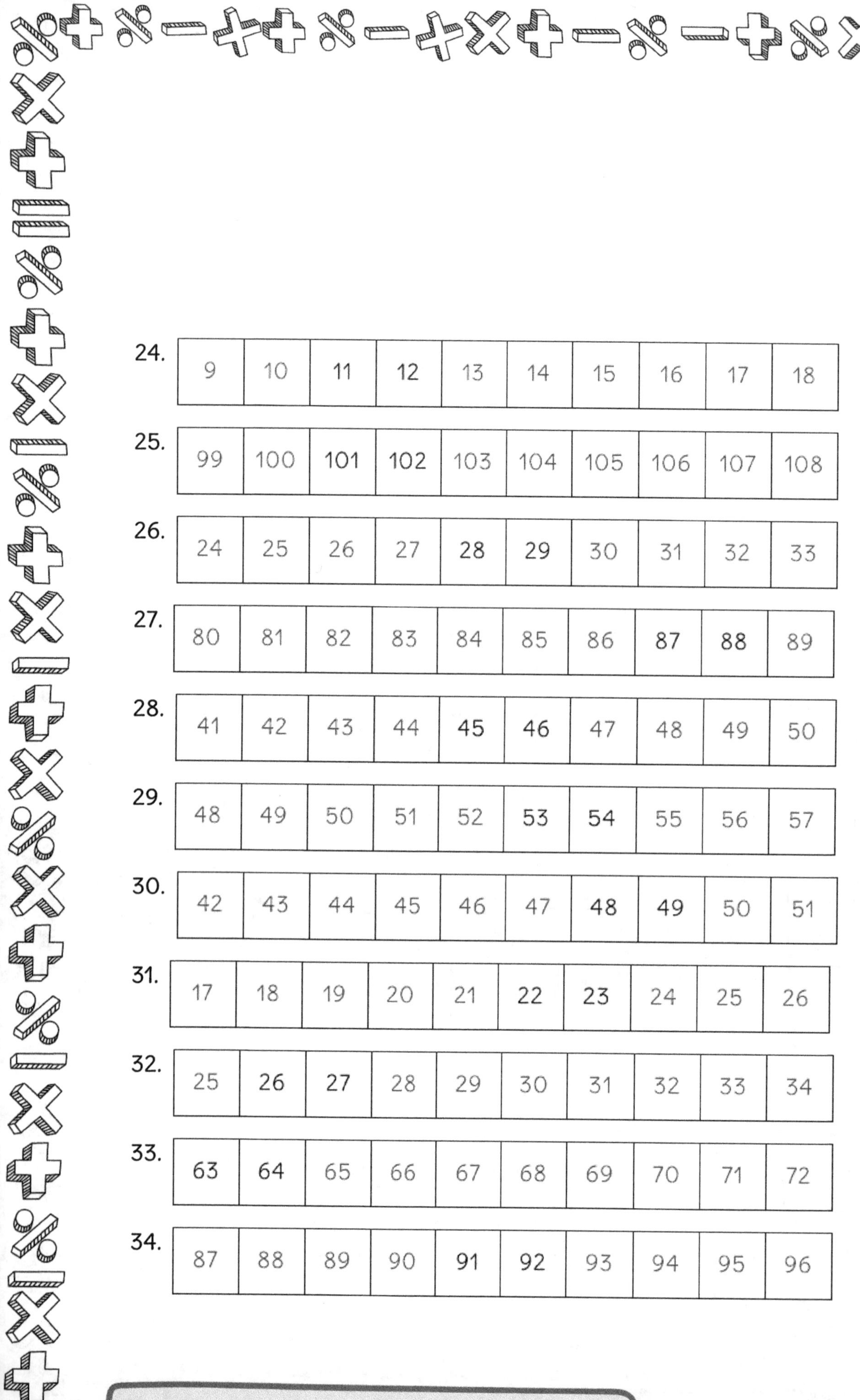

24.

| 9 | 10 | 11 | 12 | 13 | 14 | 15 | 16 | 17 | 18 |

25.

| 99 | 100 | 101 | 102 | 103 | 104 | 105 | 106 | 107 | 108 |

26.

| 24 | 25 | 26 | 27 | 28 | 29 | 30 | 31 | 32 | 33 |

27.

| 80 | 81 | 82 | 83 | 84 | 85 | 86 | 87 | 88 | 89 |

28.

| 41 | 42 | 43 | 44 | 45 | 46 | 47 | 48 | 49 | 50 |

29.

| 48 | 49 | 50 | 51 | 52 | 53 | 54 | 55 | 56 | 57 |

30.

| 42 | 43 | 44 | 45 | 46 | 47 | 48 | 49 | 50 | 51 |

31.

| 17 | 18 | 19 | 20 | 21 | 22 | 23 | 24 | 25 | 26 |

32.

| 25 | 26 | 27 | 28 | 29 | 30 | 31 | 32 | 33 | 34 |

33.

| 63 | 64 | 65 | 66 | 67 | 68 | 69 | 70 | 71 | 72 |

34.

| 87 | 88 | 89 | 90 | 91 | 92 | 93 | 94 | 95 | 96 |

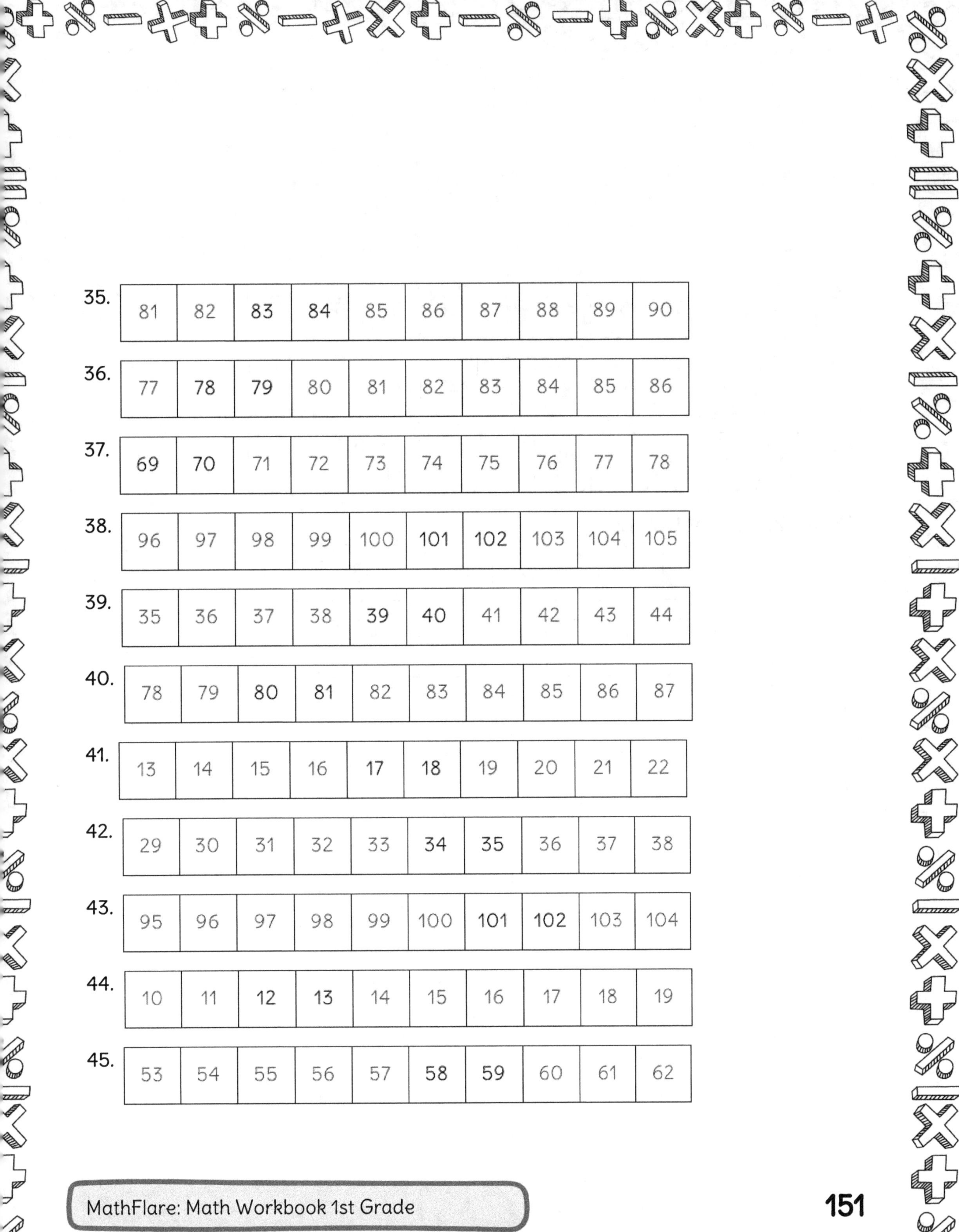

35.

| 81 | 82 | 83 | 84 | 85 | 86 | 87 | 88 | 89 | 90 |

36.

| 77 | 78 | 79 | 80 | 81 | 82 | 83 | 84 | 85 | 86 |

37.

| 69 | 70 | 71 | 72 | 73 | 74 | 75 | 76 | 77 | 78 |

38.

| 96 | 97 | 98 | 99 | 100 | 101 | 102 | 103 | 104 | 105 |

39.

| 35 | 36 | 37 | 38 | 39 | 40 | 41 | 42 | 43 | 44 |

40.

| 78 | 79 | 80 | 81 | 82 | 83 | 84 | 85 | 86 | 87 |

41.

| 13 | 14 | 15 | 16 | 17 | 18 | 19 | 20 | 21 | 22 |

42.

| 29 | 30 | 31 | 32 | 33 | 34 | 35 | 36 | 37 | 38 |

43.

| 95 | 96 | 97 | 98 | 99 | 100 | 101 | 102 | 103 | 104 |

44.

| 10 | 11 | 12 | 13 | 14 | 15 | 16 | 17 | 18 | 19 |

45.

| 53 | 54 | 55 | 56 | 57 | 58 | 59 | 60 | 61 | 62 |

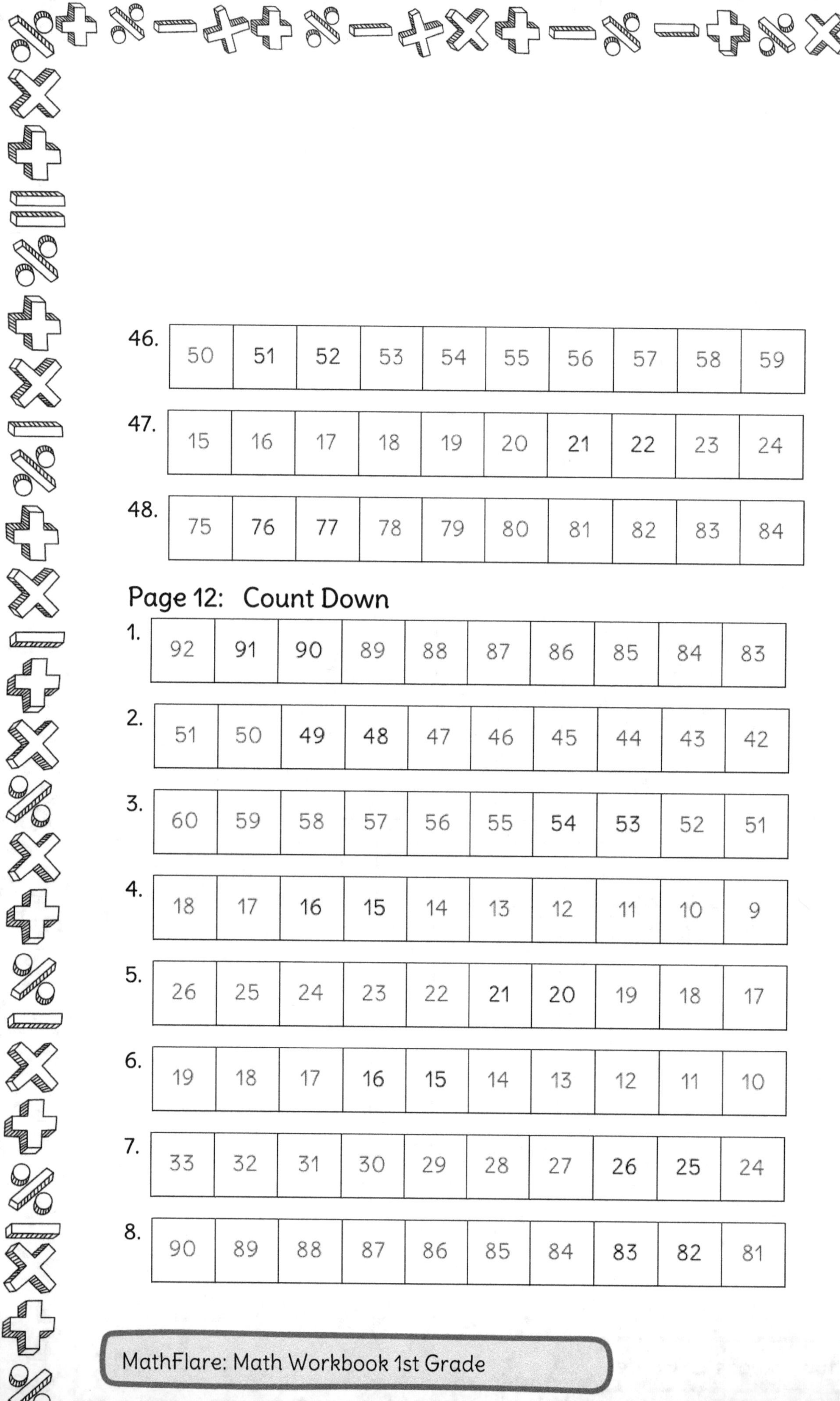

46.

| 50 | 51 | 52 | 53 | 54 | 55 | 56 | 57 | 58 | 59 |

47.

| 15 | 16 | 17 | 18 | 19 | 20 | 21 | 22 | 23 | 24 |

48.

| 75 | 76 | 77 | 78 | 79 | 80 | 81 | 82 | 83 | 84 |

Page 12:   Count Down

1.

| 92 | 91 | 90 | 89 | 88 | 87 | 86 | 85 | 84 | 83 |

2.

| 51 | 50 | 49 | 48 | 47 | 46 | 45 | 44 | 43 | 42 |

3.

| 60 | 59 | 58 | 57 | 56 | 55 | 54 | 53 | 52 | 51 |

4.

| 18 | 17 | 16 | 15 | 14 | 13 | 12 | 11 | 10 | 9 |

5.

| 26 | 25 | 24 | 23 | 22 | 21 | 20 | 19 | 18 | 17 |

6.

| 19 | 18 | 17 | 16 | 15 | 14 | 13 | 12 | 11 | 10 |

7.

| 33 | 32 | 31 | 30 | 29 | 28 | 27 | 26 | 25 | 24 |

8.

| 90 | 89 | 88 | 87 | 86 | 85 | 84 | 83 | 82 | 81 |

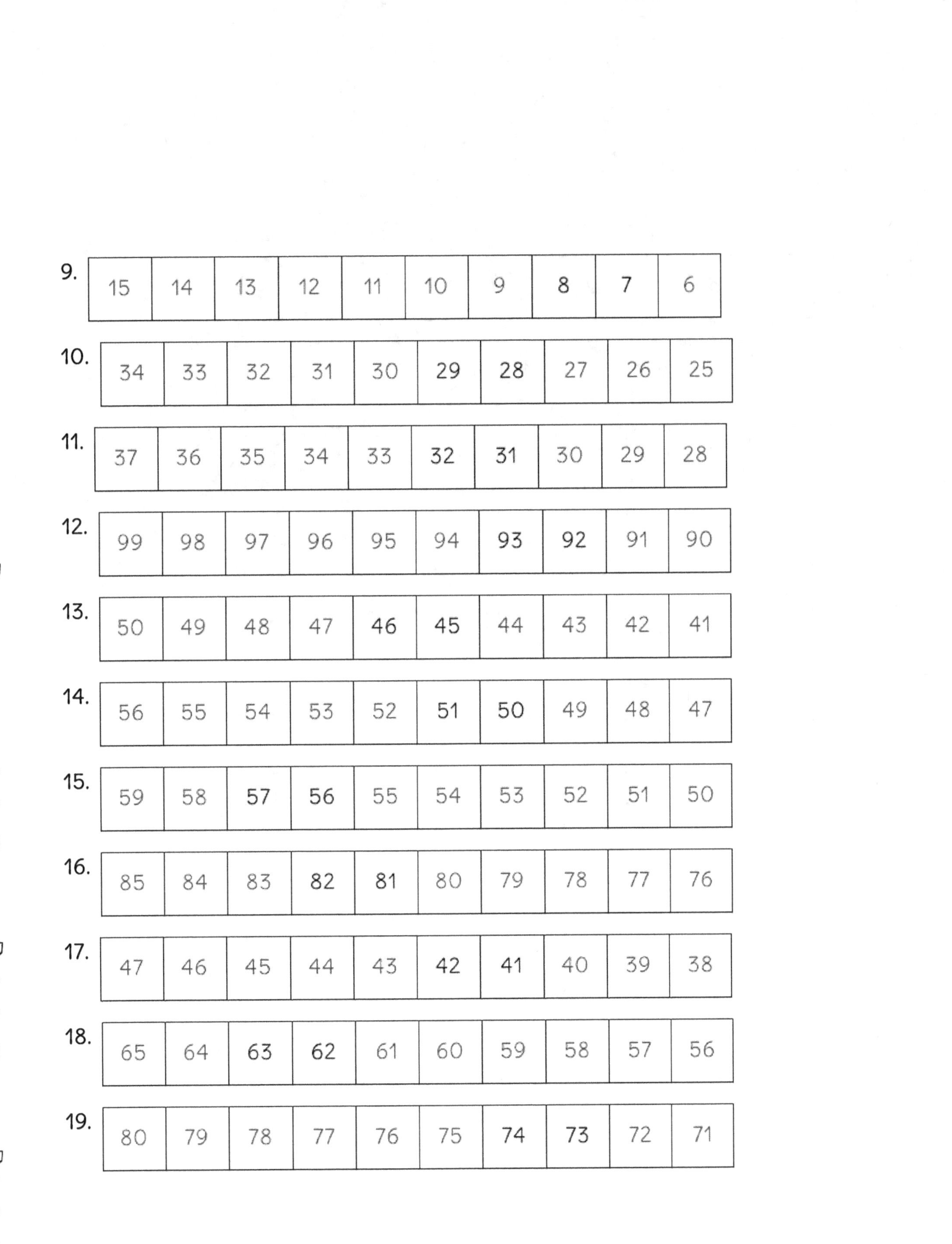

9. | 15 | 14 | 13 | 12 | 11 | 10 | 9 | 8 | 7 | 6 |

10. | 34 | 33 | 32 | 31 | 30 | 29 | 28 | 27 | 26 | 25 |

11. | 37 | 36 | 35 | 34 | 33 | 32 | 31 | 30 | 29 | 28 |

12. | 99 | 98 | 97 | 96 | 95 | 94 | 93 | 92 | 91 | 90 |

13. | 50 | 49 | 48 | 47 | 46 | 45 | 44 | 43 | 42 | 41 |

14. | 56 | 55 | 54 | 53 | 52 | 51 | 50 | 49 | 48 | 47 |

15. | 59 | 58 | 57 | 56 | 55 | 54 | 53 | 52 | 51 | 50 |

16. | 85 | 84 | 83 | 82 | 81 | 80 | 79 | 78 | 77 | 76 |

17. | 47 | 46 | 45 | 44 | 43 | 42 | 41 | 40 | 39 | 38 |

18. | 65 | 64 | 63 | 62 | 61 | 60 | 59 | 58 | 57 | 56 |

19. | 80 | 79 | 78 | 77 | 76 | 75 | 74 | 73 | 72 | 71 |

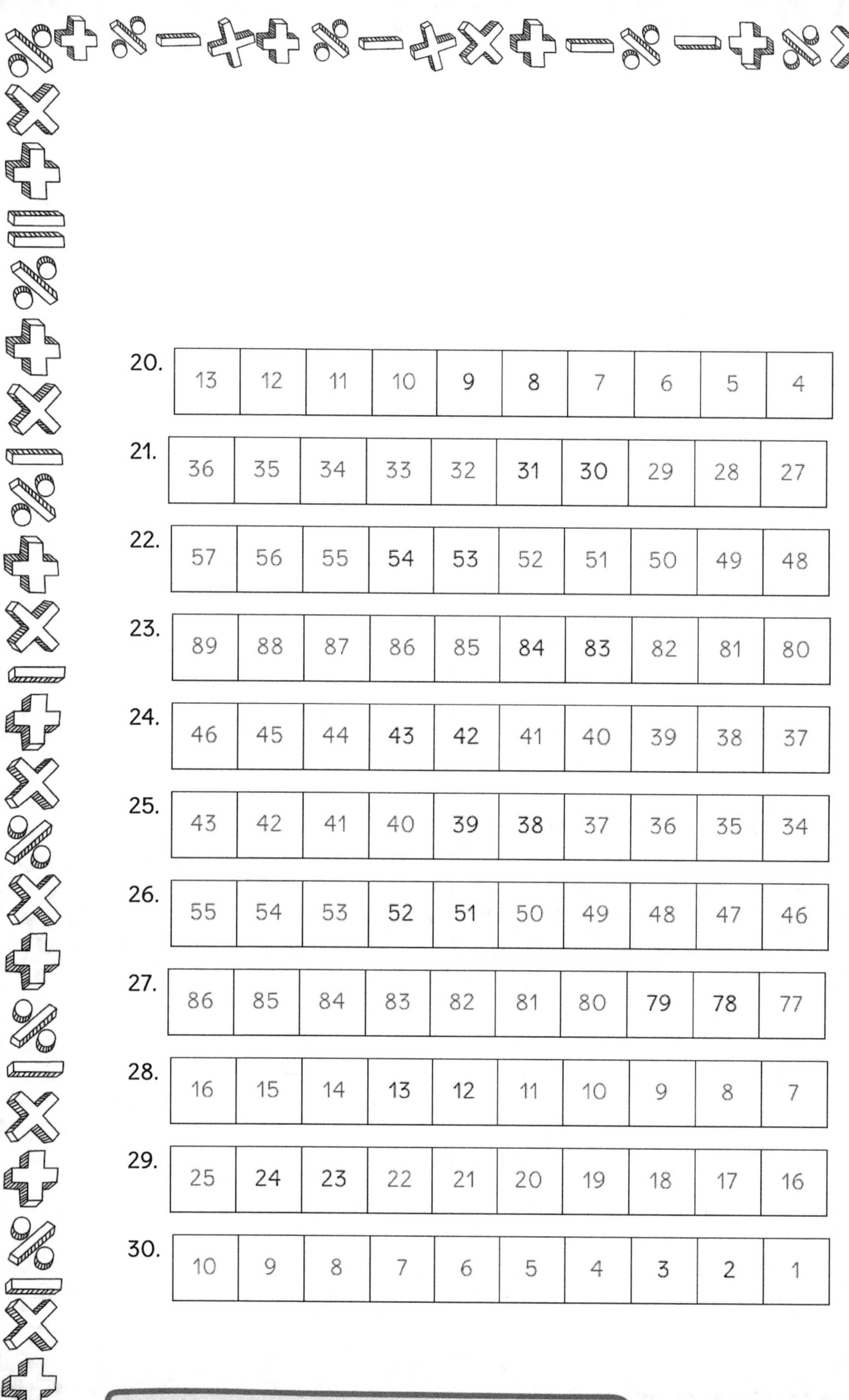

20.

| 13 | 12 | 11 | 10 | 9 | 8 | 7 | 6 | 5 | 4 |

21.

| 36 | 35 | 34 | 33 | 32 | 31 | 30 | 29 | 28 | 27 |

22.

| 57 | 56 | 55 | 54 | 53 | 52 | 51 | 50 | 49 | 48 |

23.

| 89 | 88 | 87 | 86 | 85 | 84 | 83 | 82 | 81 | 80 |

24.

| 46 | 45 | 44 | 43 | 42 | 41 | 40 | 39 | 38 | 37 |

25.

| 43 | 42 | 41 | 40 | 39 | 38 | 37 | 36 | 35 | 34 |

26.

| 55 | 54 | 53 | 52 | 51 | 50 | 49 | 48 | 47 | 46 |

27.

| 86 | 85 | 84 | 83 | 82 | 81 | 80 | 79 | 78 | 77 |

28.

| 16 | 15 | 14 | 13 | 12 | 11 | 10 | 9 | 8 | 7 |

29.

| 25 | 24 | 23 | 22 | 21 | 20 | 19 | 18 | 17 | 16 |

30.

| 10 | 9 | 8 | 7 | 6 | 5 | 4 | 3 | 2 | 1 |

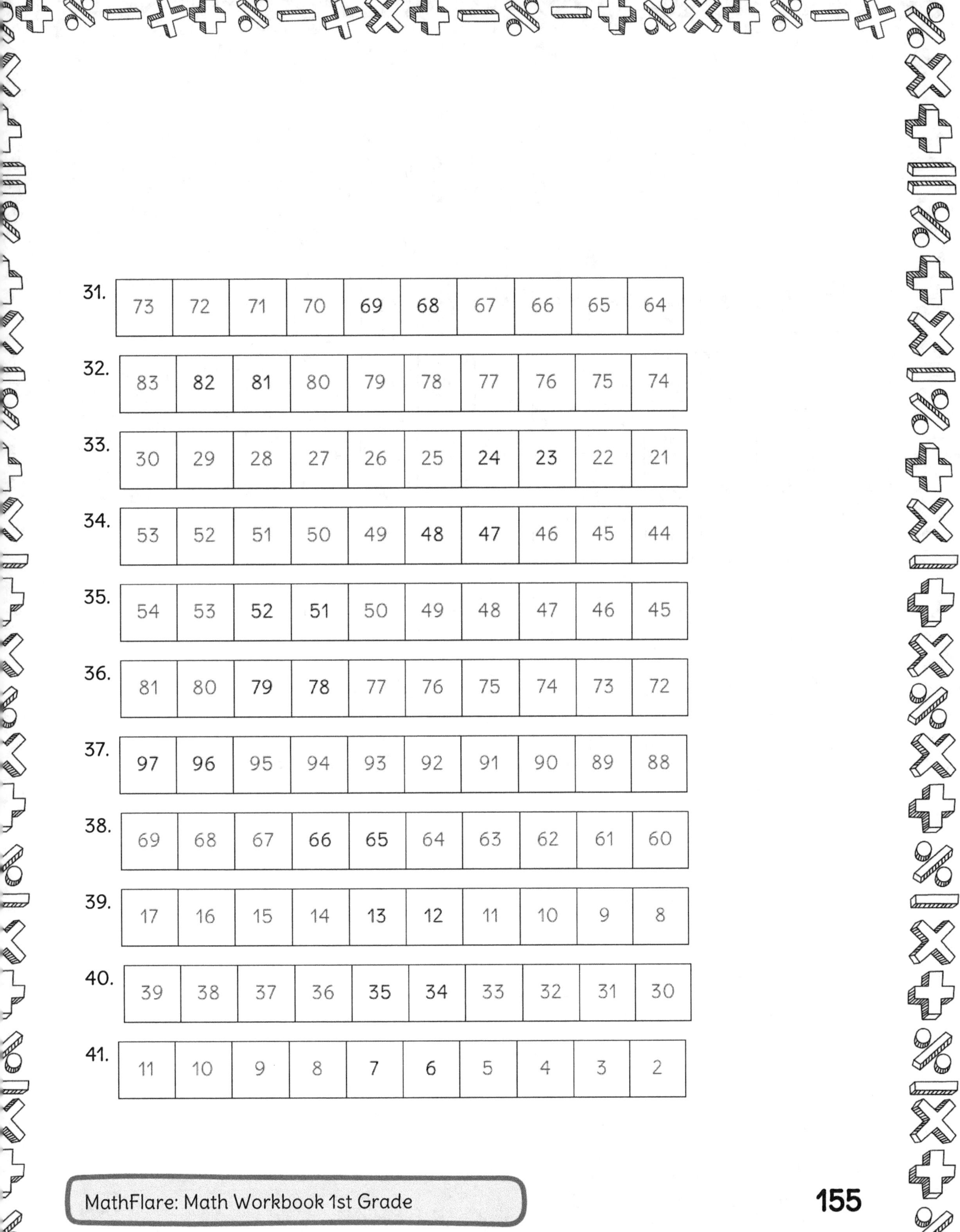

31. 73 72 71 70 69 68 67 66 65 64

32. 83 82 81 80 79 78 77 76 75 74

33. 30 29 28 27 26 25 24 23 22 21

34. 53 52 51 50 49 48 47 46 45 44

35. 54 53 52 51 50 49 48 47 46 45

36. 81 80 79 78 77 76 75 74 73 72

37. 97 96 95 94 93 92 91 90 89 88

38. 69 68 67 66 65 64 63 62 61 60

39. 17 16 15 14 13 12 11 10 9 8

40. 39 38 37 36 35 34 33 32 31 30

41. 11 10 9 8 7 6 5 4 3 2

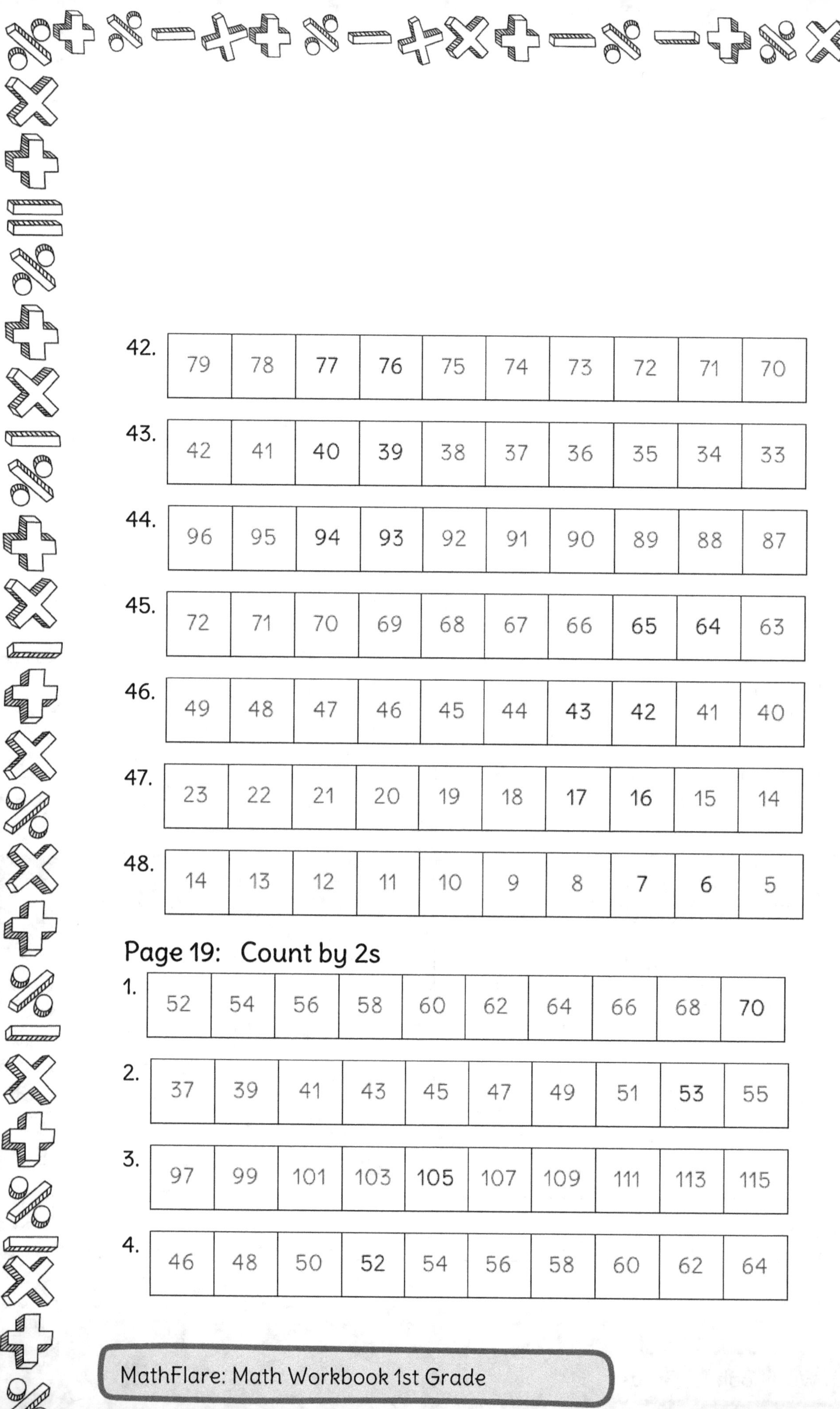

42.

| 79 | 78 | 77 | 76 | 75 | 74 | 73 | 72 | 71 | 70 |

43.

| 42 | 41 | 40 | 39 | 38 | 37 | 36 | 35 | 34 | 33 |

44.

| 96 | 95 | 94 | 93 | 92 | 91 | 90 | 89 | 88 | 87 |

45.

| 72 | 71 | 70 | 69 | 68 | 67 | 66 | 65 | 64 | 63 |

46.

| 49 | 48 | 47 | 46 | 45 | 44 | 43 | 42 | 41 | 40 |

47.

| 23 | 22 | 21 | 20 | 19 | 18 | 17 | 16 | 15 | 14 |

48.

| 14 | 13 | 12 | 11 | 10 | 9 | 8 | 7 | 6 | 5 |

Page 19:   Count by 2s

1.

| 52 | 54 | 56 | 58 | 60 | 62 | 64 | 66 | 68 | 70 |

2.

| 37 | 39 | 41 | 43 | 45 | 47 | 49 | 51 | 53 | 55 |

3.

| 97 | 99 | 101 | 103 | 105 | 107 | 109 | 111 | 113 | 115 |

4.

| 46 | 48 | 50 | 52 | 54 | 56 | 58 | 60 | 62 | 64 |

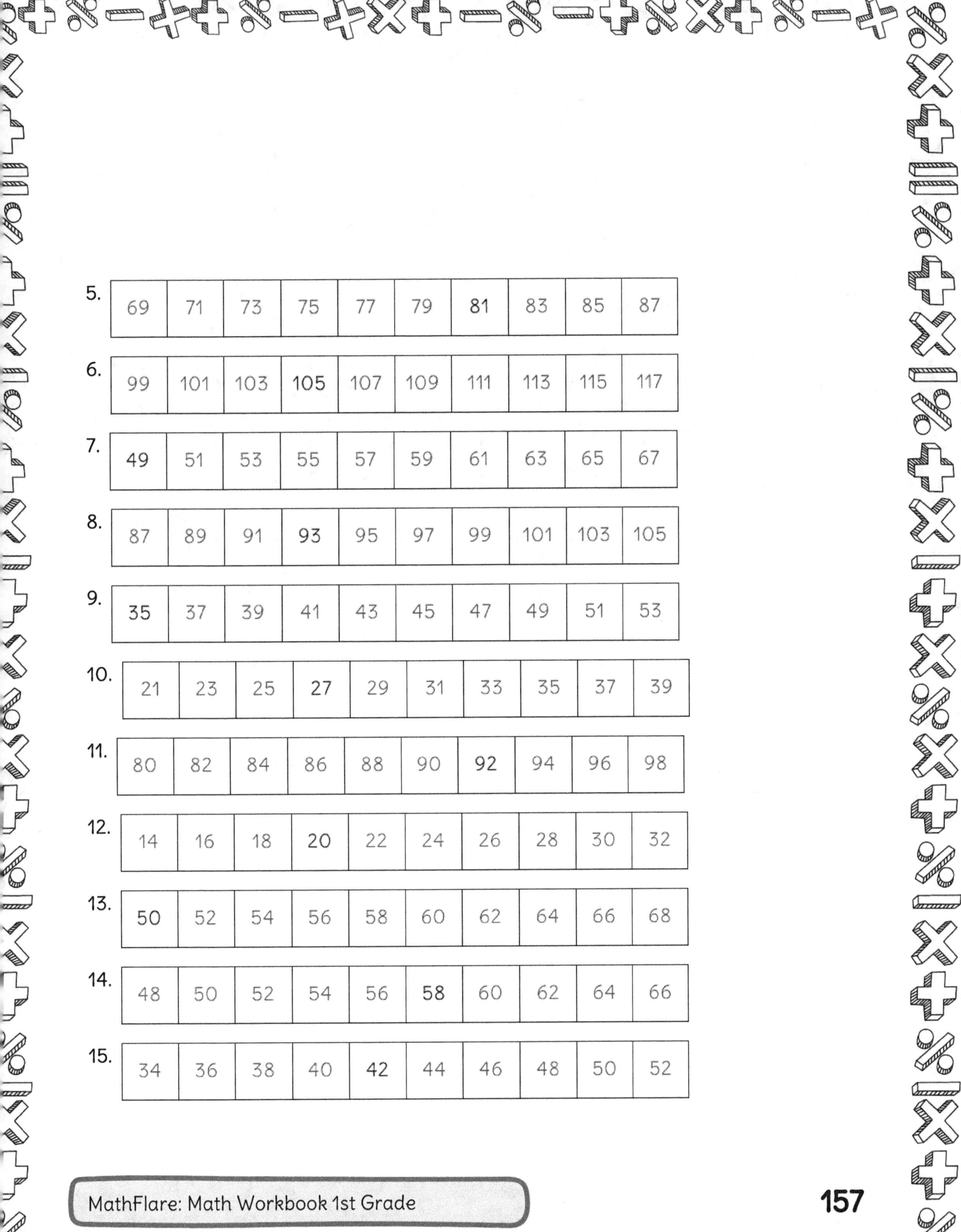

5.

| 69 | 71 | 73 | 75 | 77 | 79 | 81 | 83 | 85 | 87 |

6.

| 99 | 101 | 103 | 105 | 107 | 109 | 111 | 113 | 115 | 117 |

7.

| 49 | 51 | 53 | 55 | 57 | 59 | 61 | 63 | 65 | 67 |

8.

| 87 | 89 | 91 | 93 | 95 | 97 | 99 | 101 | 103 | 105 |

9.

| 35 | 37 | 39 | 41 | 43 | 45 | 47 | 49 | 51 | 53 |

10.

| 21 | 23 | 25 | 27 | 29 | 31 | 33 | 35 | 37 | 39 |

11.

| 80 | 82 | 84 | 86 | 88 | 90 | 92 | 94 | 96 | 98 |

12.

| 14 | 16 | 18 | 20 | 22 | 24 | 26 | 28 | 30 | 32 |

13.

| 50 | 52 | 54 | 56 | 58 | 60 | 62 | 64 | 66 | 68 |

14.

| 48 | 50 | 52 | 54 | 56 | 58 | 60 | 62 | 64 | 66 |

15.

| 34 | 36 | 38 | 40 | 42 | 44 | 46 | 48 | 50 | 52 |

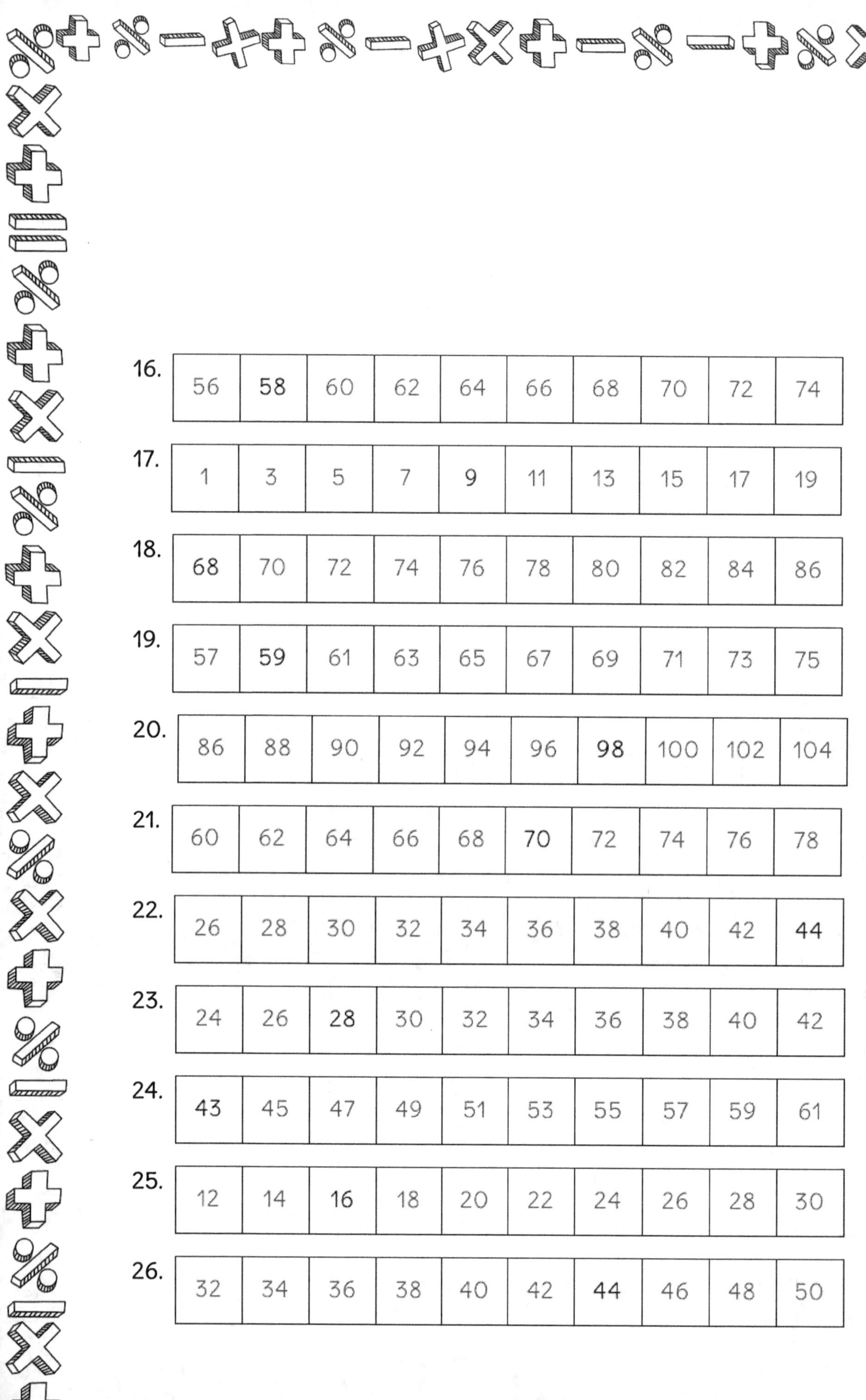

16.

| 56 | 58 | 60 | 62 | 64 | 66 | 68 | 70 | 72 | 74 |

17.

| 1 | 3 | 5 | 7 | 9 | 11 | 13 | 15 | 17 | 19 |

18.

| 68 | 70 | 72 | 74 | 76 | 78 | 80 | 82 | 84 | 86 |

19.

| 57 | 59 | 61 | 63 | 65 | 67 | 69 | 71 | 73 | 75 |

20.

| 86 | 88 | 90 | 92 | 94 | 96 | 98 | 100 | 102 | 104 |

21.

| 60 | 62 | 64 | 66 | 68 | 70 | 72 | 74 | 76 | 78 |

22.

| 26 | 28 | 30 | 32 | 34 | 36 | 38 | 40 | 42 | 44 |

23.

| 24 | 26 | 28 | 30 | 32 | 34 | 36 | 38 | 40 | 42 |

24.

| 43 | 45 | 47 | 49 | 51 | 53 | 55 | 57 | 59 | 61 |

25.

| 12 | 14 | 16 | 18 | 20 | 22 | 24 | 26 | 28 | 30 |

26.

| 32 | 34 | 36 | 38 | 40 | 42 | 44 | 46 | 48 | 50 |

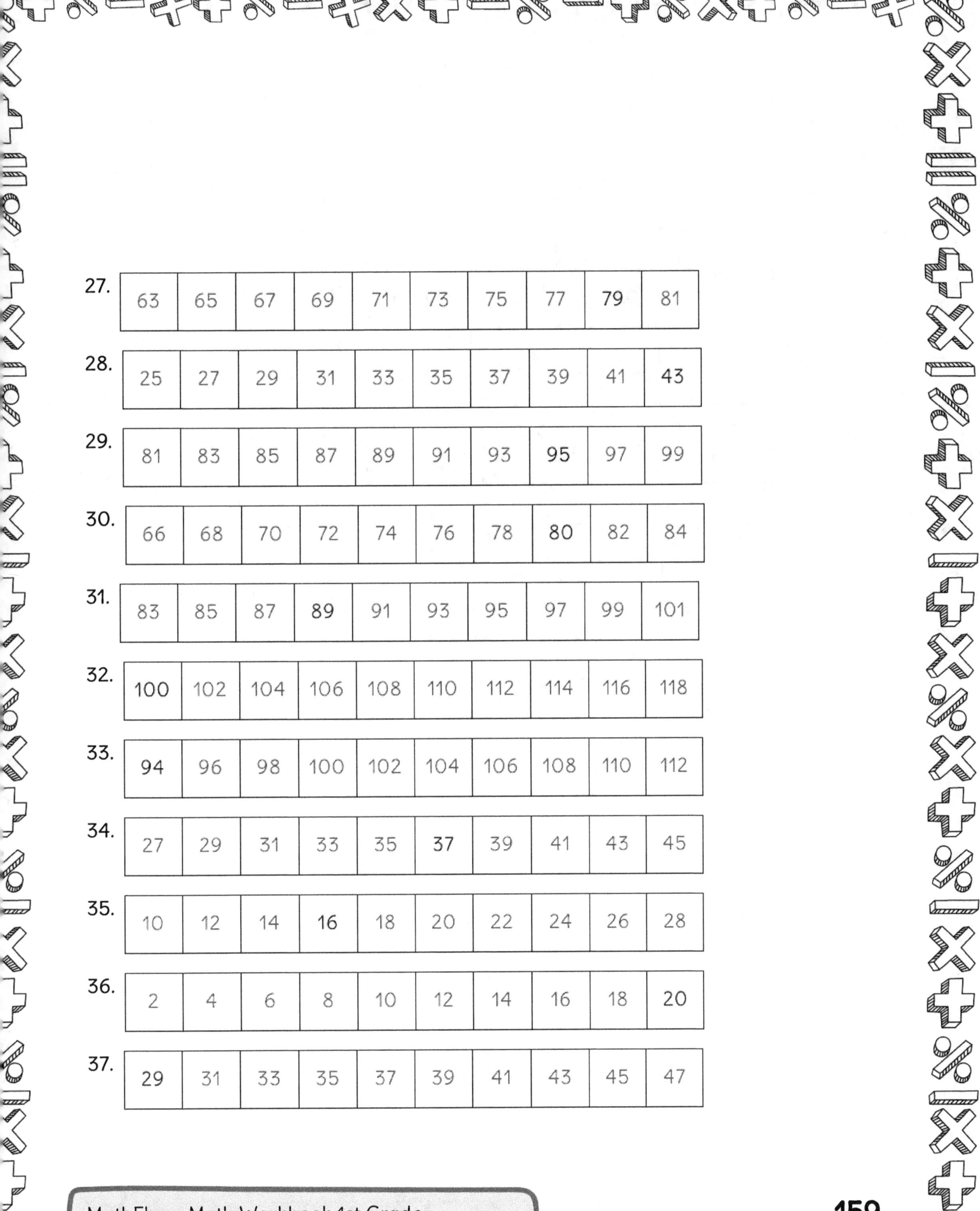

27.

| 63 | 65 | 67 | 69 | 71 | 73 | 75 | 77 | 79 | 81 |

28.

| 25 | 27 | 29 | 31 | 33 | 35 | 37 | 39 | 41 | 43 |

29.

| 81 | 83 | 85 | 87 | 89 | 91 | 93 | 95 | 97 | 99 |

30.

| 66 | 68 | 70 | 72 | 74 | 76 | 78 | 80 | 82 | 84 |

31.

| 83 | 85 | 87 | 89 | 91 | 93 | 95 | 97 | 99 | 101 |

32.

| 100 | 102 | 104 | 106 | 108 | 110 | 112 | 114 | 116 | 118 |

33.

| 94 | 96 | 98 | 100 | 102 | 104 | 106 | 108 | 110 | 112 |

34.

| 27 | 29 | 31 | 33 | 35 | 37 | 39 | 41 | 43 | 45 |

35.

| 10 | 12 | 14 | 16 | 18 | 20 | 22 | 24 | 26 | 28 |

36.

| 2 | 4 | 6 | 8 | 10 | 12 | 14 | 16 | 18 | 20 |

37.

| 29 | 31 | 33 | 35 | 37 | 39 | 41 | 43 | 45 | 47 |

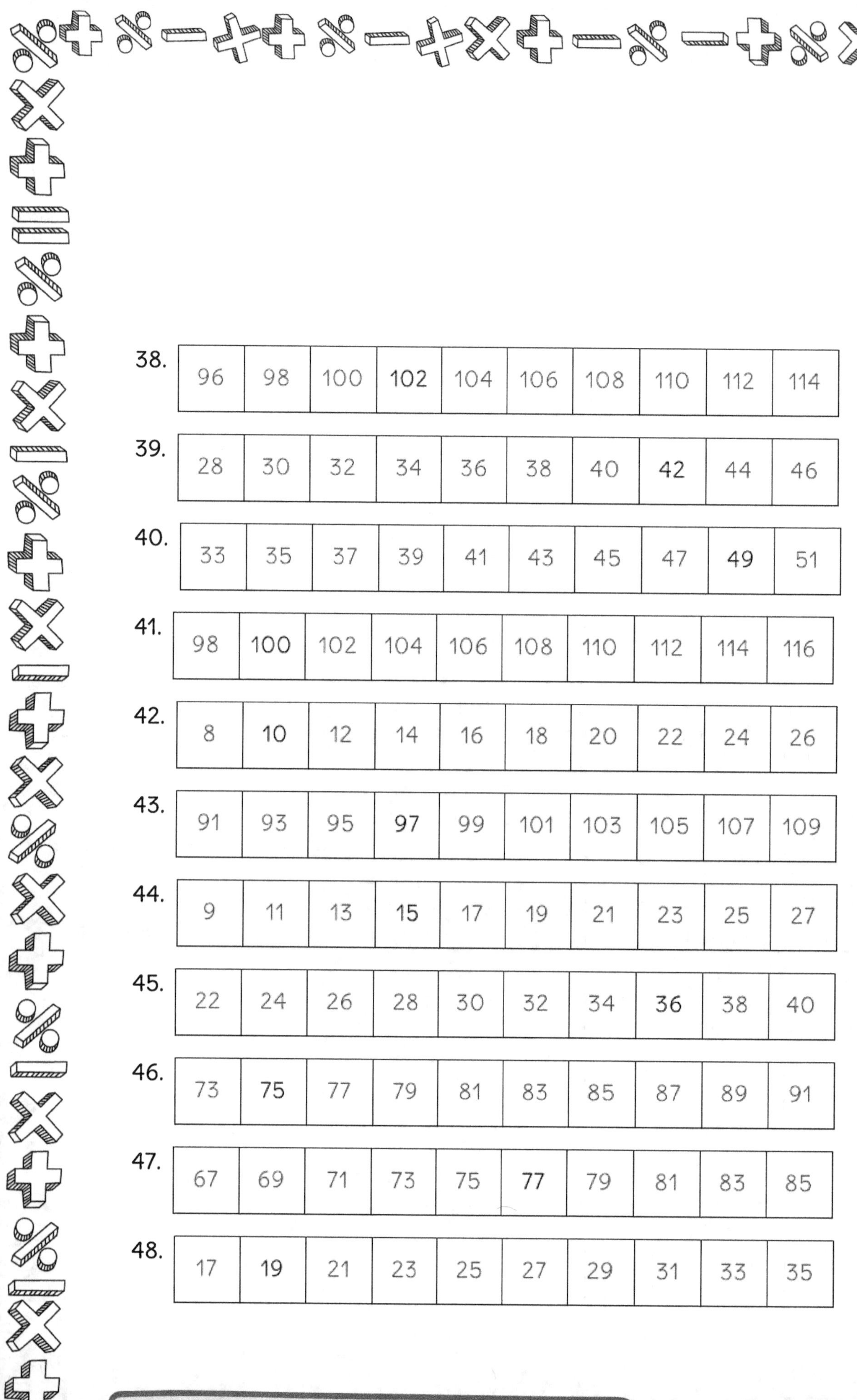

38.

| 96 | 98 | 100 | **102** | 104 | 106 | 108 | 110 | 112 | 114 |

39.

| 28 | 30 | 32 | 34 | 36 | 38 | 40 | **42** | 44 | 46 |

40.

| 33 | 35 | 37 | 39 | 41 | 43 | 45 | 47 | **49** | 51 |

41.

| 98 | **100** | 102 | 104 | 106 | 108 | 110 | 112 | 114 | 116 |

42.

| 8 | **10** | 12 | 14 | 16 | 18 | 20 | 22 | 24 | 26 |

43.

| 91 | 93 | 95 | **97** | 99 | 101 | 103 | 105 | 107 | 109 |

44.

| 9 | 11 | 13 | **15** | 17 | 19 | 21 | 23 | 25 | 27 |

45.

| 22 | 24 | 26 | 28 | 30 | 32 | 34 | **36** | 38 | 40 |

46.

| 73 | **75** | 77 | 79 | 81 | 83 | 85 | 87 | 89 | 91 |

47.

| 67 | 69 | 71 | 73 | 75 | **77** | 79 | 81 | 83 | 85 |

48.

| 17 | **19** | 21 | 23 | 25 | 27 | 29 | 31 | 33 | 35 |

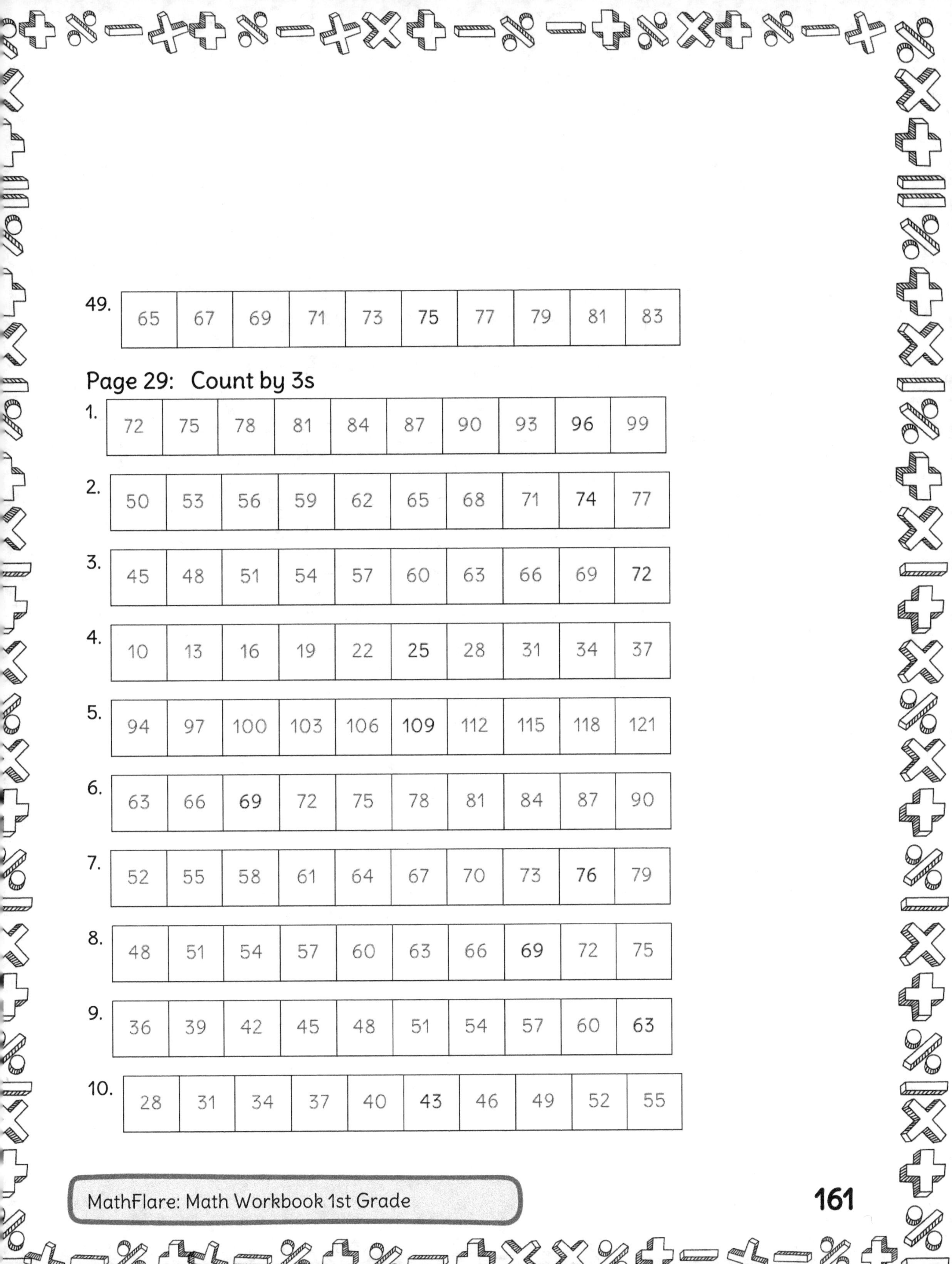

49.

| 65 | 67 | 69 | 71 | 73 | **75** | 77 | 79 | 81 | 83 |

Page 29: Count by 3s

1.

| 72 | 75 | 78 | 81 | 84 | 87 | 90 | 93 | **96** | 99 |

2.

| 50 | 53 | 56 | 59 | 62 | 65 | 68 | 71 | **74** | 77 |

3.

| 45 | 48 | 51 | 54 | 57 | 60 | 63 | 66 | 69 | **72** |

4.

| 10 | 13 | 16 | 19 | 22 | **25** | 28 | 31 | 34 | 37 |

5.

| 94 | 97 | 100 | 103 | 106 | **109** | 112 | 115 | 118 | 121 |

6.

| 63 | 66 | **69** | 72 | 75 | 78 | 81 | 84 | 87 | 90 |

7.

| 52 | 55 | 58 | 61 | 64 | 67 | 70 | 73 | **76** | 79 |

8.

| 48 | 51 | 54 | 57 | 60 | 63 | 66 | **69** | 72 | 75 |

9.

| 36 | 39 | 42 | 45 | 48 | 51 | 54 | 57 | 60 | **63** |

10.

| 28 | 31 | 34 | 37 | 40 | **43** | 46 | 49 | 52 | 55 |

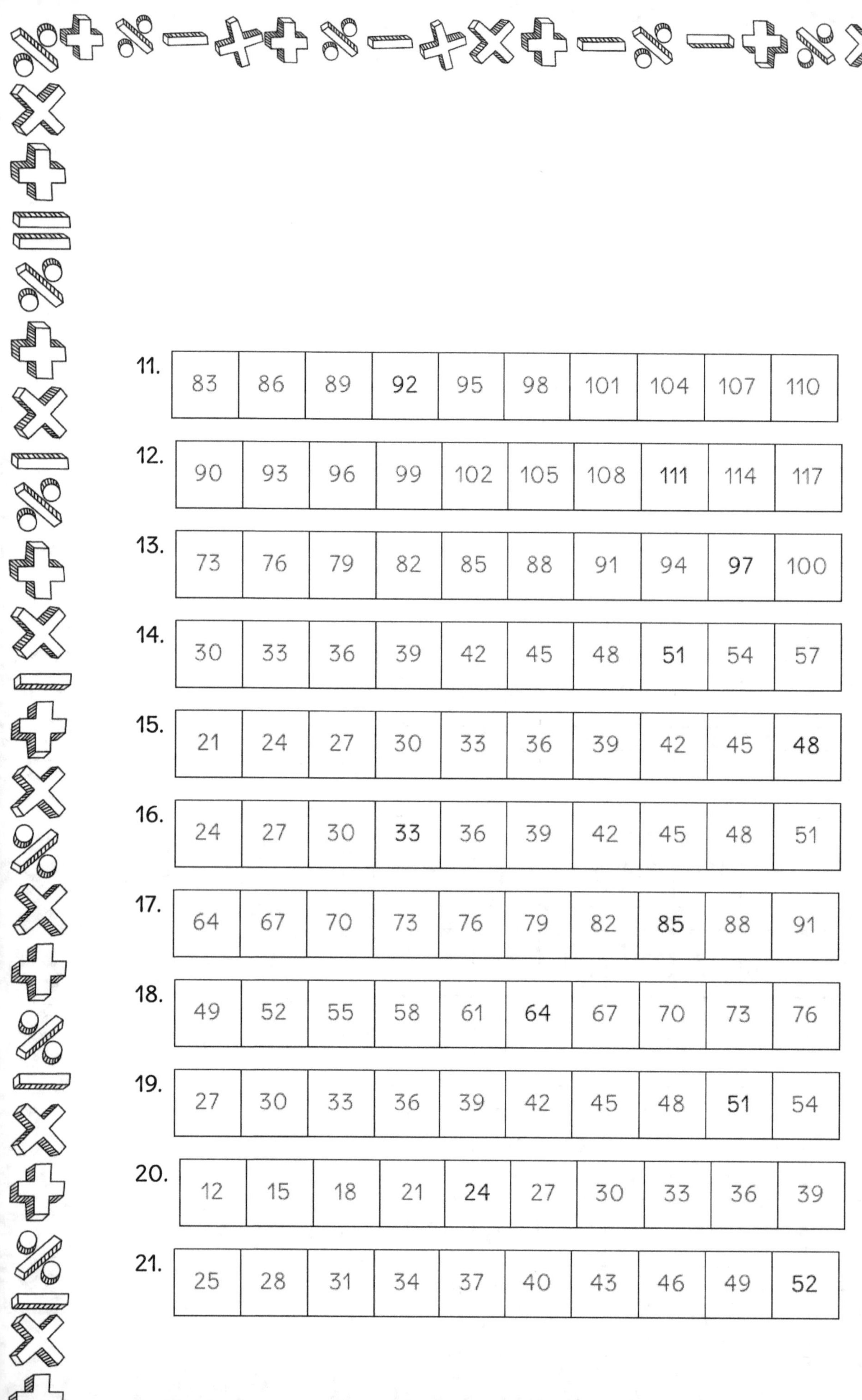

11.	83	86	89	**92**	95	98	101	104	107	110
12.	90	93	96	99	102	105	108	**111**	114	117
13.	73	76	79	82	85	88	91	94	**97**	100
14.	30	33	36	39	42	45	48	**51**	54	57
15.	21	24	27	30	33	36	39	42	45	**48**
16.	24	27	30	**33**	36	39	42	45	48	51
17.	64	67	70	73	76	79	82	**85**	88	91
18.	49	52	55	58	61	**64**	67	70	73	76
19.	27	30	33	36	39	42	45	48	**51**	54
20.	12	15	18	21	**24**	27	30	33	36	39
21.	25	28	31	34	37	40	43	46	49	**52**

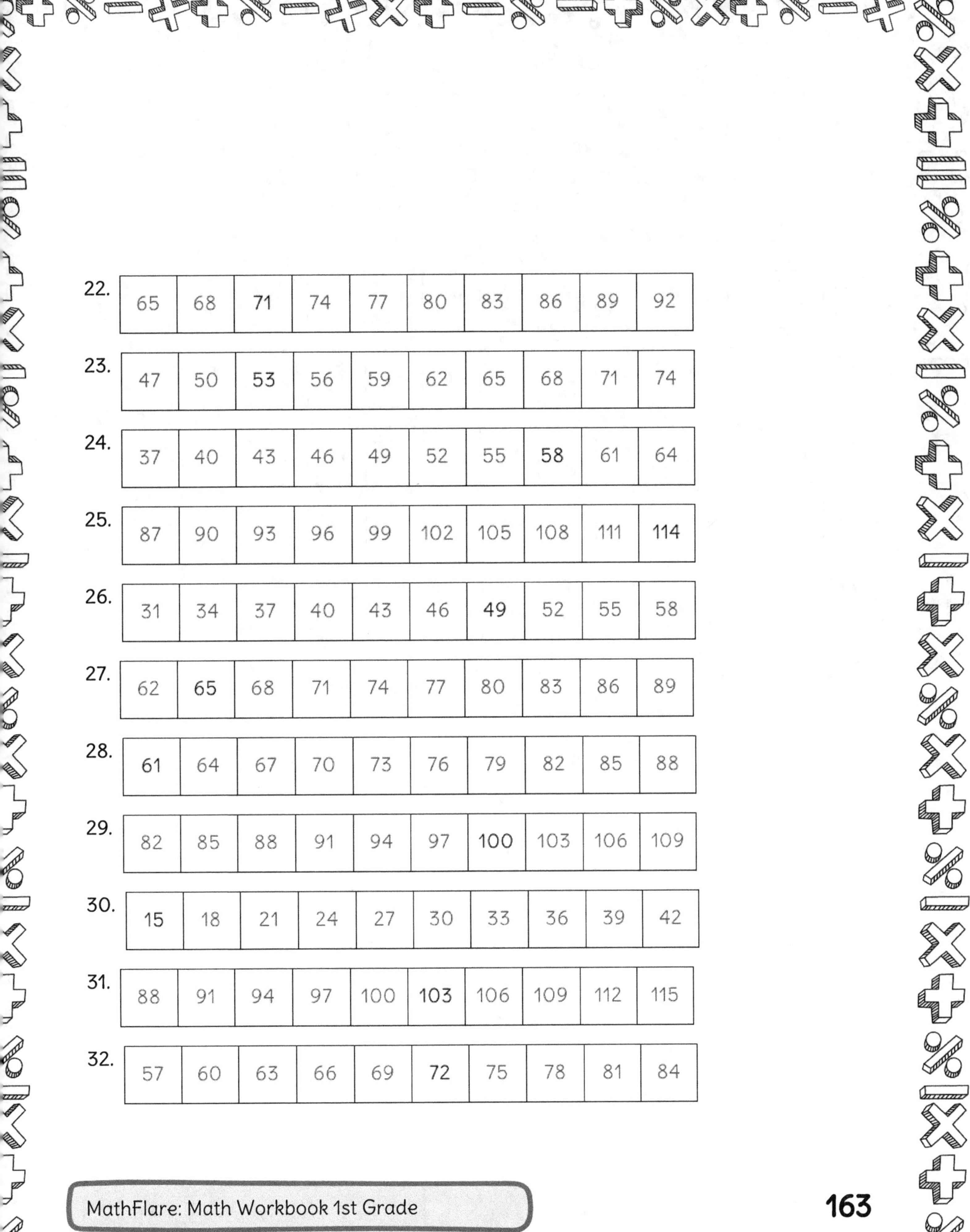

22. | 65 | 68 | **71** | 74 | 77 | 80 | 83 | 86 | 89 | 92 |

23. | 47 | 50 | **53** | 56 | 59 | 62 | 65 | 68 | 71 | 74 |

24. | 37 | 40 | 43 | 46 | 49 | 52 | 55 | **58** | 61 | 64 |

25. | 87 | 90 | 93 | 96 | 99 | 102 | 105 | 108 | 111 | **114** |

26. | 31 | 34 | 37 | 40 | 43 | 46 | **49** | 52 | 55 | 58 |

27. | 62 | **65** | 68 | 71 | 74 | 77 | 80 | 83 | 86 | 89 |

28. | 61 | 64 | 67 | 70 | 73 | 76 | 79 | 82 | 85 | 88 |

29. | 82 | 85 | 88 | 91 | 94 | 97 | **100** | 103 | 106 | 109 |

30. | 15 | 18 | 21 | 24 | 27 | 30 | 33 | 36 | 39 | 42 |

31. | 88 | 91 | 94 | 97 | 100 | **103** | 106 | 109 | 112 | 115 |

32. | 57 | 60 | 63 | 66 | 69 | **72** | 75 | 78 | 81 | 84 |

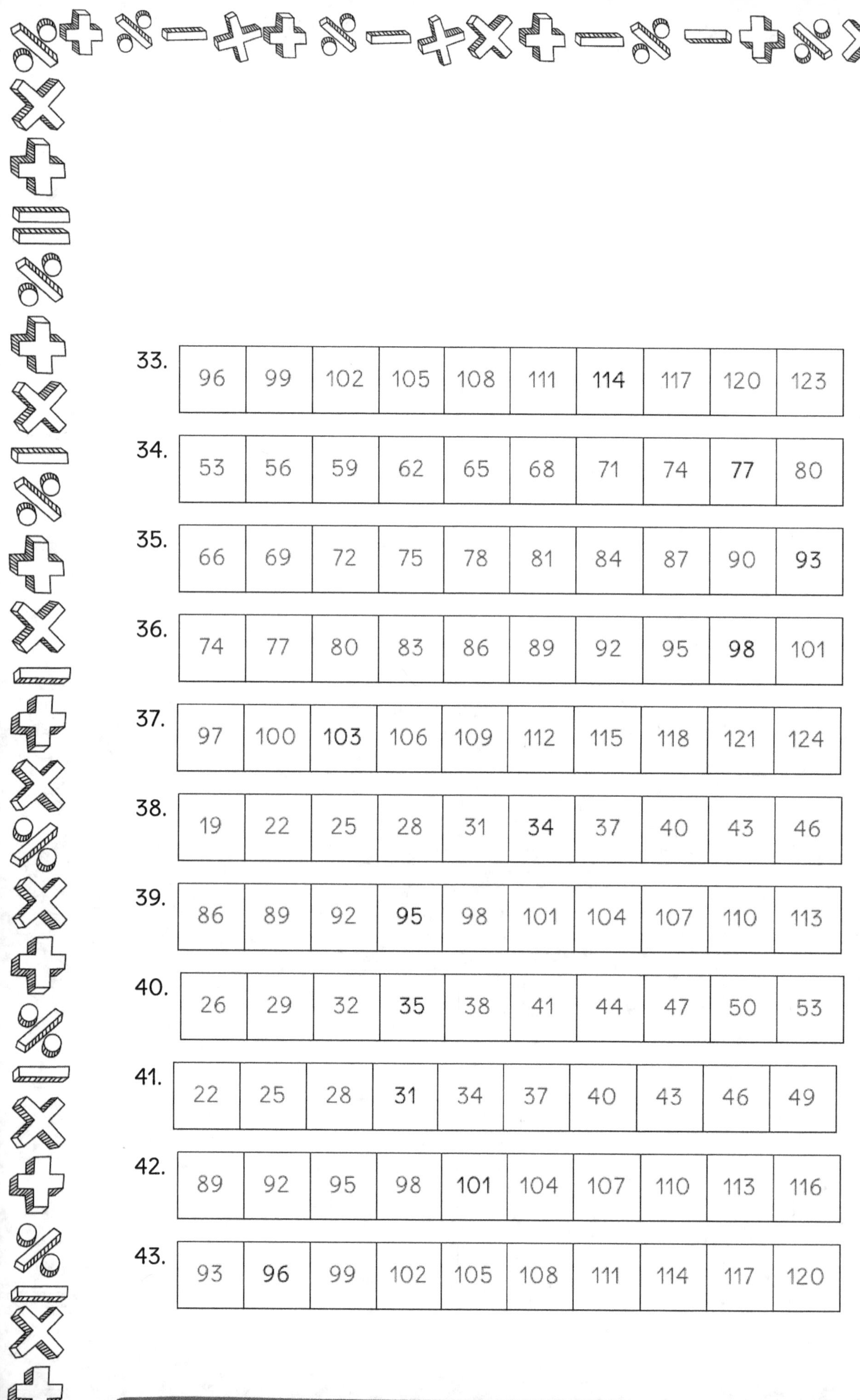

33. | 96 | 99 | 102 | 105 | 108 | 111 | **114** | 117 | 120 | 123 |

34. | 53 | 56 | 59 | 62 | 65 | 68 | 71 | 74 | **77** | 80 |

35. | 66 | 69 | 72 | 75 | 78 | 81 | 84 | 87 | 90 | **93** |

36. | 74 | 77 | 80 | 83 | 86 | 89 | 92 | 95 | **98** | 101 |

37. | 97 | 100 | **103** | 106 | 109 | 112 | 115 | 118 | 121 | 124 |

38. | 19 | 22 | 25 | 28 | 31 | **34** | 37 | 40 | 43 | 46 |

39. | 86 | 89 | 92 | **95** | 98 | 101 | 104 | 107 | 110 | 113 |

40. | 26 | 29 | 32 | **35** | 38 | 41 | 44 | 47 | 50 | 53 |

41. | 22 | 25 | 28 | **31** | 34 | 37 | 40 | 43 | 46 | 49 |

42. | 89 | 92 | 95 | 98 | **101** | 104 | 107 | 110 | 113 | 116 |

43. | 93 | **96** | 99 | 102 | 105 | 108 | 111 | 114 | 117 | 120 |

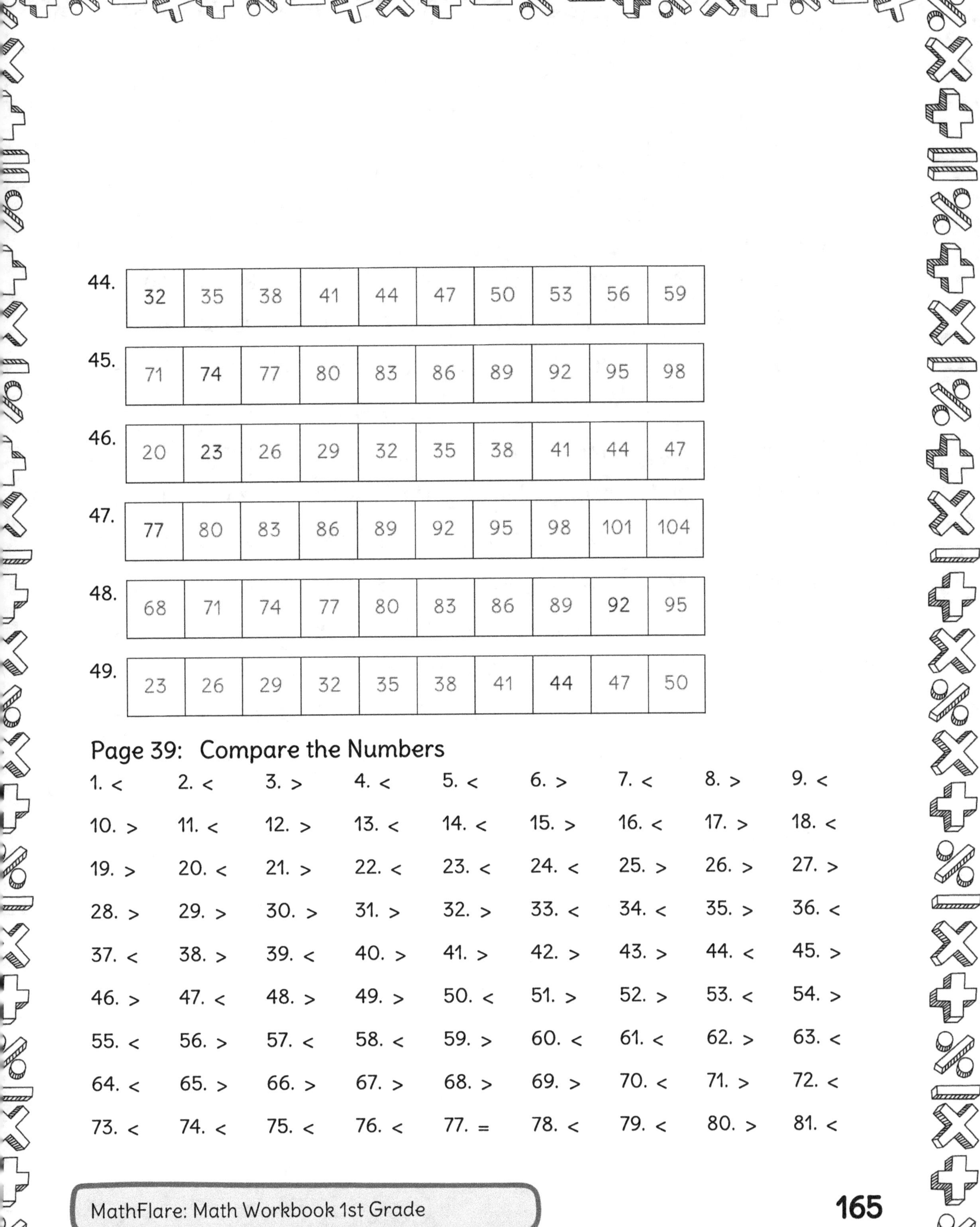

44.

| 32 | 35 | 38 | 41 | 44 | 47 | 50 | 53 | 56 | 59 |

45.

| 71 | 74 | 77 | 80 | 83 | 86 | 89 | 92 | 95 | 98 |

46.

| 20 | 23 | 26 | 29 | 32 | 35 | 38 | 41 | 44 | 47 |

47.

| 77 | 80 | 83 | 86 | 89 | 92 | 95 | 98 | 101 | 104 |

48.

| 68 | 71 | 74 | 77 | 80 | 83 | 86 | 89 | 92 | 95 |

49.

| 23 | 26 | 29 | 32 | 35 | 38 | 41 | 44 | 47 | 50 |

Page 39: Compare the Numbers

1. <   2. <   3. >   4. <   5. <   6. >   7. <   8. >   9. <

10. >   11. <   12. >   13. <   14. <   15. >   16. <   17. >   18. <

19. >   20. <   21. >   22. <   23. <   24. <   25. >   26. >   27. >

28. >   29. >   30. >   31. >   32. >   33. <   34. <   35. >   36. <

37. <   38. >   39. <   40. >   41. >   42. >   43. >   44. <   45. >

46. >   47. <   48. >   49. >   50. <   51. >   52. >   53. <   54. >

55. <   56. >   57. <   58. <   59. >   60. <   61. <   62. >   63. <

64. <   65. >   66. >   67. >   68. >   69. >   70. <   71. >   72. <

73. <   74. <   75. <   76. <   77. =   78. <   79. <   80. >   81. <

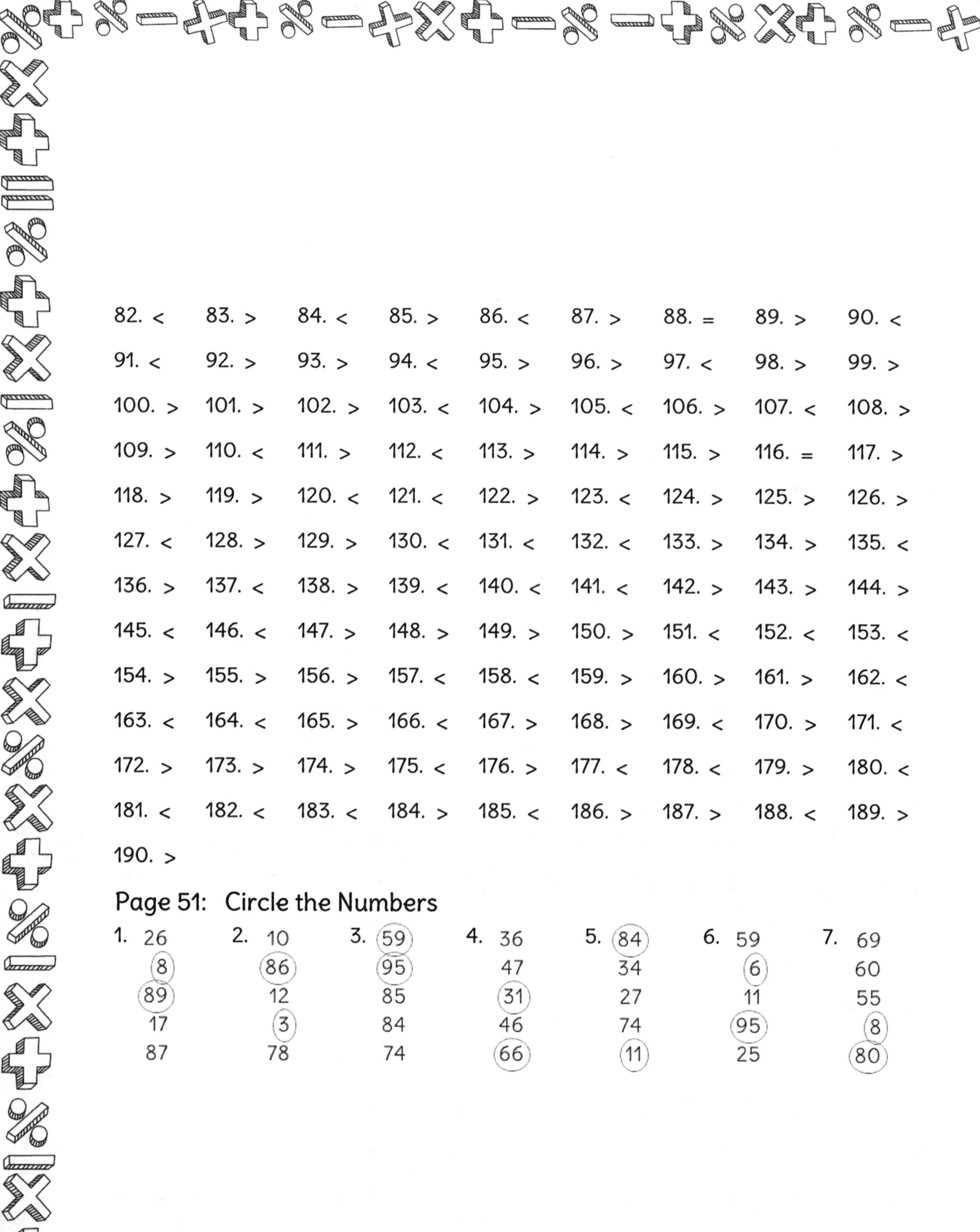

82. <   83. >   84. <   85. >   86. <   87. >   88. =   89. >   90. <

91. <   92. >   93. >   94. <   95. >   96. >   97. <   98. >   99. >

100. >   101. >   102. >   103. <   104. >   105. <   106. >   107. <   108. >

109. >   110. <   111. >   112. <   113. >   114. >   115. >   116. =   117. >

118. >   119. >   120. <   121. <   122. >   123. <   124. >   125. >   126. >

127. <   128. >   129. >   130. <   131. <   132. <   133. >   134. >   135. <

136. >   137. <   138. >   139. <   140. <   141. <   142. >   143. >   144. >

145. <   146. <   147. >   148. >   149. >   150. >   151. <   152. <   153. <

154. >   155. >   156. >   157. <   158. <   159. >   160. >   161. >   162. <

163. <   164. <   165. >   166. <   167. >   168. >   169. <   170. >   171. <

172. >   173. >   174. >   175. <   176. >   177. <   178. <   179. >   180. <

181. <   182. <   183. <   184. >   185. <   186. >   187. >   188. <   189. >

190. >

Page 51:   Circle the Numbers

1.	2.	3.	4.	5.	6.	7.
26	10	(59)	36	(84)	59	69
(8)	(86)	(95)	47	34	(6)	60
(89)	12	85	(31)	27	11	55
17	(3)	84	46	74	(95)	(8)
87	78	74	(66)	(11)	25	(80)

8. 60 (94) (41) 81 92

9. (2) 73 12 16 (85)

10. 60 65 69 (97) (26)

11. 53 33 (72) 61 (15)

12. (93) 82 15 (6) 28

13. (5) 75 17 (78) 10

14. (100) 41 78 (5) 15

15. 42 (7) 50 55 (64)

16. 12 22 (11) (90) 52

17. (95) 37 (14) 69 73

18. (36) 89 (94) 93 88

19. 78 80 (36) 53 (87)

20. 27 56 34 (7) (86)

21. (20) (87) 64 83 85

22. 47 84 17 (98) (4)

23. 71 (72) (26) 55 34

24. 68 62 48 (6) (74)

25. (11) 47 (86) 18 38

26. 62 71 (97) 69 (37)

27. 56 (89) (4) 5 32

28. (8) 74 32 (85) 26

29. 53 72 (97) 89 (18)

30. (6) 55 (81) 20 19

31. 66 (9) 28 33 (75)

32. (73) (2) 47 46 23

33. 76 (87) 49 61 (48)

34. (82) 69 (21) 24 27

35. (95) 30 64 81 (21)

36. 40 51 (97) (1) 32

37. (8) (91) 78 50 71

38. 48 61 (71) (31) 59

39. (7) 27 (87) 62 50

40. (67) (24) 36 42 38

41. 34 58 (94) (24) 37

42. 45 (47) (13) 36 23

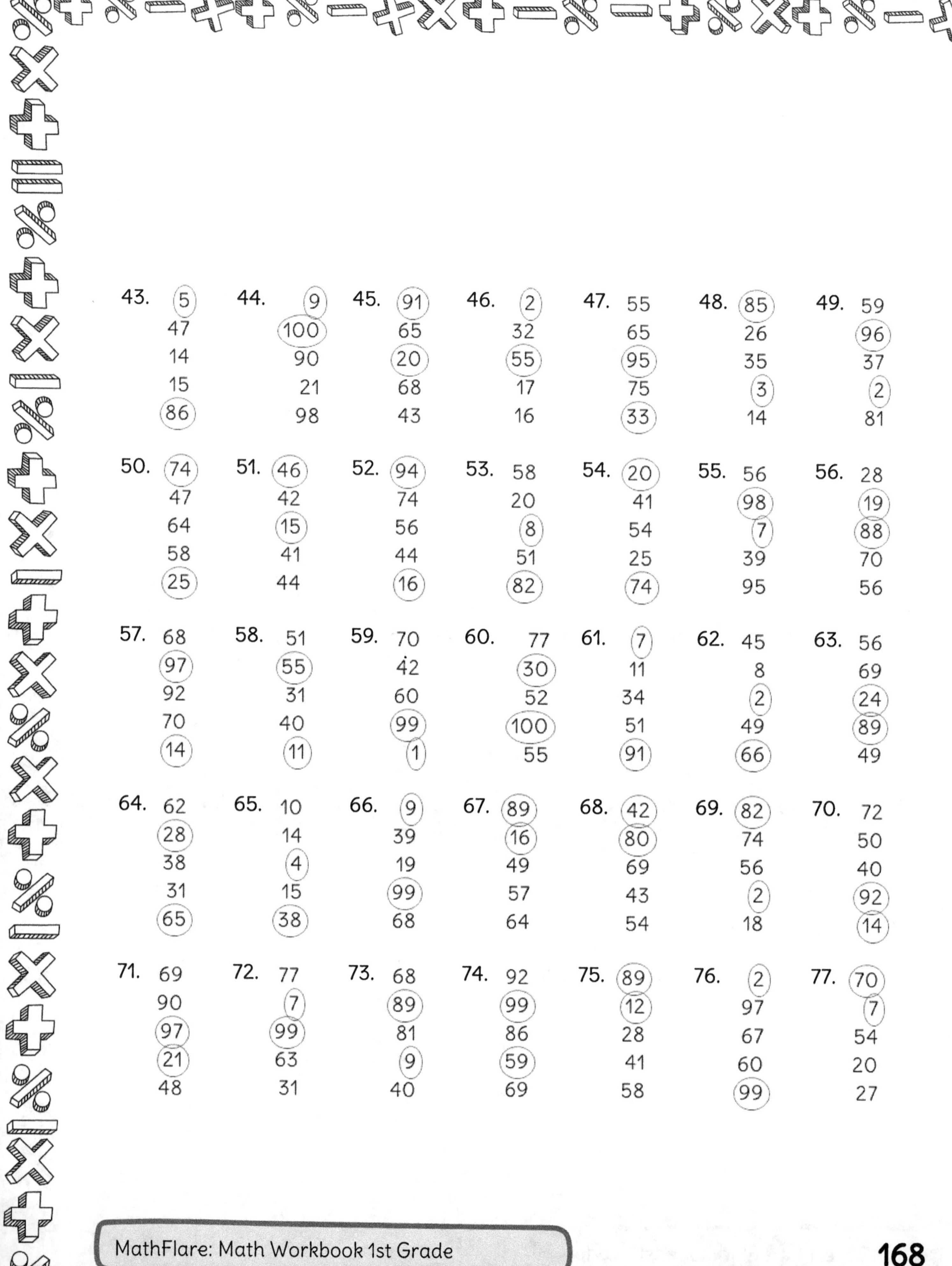

43.	44.	45.	46.	47.	48.	49.
(5)	9	(91)	(2)	55	(85)	59
47	(100)	65	32	65	26	(96)
14	90	(20)	(55)	(95)	35	37
15	21	68	17	75	(3)	(2)
(86)	98	43	16	(33)	14	81

50.	51.	52.	53.	54.	55.	56.
(74)	(46)	(94)	58	(20)	56	28
47	42	74	20	41	(98)	(19)
64	(15)	56	(8)	54	(7)	(88)
58	41	44	51	25	39	70
(25)	44	(16)	(82)	(74)	95	56

57.	58.	59.	60.	61.	62.	63.
68	51	70	77	(7)	45	56
(97)	(55)	42	(30)	11	8	69
92	31	60	52	34	(2)	(24)
70	40	(99)	(100)	51	49	(89)
(14)	(11)	(1)	55	(91)	(66)	49

64.	65.	66.	67.	68.	69.	70.
62	10	(9)	(89)	(42)	(82)	72
(28)	14	39	(16)	(80)	74	50
38	(4)	19	49	69	56	40
31	15	(99)	57	43	(2)	(92)
(65)	(38)	68	64	54	18	(14)

71.	72.	73.	74.	75.	76.	77.
69	77	68	92	(89)	(2)	(70)
90	(7)	(89)	(99)	(12)	97	(7)
(97)	(99)	81	86	28	67	54
(21)	63	(9)	(59)	41	60	20
48	31	40	69	58	(99)	27

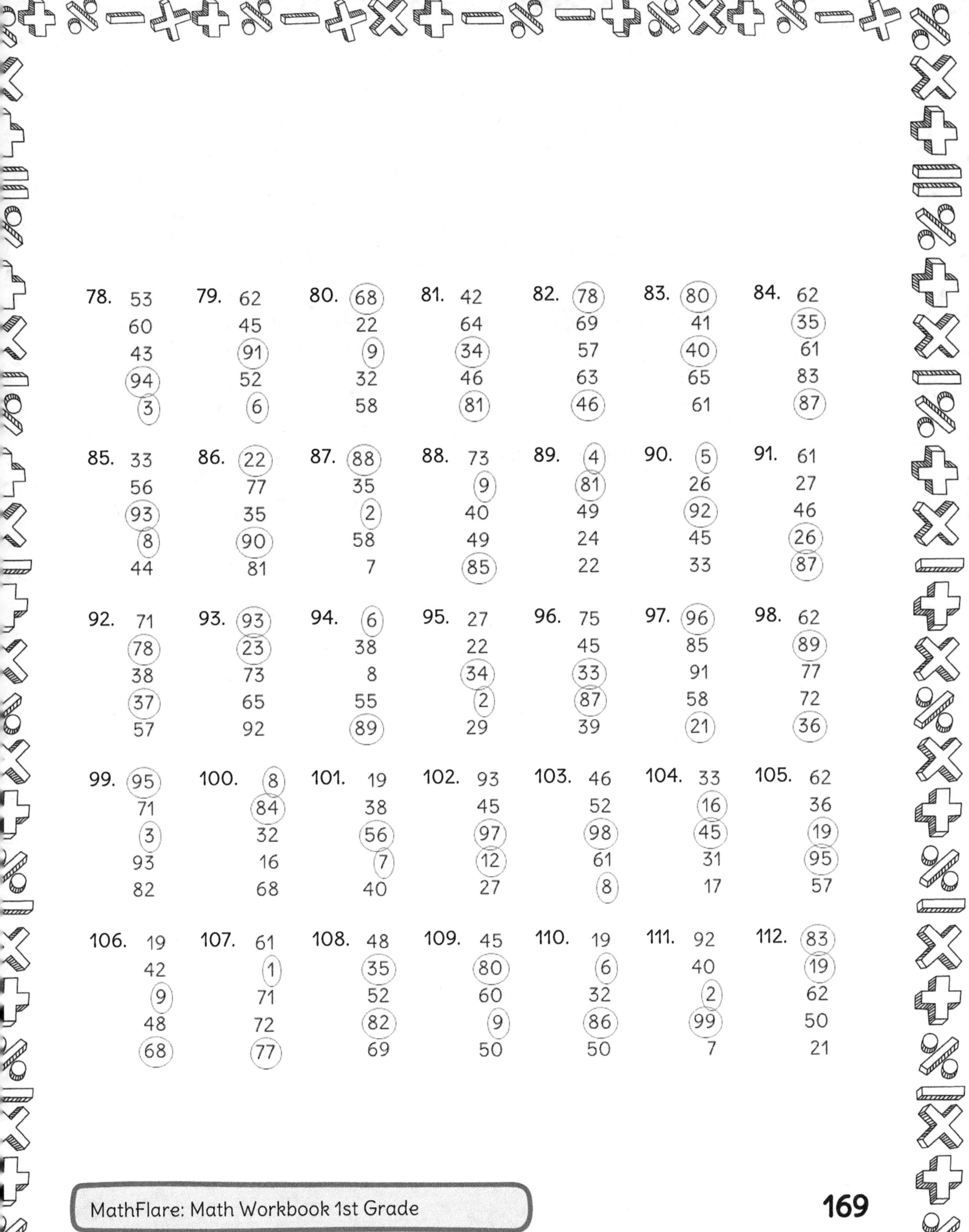

78.	79.	80.	81.	82.	83.	84.
53	62	(68)	42	(78)	(80)	62
60	45	22	64	69	41	(35)
43	(91)	(9)	(34)	57	(40)	61
(94)	52	32	46	63	65	83
(3)	(6)	58	(81)	(46)	61	(87)

85.	86.	87.	88.	89.	90.	91.
33	(22)	(88)	73	(4)	(5)	61
56	77	35	(9)	(81)	26	27
(93)	35	(2)	40	49	(92)	46
(8)	(90)	58	49	24	45	(26)
44	81	7	(85)	22	33	(87)

92.	93.	94.	95.	96.	97.	98.
71	(93)	(6)	27	75	(96)	62
(78)	(23)	38	22	45	85	(89)
38	73	8	(34)	(33)	91	77
(37)	65	55	(2)	(87)	58	72
57	92	(89)	29	39	(21)	(36)

99.	100.	101.	102.	103.	104.	105.
(95)	(8)	19	93	46	33	62
71	(84)	38	45	52	(16)	36
(3)	32	(56)	(97)	(98)	(45)	(19)
93	16	(7)	(12)	61	31	(95)
82	68	40	27	(8)	17	57

106.	107.	108.	109.	110.	111.	112.
19	61	48	45	19	92	(83)
42	(1)	(35)	(80)	(6)	40	(19)
(9)	71	52	60	32	(2)	62
48	72	(82)	(9)	(86)	(99)	50
(68)	(77)	69	50	50	7	21

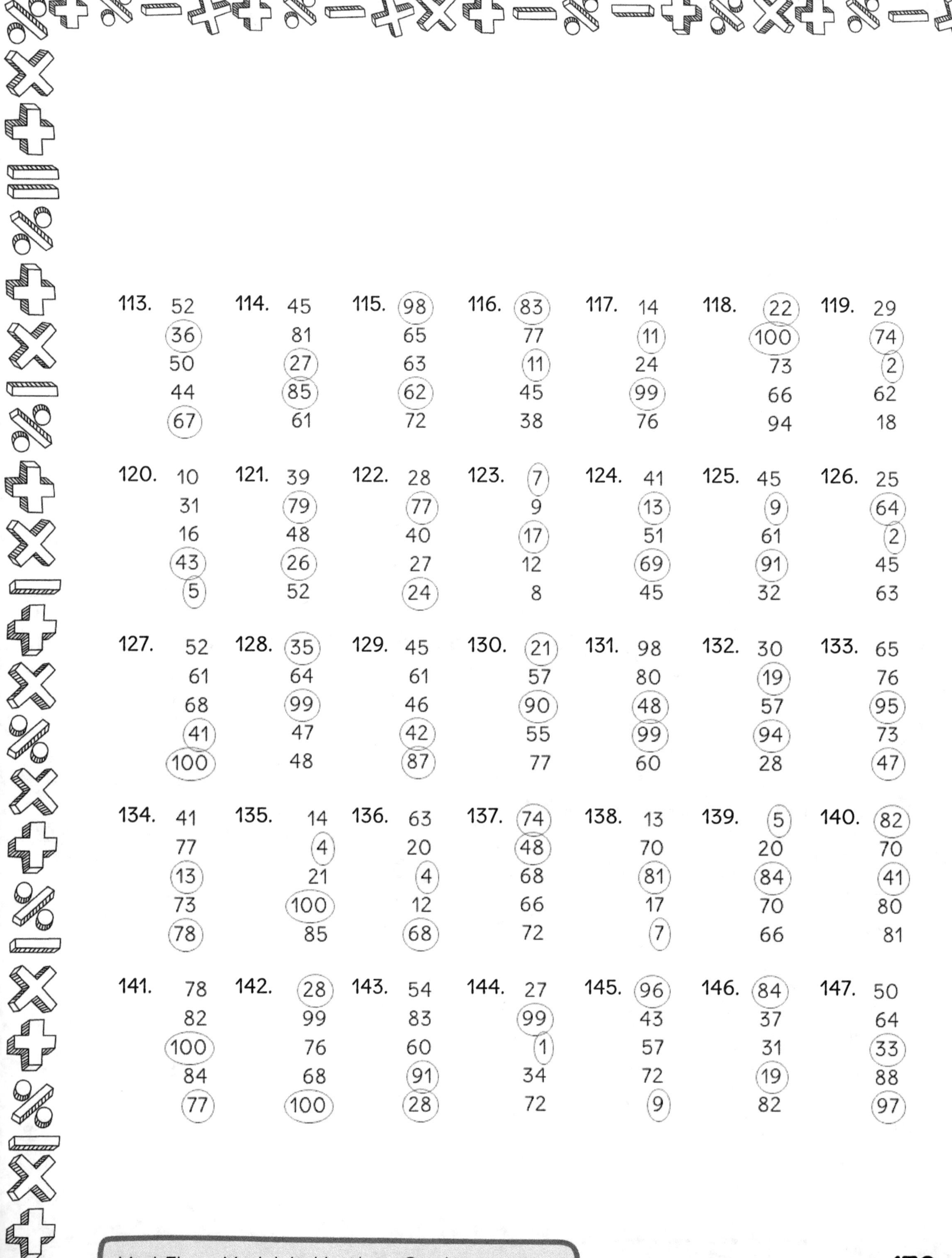

113.	114.	115.	116.	117.	118.	119.
52	45	(98)	(83)	14	(22)	29
(36)	81	65	77	(11)	(100)	(74)
50	(27)	63	(11)	24	73	(2)
44	(85)	(62)	45	(99)	66	62
(67)	61	72	38	76	94	18

120.	121.	122.	123.	124.	125.	126.
10	39	28	(7)	41	45	25
31	(79)	(77)	9	(13)	(9)	(64)
16	48	40	(17)	51	61	(2)
(43)	(26)	27	12	(69)	(91)	45
(5)	52	(24)	8	45	32	63

127.	128.	129.	130.	131.	132.	133.
52	(35)	45	(21)	98	30	65
61	64	61	57	80	(19)	76
68	(99)	46	(90)	(48)	57	(95)
(41)	47	(42)	55	(99)	(94)	73
(100)	48	(87)	77	60	28	(47)

134.	135.	136.	137.	138.	139.	140.
41	14	63	(74)	13	(5)	(82)
77	(4)	20	(48)	70	20	70
(13)	21	(4)	68	(81)	(84)	(41)
73	(100)	12	66	17	70	80
(78)	85	(68)	72	(7)	66	81

141.	142.	143.	144.	145.	146.	147.
78	(28)	54	27	(96)	(84)	50
82	99	83	(99)	43	37	64
(100)	76	60	(1)	57	31	(33)
84	68	(91)	34	72	(19)	88
(77)	(100)	(28)	72	(9)	82	(97)

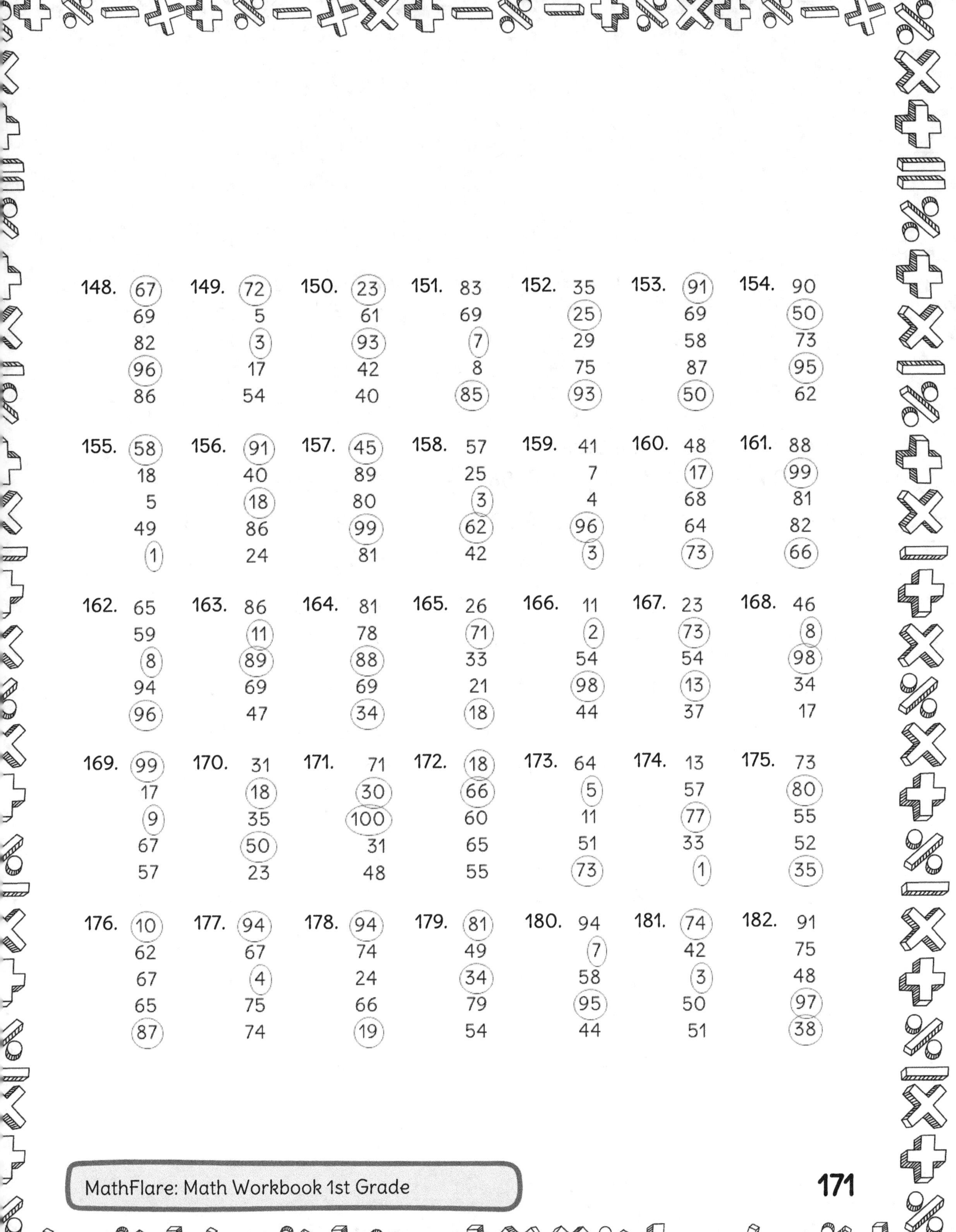

148.	149.	150.	151.	152.	153.	154.
(67)	(72)	(23)	83	35	(91)	90
69	5	61	69	(25)	69	(50)
82	(3)	(93)	(7)	29	58	73
(96)	17	42	8	75	87	(95)
86	54	40	(85)	(93)	(50)	62

155.	156.	157.	158.	159.	160.	161.
(58)	(91)	(45)	57	41	48	88
18	40	89	25	7	(17)	(99)
5	(18)	80	(3)	4	68	81
49	86	(99)	(62)	(96)	64	82
(1)	24	81	42	(3)	(73)	(66)

162.	163.	164.	165.	166.	167.	168.
65	86	81	26	11	23	46
59	(11)	78	(71)	(2)	(73)	(8)
(8)	(89)	(88)	33	54	54	(98)
94	69	69	21	(98)	(13)	34
(96)	47	(34)	(18)	44	37	17

169.	170.	171.	172.	173.	174.	175.
(99)	31	71	(18)	64	13	73
17	(18)	(30)	(66)	(5)	57	(80)
(9)	35	(100)	60	11	(77)	55
67	(50)	31	65	51	33	52
57	23	48	55	(73)	(1)	(35)

176.	177.	178.	179.	180.	181.	182.
(10)	(94)	(94)	(81)	94	(74)	91
62	67	74	49	(7)	42	75
67	(4)	24	(34)	58	(3)	48
65	75	66	79	(95)	50	(97)
(87)	74	(19)	54	44	51	(38)

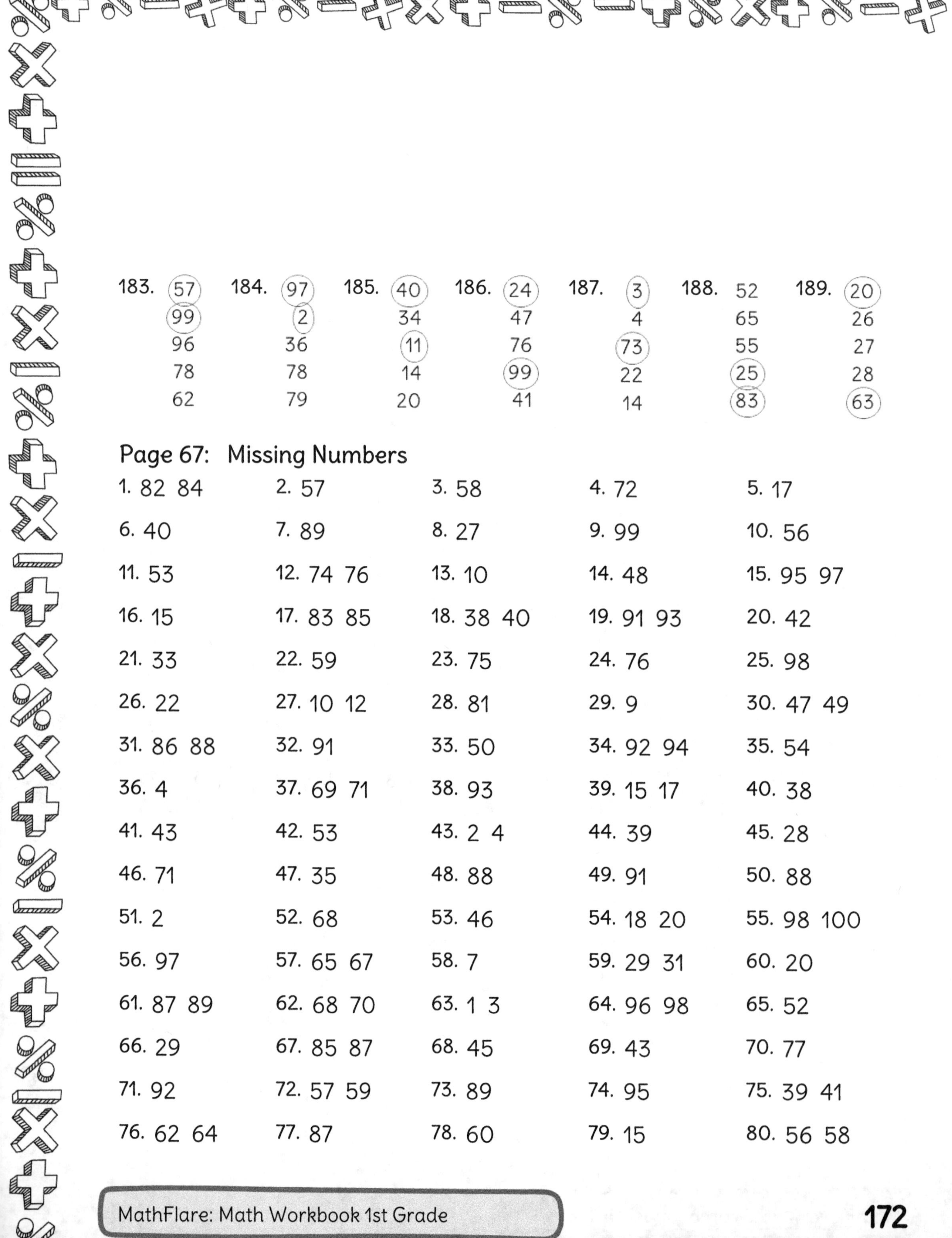

183.	184.	185.	186.	187.	188.	189.
(57)	(97)	(40)	(24)	(3)	52	(20)
(99)	(2)	34	47	4	65	26
96	36	(11)	76	(73)	55	27
78	78	14	(99)	22	(25)	28
62	79	20	41	14	(83)	(63)

Page 67:   Missing Numbers

1. 82 84   2. 57   3. 58   4. 72   5. 17

6. 40   7. 89   8. 27   9. 99   10. 56

11. 53   12. 74 76   13. 10   14. 48   15. 95 97

16. 15   17. 83 85   18. 38 40   19. 91 93   20. 42

21. 33   22. 59   23. 75   24. 76   25. 98

26. 22   27. 10 12   28. 81   29. 9   30. 47 49

31. 86 88   32. 91   33. 50   34. 92 94   35. 54

36. 4   37. 69 71   38. 93   39. 15 17   40. 38

41. 43   42. 53   43. 2 4   44. 39   45. 28

46. 71   47. 35   48. 88   49. 91   50. 88

51. 2   52. 68   53. 46   54. 18 20   55. 98 100

56. 97   57. 65 67   58. 7   59. 29 31   60. 20

61. 87 89   62. 68 70   63. 1 3   64. 96 98   65. 52

66. 29   67. 85 87   68. 45   69. 43   70. 77

71. 92   72. 57 59   73. 89   74. 95   75. 39 41

76. 62 64   77. 87   78. 60   79. 15   80. 56 58

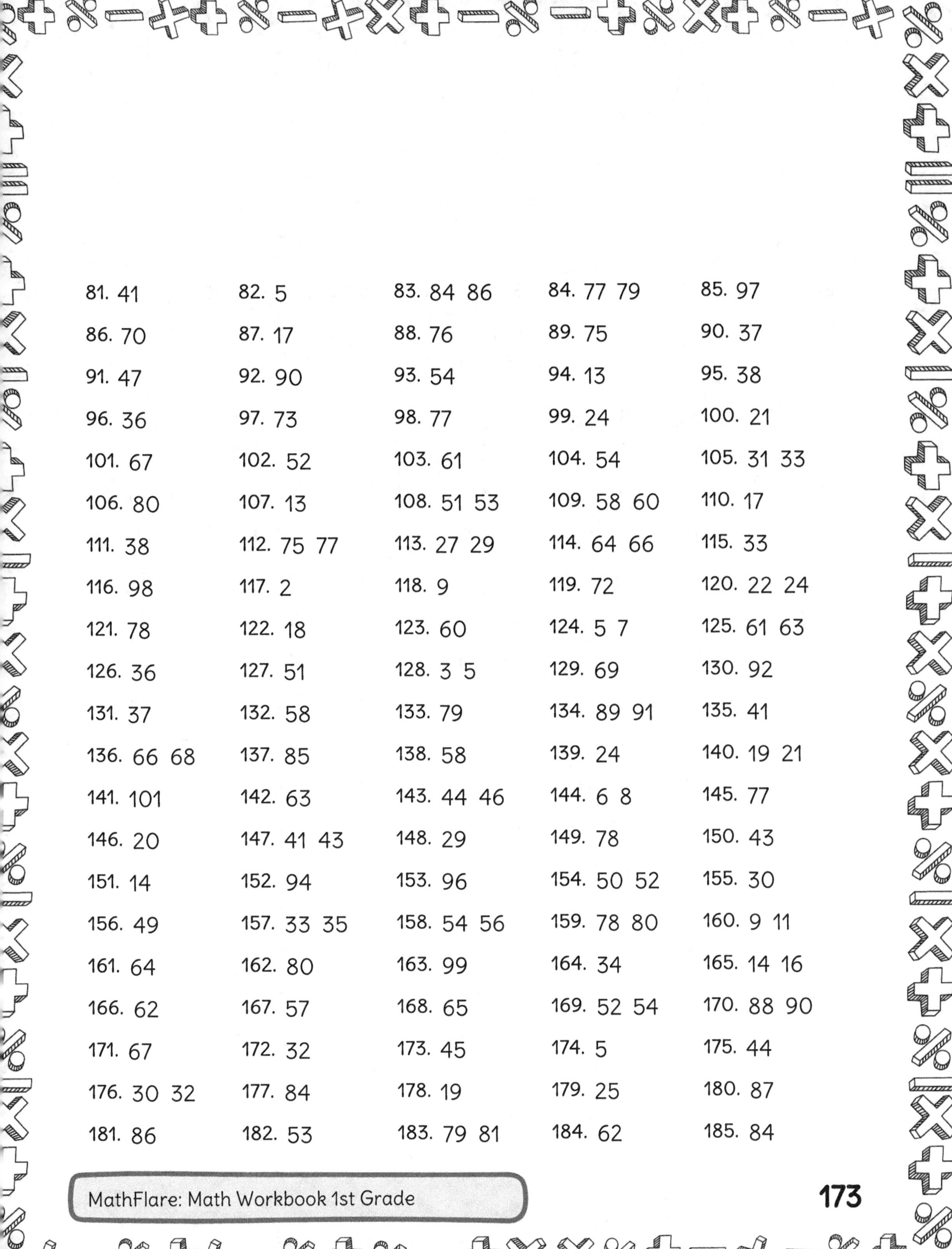

81. 41	82. 5	83. 84 86	84. 77 79	85. 97
86. 70	87. 17	88. 76	89. 75	90. 37
91. 47	92. 90	93. 54	94. 13	95. 38
96. 36	97. 73	98. 77	99. 24	100. 21
101. 67	102. 52	103. 61	104. 54	105. 31 33
106. 80	107. 13	108. 51 53	109. 58 60	110. 17
111. 38	112. 75 77	113. 27 29	114. 64 66	115. 33
116. 98	117. 2	118. 9	119. 72	120. 22 24
121. 78	122. 18	123. 60	124. 5 7	125. 61 63
126. 36	127. 51	128. 3 5	129. 69	130. 92
131. 37	132. 58	133. 79	134. 89 91	135. 41
136. 66 68	137. 85	138. 58	139. 24	140. 19 21
141. 101	142. 63	143. 44 46	144. 6 8	145. 77
146. 20	147. 41 43	148. 29	149. 78	150. 43
151. 14	152. 94	153. 96	154. 50 52	155. 30
156. 49	157. 33 35	158. 54 56	159. 78 80	160. 9 11
161. 64	162. 80	163. 99	164. 34	165. 14 16
166. 62	167. 57	168. 65	169. 52 54	170. 88 90
171. 67	172. 32	173. 45	174. 5	175. 44
176. 30 32	177. 84	178. 19	179. 25	180. 87
181. 86	182. 53	183. 79 81	184. 62	185. 84

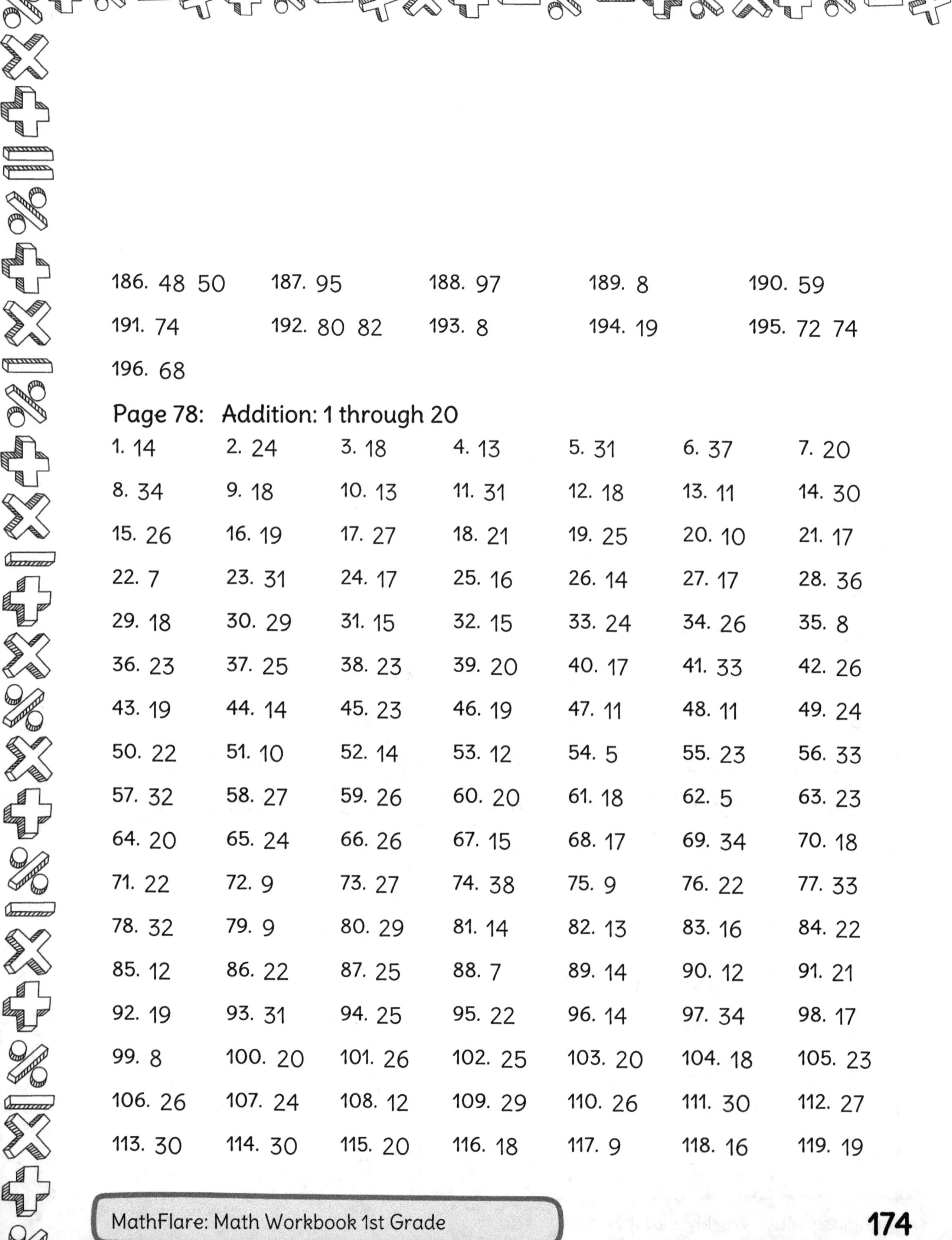

186. 48 50   187. 95   188. 97   189. 8   190. 59

191. 74   192. 80 82   193. 8   194. 19   195. 72 74

196. 68

Page 78:   Addition: 1 through 20

1. 14   2. 24   3. 18   4. 13   5. 31   6. 37   7. 20

8. 34   9. 18   10. 13   11. 31   12. 18   13. 11   14. 30

15. 26   16. 19   17. 27   18. 21   19. 25   20. 10   21. 17

22. 7   23. 31   24. 17   25. 16   26. 14   27. 17   28. 36

29. 18   30. 29   31. 15   32. 15   33. 24   34. 26   35. 8

36. 23   37. 25   38. 23   39. 20   40. 17   41. 33   42. 26

43. 19   44. 14   45. 23   46. 19   47. 11   48. 11   49. 24

50. 22   51. 10   52. 14   53. 12   54. 5   55. 23   56. 33

57. 32   58. 27   59. 26   60. 20   61. 18   62. 5   63. 23

64. 20   65. 24   66. 26   67. 15   68. 17   69. 34   70. 18

71. 22   72. 9   73. 27   74. 38   75. 9   76. 22   77. 33

78. 32   79. 9   80. 29   81. 14   82. 13   83. 16   84. 22

85. 12   86. 22   87. 25   88. 7   89. 14   90. 12   91. 21

92. 19   93. 31   94. 25   95. 22   96. 14   97. 34   98. 17

99. 8   100. 20   101. 26   102. 25   103. 20   104. 18   105. 23

106. 26   107. 24   108. 12   109. 29   110. 26   111. 30   112. 27

113. 30   114. 30   115. 20   116. 18   117. 9   118. 16   119. 19

120. 10   121. 21   122. 30   123. 28   124. 18   125. 16   126. 37

127. 29   128. 15   129. 27   130. 18   131. 7   132. 11   133. 24

134. 16   135. 23   136. 17   137. 16   138. 4   139. 11   140. 12

141. 24   142. 28   143. 28   144. 13   145. 30   146. 15   147. 24

148. 33   149. 23   150. 17   151. 15   152. 11   153. 21   154. 33

155. 20   156. 36   157. 5   158. 38   159. 16   160. 21   161. 23

162. 25   163. 8   164. 18   165. 19   166. 39   167. 20   168. 11

169. 13   170. 17   171. 21   172. 23   173. 24   174. 18   175. 21

176. 21   177. 15   178. 32   179. 32   180. 29   181. 9   182. 20

183. 19   184. 16   185. 22   186. 25   187. 22   188. 28   189. 4

190. 16   191. 20   192. 14   193. 27   194. 23

Page 86: Subtraction: 1 through 20

1. 4   2. 6   3. 2   4. 11   5. 5   6. 0   7. 11   8. 3

9. 3   10. 10   11. 0   12. 2   13. 8   14. 12   15. 1   16. 1

17. 1   18. 7   19. 2   20. 12   21. 1   22. 7   23. 2   24. 5

25. 6   26. 3   27. 7   28. 4   29. 1   30. 19   31. 14   32. 10

33. 1   34. 9   35. 13   36. 2   37. 15   38. 4   39. 6   40. 11

41. 1   42. 6   43. 14   44. 4   45. 0   46. 2   47. 2   48. 4

49. 4   50. 8   51. 0   52. 1   53. 1   54. 3   55. 0   56. 9

57. 6   58. 8   59. 3   60. 0   61. 2   62. 13   63. 3   64. 3

65. 7   66. 9   67. 1   68. 8   69. 12   70. 13   71. 18   72. 5

73. 11   74. 4   75. 3   76. 4   77. 2   78. 9   79. 8   80. 7

81. 13   82. 11   83. 10   84. 6   85. 15   86. 16   87. 7   88. 2

89. 4   90. 0   91. 12   92. 1   93. 7   94. 0   95. 9   96. 7

97. 10   98. 3   99. 1   100. 6   101. 4   102. 2   103. 14   104. 12

105. 2   106. 11   107. 1   108. 6   109. 9   110. 3   111. 11   112. 5

113. 4   114. 1   115. 1   116. 5   117. 5   118. 3   119. 2   120. 3

121. 0   122. 0   123. 3   124. 6   125. 16   126. 7   127. 8   128. 1

129. 14   130. 6   131. 5   132. 5   133. 2   134. 8   135. 15   136. 9

137. 5   138. 6   139. 9   140. 5   141. 7   142. 0   143. 10   144. 3

145. 8   146. 13   147. 4   148. 2   149. 9   150. 10   151. 3   152. 3

153. 17   154. 5   155. 9   156. 6   157. 4   158. 14   159. 8   160. 10

161. 5   162. 7   163. 5   164. 4   165. 4   166. 11   167. 8   168. 1

169. 7   170. 6   171. 2   172. 1   173. 2   174. 10   175. 5   176. 15

177. 0   178. 16   179. 13   180. 1   181. 11   182. 12   183. 0   184. 5

185. 3   186. 10   187. 0   188. 12   189. 0   190. 6   191. 0   192. 17

193. 18   194. 0   195. 8

Page 94:   Commutative Property

1. 9   2. 3   3. 2   4. 4   5. 10   6. 1   7. 5   8. 2   9. 4

10. 10   11. 6   12. 3   13. 9   14. 3   15. 10   16. 7   17. 8   18. 6

19. 5   20. 1   21. 3   22. 5   23. 2   24. 9   25. 5   26. 7   27. 3

28. 10   29. 2   30. 8   31. 1   32. 9   33. 3   34. 2   35. 7   36. 6

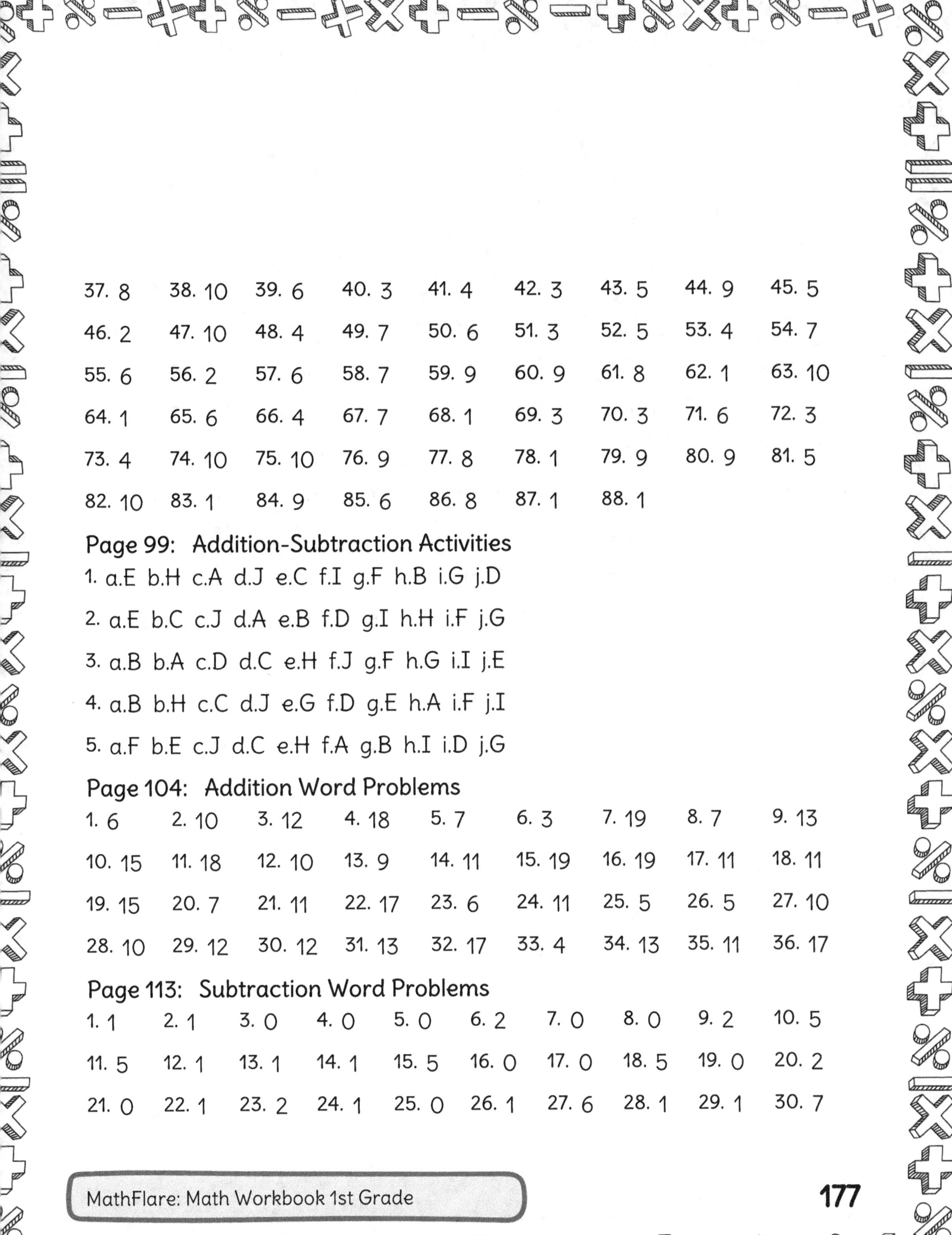

37. 8	38. 10	39. 6	40. 3	41. 4	42. 3	43. 5	44. 9	45. 5
46. 2	47. 10	48. 4	49. 7	50. 6	51. 3	52. 5	53. 4	54. 7
55. 6	56. 2	57. 6	58. 7	59. 9	60. 9	61. 8	62. 1	63. 10
64. 1	65. 6	66. 4	67. 7	68. 1	69. 3	70. 3	71. 6	72. 3
73. 4	74. 10	75. 10	76. 9	77. 8	78. 1	79. 9	80. 9	81. 5
82. 10	83. 1	84. 9	85. 6	86. 8	87. 1	88. 1		

Page 99: Addition-Subtraction Activities

1. a.E b.H c.A d.J e.C f.I g.F h.B i.G j.D

2. a.E b.C c.J d.A e.B f.D g.I h.H i.F j.G

3. a.B b.A c.D d.C e.H f.J g.F h.G i.I j.E

4. a.B b.H c.C d.J e.G f.D g.E h.A i.F j.I

5. a.F b.E c.J d.C e.H f.A g.B h.I i.D j.G

Page 104: Addition Word Problems

1. 6	2. 10	3. 12	4. 18	5. 7	6. 3	7. 19	8. 7	9. 13
10. 15	11. 18	12. 10	13. 9	14. 11	15. 19	16. 19	17. 11	18. 11
19. 15	20. 7	21. 11	22. 17	23. 6	24. 11	25. 5	26. 5	27. 10
28. 10	29. 12	30. 12	31. 13	32. 17	33. 4	34. 13	35. 11	36. 17

Page 113: Subtraction Word Problems

1. 1	2. 1	3. 0	4. 0	5. 0	6. 2	7. 0	8. 0	9. 2	10. 5
11. 5	12. 1	13. 1	14. 1	15. 5	16. 0	17. 0	18. 5	19. 0	20. 2
21. 0	22. 1	23. 2	24. 1	25. 0	26. 1	27. 6	28. 1	29. 1	30. 7

31. 0   32. 1   33. 4   34. 0   35. 2   36. 4   37. 8   38. 8   39. 0   40. 0

Page 123:   Place Value

1. 4 ones	2. 7 ones	3. 6 tens	4. 3 ones	5. 5 tens
6. 4 ones	7. 3 ones	8. 9 ones	9. 4 tens	10. 7 ones
11. 2 tens	12. 2 ones	13. 9 ones	14. 9 ones	15. 6 tens
16. 7 tens	17. 1 one	18. 0 ones	19. 7 tens	20. 3 ones
21. 1 one	22. 8 ones	23. 5 tens	24. 3 tens	25. 4 ones
26. 9 ones	27. 9 ones	28. 9 tens	29. 3 ones	30. 7 ones
31. 7 ones	32. 8 ones	33. 7 tens	34. 4 tens	35. 7 tens
36. 8 tens	37. 1 ten	38. 5 tens	39. 6 ones	40. 5 tens
41. 8 ones	42. 7 tens	43. 2 ones	44. 1 one	45. 9 tens
46. 4 ones	47. 6 tens	48. 9 tens	49. 9 ones	50. 6 ones
51. 2 ones	52. 7 tens	53. 7 tens	54. 8 ones	55. 8 tens
56. 8 ones	57. 5 ones	58. 3 ones	59. 8 ones	60. 5 ones
61. 6 ones	62. 8 tens	63. 4 tens	64. 0 ones	65. 3 tens
66. 6 tens	67. 7 ones	68. 8 ones	69. 5 ones	70. 8 ones
71. 8 tens	72. 7 ones	73. 7 ones	74. 6 ones	75. 3 ones
76. 2 tens	77. 5 ones	78. 5 tens	79. 3 ones	80. 6 ones
81. 3 tens	82. 4 tens	83. 8 tens	84. 1 one	85. 0 ones
86. 2 ones	87. 1 ten	88. 6 ones		

Page 128:   Place Value: Expanded Notation

1. 80   2. 18   3. 4   4. 33   5. 21   6. 35   7. 89

8. 25   9. 38   10. 8   11. 23   12. 84   13. 57   14. 12

15. 54   16. 17   17. 19   18. 53   19. 41   20. 2   21. 3

22. 9   23. 60   24. 66   25. 72   26. 96   27. 83   28. 85

29. 68   30. 51   31. 86   32. 63   33. 1   34. 49   35. 95

36. 90   37. 30   38. 59   39. 29   40. 15   41. 52   42. 44

43. 79   44. 16   45. 50   46. 13   47. 75   48. 24   49. 55

50. 27   51. 43   52. 100   53. 67   54. 36   55. 94   56. 58

57. 45   58. 6   59. 39   60. 37   61. 88   62. 77   63. 32

64. 42   65. 64   66. 70   67. 62   68. 5   69. 28   70. 93

71. 56   72. 61   73. 26   74. 73   75. 20   76. 7   77. 22

78. 31   79. 97   80. 78   81. 91   82. 34   83. 98   84. 92

85. 48   86. 71   87. 81   88. 11

Page 133:   Place Value: Expanded Notation

1. 3 tens + 1 one   2. 2 tens + 3 ones   3. 3 ones

4. 3 tens + 4 ones   5. 1 ten + 9 ones   6. 7 tens

7. 7 ones   8. 5 tens + 6 ones   9. 8 ones

10. 9 ones   11. 6 tens + 9 ones   12. 5 tens + 8 ones

13. 4 tens + 4 ones   14. 8 tens + 3 ones   15. 2 tens + 8 ones

16. 9 tens + 4 ones   17. 7 tens + 1 one   18. 4 tens + 5 ones

19. 9 tens
20. 2 tens + 7 ones
21. 2 tens + 2 ones

22. 1 hundred
23. 2 tens + 4 ones
24. 7 tens + 6 ones

25. 5 tens + 5 ones
26. 3 tens + 5 ones
27. 9 tens + 5 ones

28. 5 ones
29. 1 ten + 4 ones
30. 1 ten + 6 ones

31. 4 tens
32. 1 ten + 1 one
33. 9 tens + 6 ones

34. 4 tens + 2 ones
35. 3 tens + 8 ones
36. 8 tens + 2 ones

37. 6 tens + 7 ones
38. 9 tens + 9 ones
39. 1 ten + 5 ones

40. 4 tens + 6 ones
41. 6 tens + 5 ones
42. 6 tens + 1 one

43. 1 ten + 2 ones
44. 2 tens + 9 ones
45. 8 tens + 4 ones

46. 8 tens
47. 5 tens + 1 one
48. 7 tens + 4 ones

49. 5 tens + 2 ones
50. 3 tens
51. 5 tens + 4 ones

52. 2 tens
53. 3 tens + 3 ones
54. 6 tens

55. 3 tens + 2 ones
56. 1 ten + 8 ones
57. 5 tens + 3 ones

58. 2 tens + 6 ones
59. 8 tens + 9 ones
60. 9 tens + 1 one

61. 4 tens + 9 ones
62. 2 ones
63. 1 one

64. 1 ten + 7 ones
65. 6 tens + 8 ones
66. 8 tens + 6 ones

67. 8 tens + 5 ones
68. 3 tens + 7 ones
69. 1 ten + 3 ones

70. 6 ones
71. 6 tens + 2 ones
72. 5 tens + 7 ones

73. 4 tens + 3 ones
74. 6 tens + 4 ones
75. 6 tens + 3 ones

76. 7 tens + 7 ones
77. 4 tens + 1 one
78. 9 tens + 7 ones

79. 3 tens + 6 ones
80. 7 tens + 9 ones
81. 7 tens + 3 ones

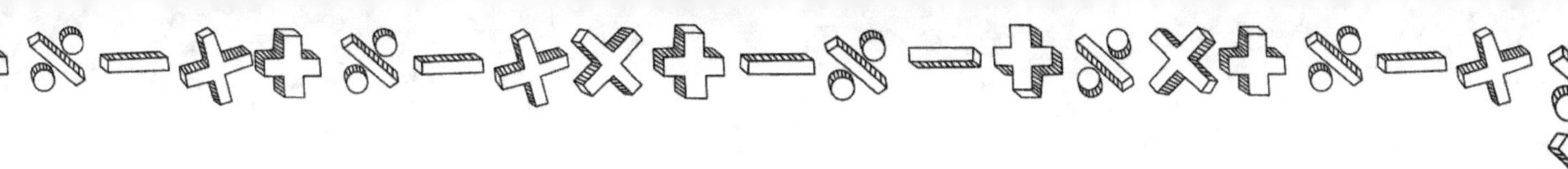

82. 9 tens + 3 ones   83. 4 tens + 7 ones   84. 9 tens + 2 ones

85. 2 tens + 5 ones   86. 3 tens + 9 ones   87. 4 tens + 8 ones

88. 8 tens + 8 ones

Page 139: Telling Time: Hours and Minutes

1.  6:00

2.  5:30

3.  3:00

4.  4:30

5.  2:00

6.  11:00

7.  2:30

8. 9:30

9.  7:30

10.  10:30

11.  12:30

12.  5:00

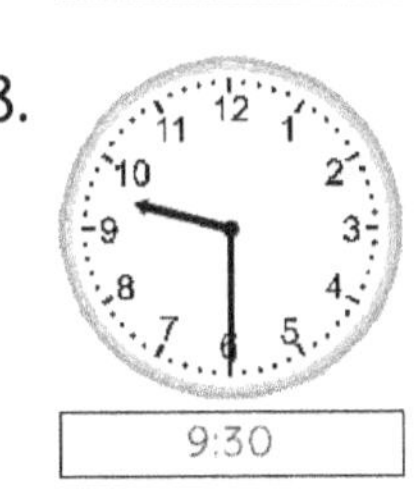

Page 141: Measure the Lines

1. 11   2. 3   3. 15   4. 13   5. 8   6. 12   7. 7   8. 14   9. 9

10. 10   11. 6   12. 4   13. 5   14. 12   15. 7   16. 8   17. 7   18. 8

19. 12   20. 4   21. 7   22. 3   23. 14

Page 144: Measure the Rectangles

1. W=4 H=3   2. W=1 H=3   3. W=5 H=4   4. W=3 H=3

5. W=4 H=5   6. W=2 H=5   7. W=4 H=4   8. W=4 H=2

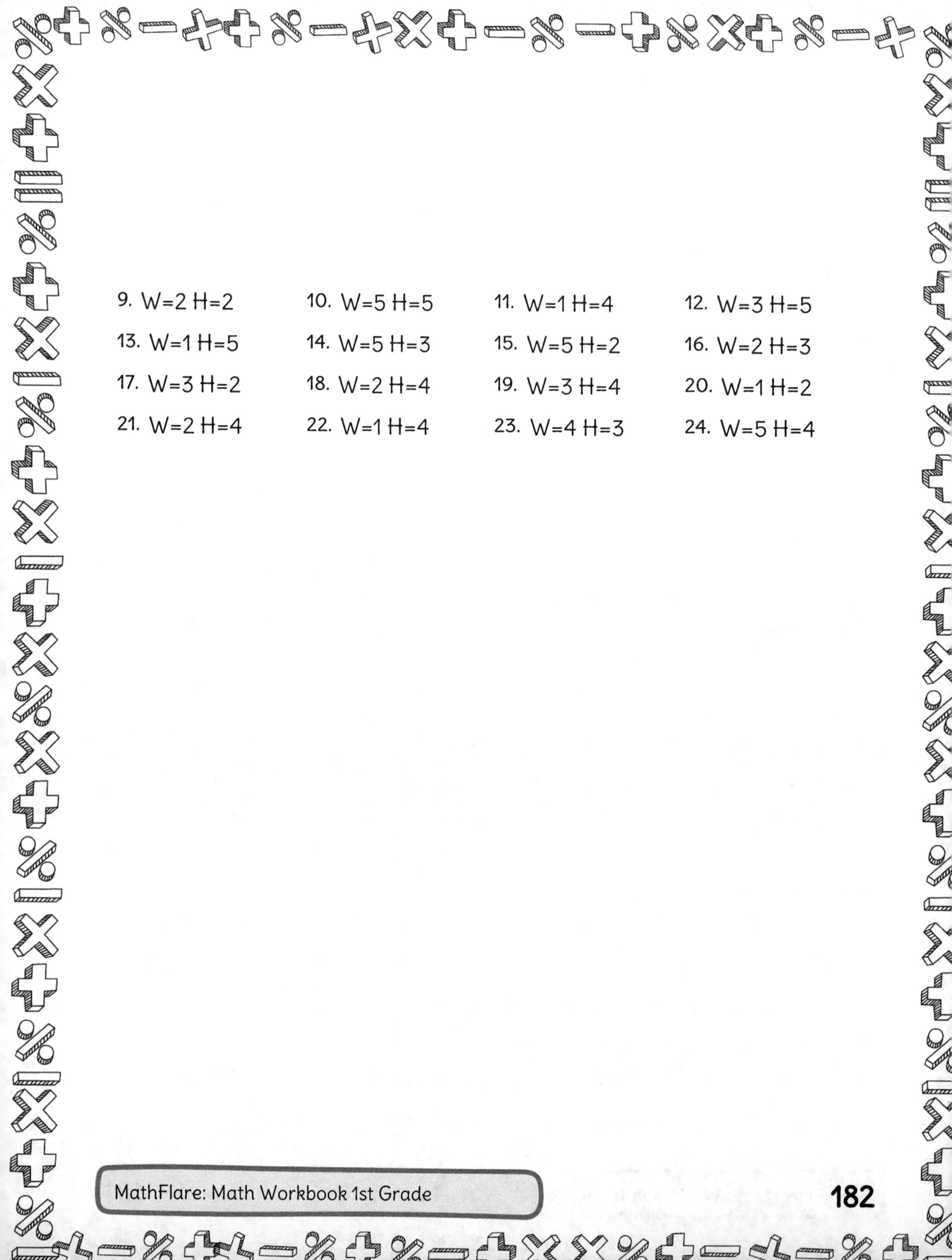

9. W=2 H=2   10. W=5 H=5   11. W=1 H=4   12. W=3 H=5

13. W=1 H=5   14. W=5 H=3   15. W=5 H=2   16. W=2 H=3

17. W=3 H=2   18. W=2 H=4   19. W=3 H=4   20. W=1 H=2

21. W=2 H=4   22. W=1 H=4   23. W=4 H=3   24. W=5 H=4